D1395515

DRONLEY
ROSEMILL, GOODS
BALDRAGON
GAGIE, GDS.
KINGENNIE
ARBROATH
EAST HAVEN
DUNDEE & ARBROATH
CARNOUSTIE
BARRY LINKS
BUDS
DUNDEE
LOCHEE
LOCHEE WEST
MARYFIELD
BARNHILL
LONGFORGAN
INVERGOWRIE
LIFF
BALDOVAN
EAST
JUNC.
WEST
INCHTURE VILLAGE
INCHTURE
TAY BRIDGE
ESPLANADE
WEST
GSA.
ERROL
NANS
MAGDALEN GREEN
TAY BRIDGE PASS
EAST NEW
TAY BRIDGE GDS
EAST NEW
FIRTH OF TAY
WORMIT
ST FORT
KILMANY
LEUCHARS
OLD STA. GDS
JUNC. STA. PASS
St Andrew's Bay
LUTHRIE
GUARD BRIDGE
ST ANDREWS
NEWBURGH
LINDORES
DAIRSIE
Lindores L.
GLENBURNIE JUNC.
CUPAR
MT MELVILLE
STRAVITHIE
BOARHILLS
Fife Ness
COLLESSIE
SPRINGFIELD
KINGSBARNS
AUCHTER-MUCHTY
LADYBANK
STRATHMIGLO
KINGSKETTLE
LARGOWARD GOODS
LOCHTY GOODS
CRAIL
SIDE
FALKLAND ROAD
MONTRAVE GOODS
KILCONQUHAR
COLINSBURGH
ANSTRUTHER
PITTENWEEM
MARKINCH
KENNOWAY GOODS
LARGO
ELIE
ST MONANS
AUCHMUTY MILLS
CAMERON BRI
LUNDIN LINKS
LESLIE
LEVEN
Isle of May
R. Leven
METHIL
THORNTON JUNC
MUIREDGE COL.
BUCKHAVEN
Elie Ness
KINGLASSIE COL.
WEMYSS CASTLE
CRAIGHEAD
WEST WEMYSS
CARDENDEN
LADY HELEN
DYSART
CHGELLY COL.
SINCLAIRTOWN
HARBOUR
AUCHTERTOOL
KIRKCALDY
GOODS
INVERTIEL JUNC.
BEATH
FIRTH OF FORTH
KINGHORN
PETTYCUR
Fidra
Craigleith
Bass Rock
BURNTISLAND
NORTH BERWICK
ABERDOUR
Inchkeith
GULLANE
DIRLETON
Inchcolm
EAST FORTUNE
Tynninghame Ho.
FIRTH
GRANTON
LEITH
ABERLADY
EAST LINTON
DUNBAR
EDINBURGH
NORTH
SOUTH
LONGNIDDRY
DREM
PRINCES STR
WAVERLEY
PORTOBELLO
JOPPA
NEW HAILES
FISHERROW GOODS
MUSSELBURGH
HADDINGTON
BELTONFORD GOODS
HAY
MARKET
GILMERTON
INVERESK
PRESTONPANS
Garvald
MERCHISTON
TRANENT
MACMERRY GOODS
SLATEFORD
BROOMIEKNOWE
ESBANK
SMEATON
WINTON GOODS
HADDINGTON
COLINTON
LASSWADE
MILLERHILL
COACH
LOANHEAD
ORMISTON
GIFFORD
CURRIE
ROSLIN
CASTLE
DALKEITH
PENCAITLAND
SALTOUN
HILLS
JUNIPER GREEN
BONNYRIGG
HARDENGREEN
COACH
Pathhead
HUMBIE
LAMMERMUIR
ENCORSE
POLTON
NEWTONGRANGE
K GAS WORKS
HAWTHORNDEN
GOREBRIDGE
SK BRIDGES
ROSSLYNLEE
FUSHIEBRIDGE
ENICUIK
AUCHENDINNY
POMATHORN
HEAD
Longformacus
Whit

Railways of Fife

The Railways of Fife

A Study of Railway development in Fife and the
adjoining counties of Perth, Kinross and
Clackmannan.

by

W. SCOTT BRUCE, B.Sc. (Lond), F.R.G.S.

with

Photographs and Maps

MELVEN PRESS
PERTH 1980

Published by:
The Melven Press
176, High Street,
Perth,
Scotland.

ISBN 0 906664 03 9

Printed in Scotland by
Macdonald Printers (Edinburgh) Ltd.,
Edgefield Road, Loanhead, Midlothian.

Acknowledgements

In preparing this book I have received much valuable assistance and advice from the staff of West Register House in Edinburgh and for this I am most grateful. I am particularly indebted to Mr A. McCall of Scone who in his 'retirement' has so eagerly deployed his skills as an engineering draftsman in the preparation of the maps and sketches. During the years spent gathering material, frequent visits were made to many newspaper offices at all of which I was received with the utmost courtesy and willingly given freedom of access to seek for any information required. Finally, I must not omit to thank most sincerely all those other persons who, even in a small way, have helped me or given that encouragement without which the idea of this book would never have been fulfilled.

The Publishers acknowledge the assistance of *Carto Graphics,* of Edinburgh in the preparation of maps and plans used in this book.

To my daughters
Alissa and Verity

Maps and Diagrams

Illustrations

Contents

Introduction

THE FIFE PENINSULA is that part of Scotland's eastern seaboard situated between the Firths of Forth and Tay. At its western extremities lie the garrisoned bridgehead towns of Stirling and Perth—both important since the days of antiquity as centres of trade and commerce. To the north-east of Stirling rise the Ochil Hills, forming an abrupt and impressive barrier reaching to over 2,000 feet in height. Despite a gradual reduction in their magnitude as they stretch towards the Tay, there are but few possible channels for land communication between the lower country to the east and the rest of Scotland.

The area outlined above and depicted in the General Map has been designated the Fife Peninsula because by far the largest part of it falls within the boundaries of the new Fife Region. Its administration is, however, shared with Tayside and Central Regions, which replace parts of the former counties of Perth, Kinross, Clackmannan and Stirling once a part of the area.

The aim of this book is to record the history of railways in these localities, examining how the railways were influenced by and played a part in the shaping of what has, over the past 130 years, become a very rapidly changing environment. In Map No. 1 where the Peninsula's present railway network is distinguished from other routes by the use of a thicker line, the intention to include two short continuations of line running north-west from the Ochils into Perth will be noted. Indeed, until nationalisation trains of the L.N.E.R. were required to run over L.M.S. metals for some two miles from Hilton Junction through the Moncrieffe tunnel and into Perth. Because the companies which shared the Moncrieffe tunnel jointly owned Perth General Station, but had their own separate locomotive and goods facilities and because the economy of a town as important as Perth greatly influenced trade on the lines to the south and east a study of railway development at Perth, although not a part of the Fife Peninsula is felt to be worthy of inclusion. For similar reasons it is considered that it would be wrong not to describe railway events south of the Forth at Stirling.

The book may be considered in three parts—each concentrating on a major stage in the evolvement of the present railways. The first concerns the growth of the network which was completed, with a few minor exceptions, by the opening of the Forth Bridge in 1890. This bridge, an improvement upon the ferry connection between Granton and Burntisland, came into use three years after the reconstructed Tay Bridge. With the establishment of permanent links between the north and south, the area was fully prepared to share in the heyday of railway travel. This heyday is the subject of part two. Like many other regions, the Fife Peninsula has since the early 1950's witnessed a rationalisation of services, involving the complete closure of many lines partially compensated by new specialised freight services and the arrival of dieselisation. These developments, together with competition originating in the 1960's from construction of the Forth and Tay Road Bridges, are examined in the concluding part.

W. S. BRUCE, 1980

1

The Beggar's Mantle

IN order to appreciate the motives which enticed Fife's landed gentry and manufacturing proprietors to sacrifice the capital necessary to construct a railway across their county, and to understand the development potential awaiting its construction, a short examination of the local geography may prove helpful. It must be especially difficult for readers familiar with the Peninsula to envisage the chapters which follow as evolving against an entirely different backcloth from that with which they are familiar. The writer will therefore comment on this, a rapidly changing scene in which people were constantly moving from place to place, either as travellers or as carriers of agricultural produce, extracted minerals and manufactured goods.

The General Map shows that the Peninsula's physical divisions conform to an essentially simple pattern of upland and lowland zones with a WSW-ENE trend.

In the north, a very narrow strip of coastal plain bordering the River Tay is backed by a range of undulating volcanic hills which occasionally exceed 600 feet. Both these divisions provide easily cultivated soils and in the eighteenth and nineteenth centuries supported numerous small, but thriving, agricultural communities.

These northern hills are separated from the equally fertile East Neuk Plateau by the Howe of Fife and Stratheden, which until the fairly recent past were low areas comprising ill-drained, water-logged soils difficult to reclaim. Monks from Lindores Abbey, near Newburgh, once cut peat around a small settlement near its centre which they named Ladybog in memory of their Abbey's dedicator. After railway plans were formulated, it was felt by the Company that Ladybank sounded a more pleasing name for what was to become an important junction. Settlements in the Howe, such as Auchtermuchty,

Pitlessie and Kingskettle, were confined to the edges of the basin. To the west, the prominent Lomond, Cleish and Benarty Hills remain the only sizeable areas of uncultivated upland.

Excellent soils derived from deposits associated with raised beaches have made the East Neuk Coastlands a highly productive agricultural division. The South-Western Coastlands, which slope from about 350 feet down to the sea increase in their agricultural quality towards the coast. Separating the South-Western Plateau and that of the East Neuk is the Leven Valley, an undulating lowland, mostly below 200 feet, where the occurrence of boulder clay made for heavy, cold soils with drainage difficulties.

To these generally favourable conditions of soil and terrain must be added those of climate. Over 70% of the Peninsula has an annual rainfall below 35 inches and the eastern coastlands average as little as 25 inches, whilst throughout, there are four months with mean temperatures above 50°F. Consequently, long before the advent of railways to assist with agricultural exports and the development of fashionable holiday resorts, east Fife had become one of the most agriculturally productive areas of Scotland. Its coastal fringes, which by the eighteenth century were studded with Royal Burghs, were the principal centres of wealth and population. Not only farm produce but rich harvests from the sea were, for lack of more suitable transport, shipped out from the many small industrious ports. Here was a hive of activity from which any potential railway would strive to benefit. Indeed, in years to come, the number and size of trains carrying fattened cattle from the East Neuk to markets in the industrial west was frequently considered worthy of comment. The traditional description of the Peninsula as 'a beggar's mantle fringed with gold' reflects upon these conditions.

The exact location of coastal settlements depended upon suitable sites for the construction of harbours. The narrow northern coastal strip with its gently shelving shores of sand and rock was unsuitable, so that apart from Newport, from where the short crossing to Angus could be made, traffic was concentrated entirely on Newburgh. In the east, from St Andrews to Fife Ness, a rocky coast and easterly exposure was unfavourable to the construction of harbours, but along the south coast secluded havens were plentiful.

By the time that grandiose railway schemes were being formulated during the 1845 'mania' four of the ports along the Forth—Anstruther, Kirkcaldy, Burntisland and Alloa—dominated seaborne trade to and from a wide hinterland. Of the four, Alloa was pre-eminent. Together with its branch ports of Stirling and Kincardine, total registered tonnage in 1842 was upwards of 19,000 tons. This figure was larger than that of any other port on the Firth excepting Leith, and even that port did not much exceed its rivals on the upper reaches.

At Alloa alone, the registered tonnage recorded was 9,662 tons. The significance of shipping here is a measure of that town's very early prosperity as an industrial centre. An early mineral railway dating from the eighteenth century brought coal from expanding workings on the Earl of Mar's estate for shipment from the port. There were also no fewer than six extensive woollen factories, two large distilleries and a glass-works—the latter extending over six acres. More than 80,000 barrels of ale were made annually at some eight breweries, much of it being exported to England, the Continent, the Americas and even Australia.

Ferries at Alloa and Kincardine provided access south of the river. That at Kincardine was considered to be under excellent management and decidedly the best on the Forth. Two steamboats plied the five minute crossing.

The following abstract about Kirkcaldy, written in 1843 for inclusion in the New Statistical Account, would just as equally have excited railway financiers with the prospect of a rewarding return on their outlay:—

The principal trade of the town is the manufacture of various types of linen, involving shipments of flax across the North Sea from the Baltic ports and the export of cloth to other parts of Britain besides oveseas. There are also the collateral branches of flax spinning, bleaching and machine making. The trade is carried on chiefly by eight factories employing 1,100 weavers.

15

Shipping registered at the port consists of 91 vessels of 8,911 tons. Two smacks ply regularly between London and Kirkcaldy and there are regular traders to Leith and by the Forth and Clyde Canal to Glasgow.

Daily coaches start from the town or pass through it to Aberdeen, Dundee, Perth, St. Andrews and Glasgow. The coach to Glasgow travels via Dunfermline to Falkirk, where it connected with boats on the Forth and Clyde Canal and more recently with the Edinburgh and Glasgow Railway. Steam vessels also ply on the Forth between Edinburgh, Kirkcaldy, Alloa and Stirling.

Clearly, any railway, especially one designed with a view to forming part of an integral East Coast route and also for securing a share of West Coast consignments, would have a very significant effect on this town's hitherto sea-based traffic pattern.

Unquestionably however, the greatest railway benefits were to be derived from acquiring a share in the lucrative trade clearly apparent to any traveller passing through Perth. The city's manufactures consisted principally of dyed-cotton goods, of which umbrella cloth was the staple. This commodity was mostly sent to London and Manchester besides other towns in Scotland.

Because of its location 22 miles up river from Dundee and the nature of the river bed, vessels of 150 tons, when deep laden, could proceed above the confluence of the River Earn to Perth only with difficulty. Until dredgers could prove effectual, many larger steam ships were obliged either to transfer their cargoes to and from lighters at Dundee or alternatively put in at Newburgh, from where goods could be taken by land.

Perth shippers, who thereby lost valuable time, could offer competing railways every prospect for a large traffic potential. In 1835 harbour records show that the quantity of seaborne coal was, from England, about 22,000 tons and from Scotland, some 11,500 tons. These tonnages were in total only slightly greater than the 27,114 tons of potatoes outward bound for the London market. Other exports comprised over 5,000 boxes of salmon, more than 40,000 quarters of various corns and a considerable quantity of timber and slates.

In the extreme north-east of the Peninsula four important

roads converged on the ferry at Newport. These included the principal turnpike road between Edinburgh and the north-east of Scotland.

For many years before 1822 there had been two public ferries to Dundee across the Tay—the principal at Woodhaven and another at Newport, about a mile further east. These ferries were small and inconvenient sailing boats. Upon the construction of a new turnpike road connecting Cupar with Newport, from where the crossing to Dundee was both shorter and more convenient, Newport succeeded Woodhaven as the principal place of resort. In 1821 a double or twin steamboat, such as those used on the American rivers, replaced as many as twenty-five smaller craft on the passage. Initially, this vessel plied alternatively from Dundee to Newport and Woodhaven, but as the latter was found to be inconvenient for passengers, calls were made only at Newport after 1822. During the following years new ferry harbours were built and traffic rapidly increased. An additional twin steamboat was obtained so as to afford an hourly passage from each side and, a large sail-boat, pinnace, and yawl were retained to provide additional accommodation when required.

The sizeable volume of traffic crossing the Tay to Dundee is indicated by the following return for 1834:—

Passengers	86,608	Cattle	4,598
Four wheeled carriages	268	Sheep	11,911
Gigs	578	Carts of goods	2,798
Horses	3,794	Barrels bulk of	
Carts	3,727	goods	3,375

It was not until 1805 that the first public conveyance was established through Fife with the introduction of a two-horse diligence which ran with 'much deliberation and leisure' between Newport and Pettycur, near Kinghorn. It travelled by way of the more circuitous route through Kennoway and apparently took the whole day about it. At Pettycur passengers were required to secure their own passage across the Forth and patiently await both the boatman's readiness and suitable weather.

17

In 1810, a four-horse coach named *The Union* and operated by Mr M'Nab, a Cupar hostler, began a through service via the Edinburgh suburb of Newhaven, across to Pettycur and thence over the Tay between Newport and Dundee. Until 1845 this coach provided the only direct public conveyance between the two cities and those intermediate towns situated east of the Great North Road linking Perth and the Queensferry. For some years it had been possible to sail direct from Edinburgh to Dundee on alternate days.

Mr M'Nab, in connection with his coach service, financed the construction of a low-water landing slip at Newhaven, and obtaining a licence established a regular ferry across the Forth by purchasing and manning sailing cutters. Other improvements were to follow upon this initial step. The establishment of steamboat services was only undertaken by existing Trustees when they found that, unless they did so, Mr M'Nab would readily oblige the public.

Because there was never sufficient traffic between Forfar and Perth to pay a coach, especially after the opening of the railway from Coupar Angus to Dundee, *The Defiance* coach from Aberdeen to Edinburgh, which hitherto ran via Forfar and Perth to Queensferry, was in March, 1845 re-routed at Forfar to Dundee and Kinghorn. This coach used a new pier opened at Granton in 1844 to accommodate a rapidly increasing ferry traffic. The pier at Granton harbour was 1,700 feet long and provided berths for no fewer than 10 steamers, some as large as 1,000 tons.

Although ferry services continued from Leith and Newhaven to Fife, especially Kirkcaldy, Granton traffic was concentrated first on Pettycur but very soon changed to the rapidly developing port at Burntisland. In June 1847, the Edinburgh and Northern Railway bought the Granton-Burntisland ferries, in readiness for its forthcoming services to the north. However, the main route north from Edinburgh continued to link Queensferry and Perth by way of Kinross. In 1841 the number of passengers who crossed at Queensferry averaged 228 each day, but often the total rose to over 450. It is reported that during the season of cattle trysts at Falkirk roads around the Ferry might be blocked both by day and night for as long as a week.

Prior to the opening of railway communications, three daily mail coaches between Perth and Edinburgh operated along the Great North Road, stopping for fresh horses at Kinross, whilst a fourth ran via Newburgh and Auchtermuchty to Pettycur. Although unsubstantiated, it is reasonable to imagine these coaches being frequently trapped in nineteenth century traffic bottlenecks.

Settlements in Fife are concentrated on the coast, few of any significance being located in the Peninsula's interior. Those that there were either acted as staging-points along the main highways or as supply bases for workers laboriously extracting mineral wealth, which had then to be carted to the coastal ports. By all accounts the roads were very busy. Of the parish of Cults, near Ladybank, the New Statistical Account states:—

> The quantity of lime sold annually exceeds 6,700 tons. About one-third of this quantity is shipped at Newburgh for Dundee and Perth, whence it is conveyed to Dunkeld, Crieff, Methven and many other places in Forfarshire and Perthshire. The lime quarries of Cults afford employment to a number of carters in conveying coals to the kilns and lime to the port of Newburgh. In the summer season, there are upwards of a hundred carters from this and neighbouring parishes regularly engaged in this occupation. The greater proportion of these are tenants of small farms, which, but for the carting of coal and lime, would not afford sufficient work for their horses.

English coal used in the north of Fife was brought to Newburgh by sea, chiefly from Newcastle and Sunderland; whilst Scottish coal was landed by coasting vessels from Dysart, Wemyss and Alloa. Considerable quantities were also conveyed in carts overland from Lochgelly, Balgonie and Balbirnie—distances of over twenty miles. As a return cargo, the English colliers loaded large quantities of planks and pit-props, cut from forests near Ladybank and Falkland. There was a lively trade and stir at the shore of Newburgh, for not only were large consignments of potatoes from Kinross and the surrounding district despatched for the London market, but vessels bound for Perth had often to wait here on the flow of tide, so giving their crews time ashore to visit alehouses—of which there were no fewer than 29.

Writing for the New Statistical Account as early as 1836, the Rev. L. Miller, minister of the adjoining parish of Abdie (formerly Lindores), comments:—

> It would greatly contribute to the comfort of the parish, could the necessary articles of coal and lime be procured at a more reasonable rate. Whether coals are bought at Newburgh shore, or sent for to the Balbirnie or other coal pits, they cost 10 shillings a single cart load. Therefore, a railway has been talked of from the New Inn to Newburgh, and I doubt not but in some future time this improvement may take place.

The New Inn is situated very close to Lochmuir Summit on the present railway.

In the same year, the minister of Cupar parish noted that the railway then in contemplation would be of great service to the town, in providing the means for carrying very essential coal supplies from the southern and western parts of the county at a more reasonable rate.

The economy before the nineteenth century had given rise to a fairly even spread of population throughout the Peninsula; that of the nineteenth century gave an overwhelming superiority to resource development and with it population growth in the west.[1]

By 1840, flax spinning, hitherto a widespread village occupation, had become almost entirely mechanised and was becoming concentrated in the larger centres, particularly Dunfermline and Kirkcaldy. The new mills attracted labour from outside the county and migration was important. Between 1801 and 1841 the populations of Fife, Clackmannan and Kinross increased by 56,700, raising the total to 168,000. Their continuing rapid rise gave railway developers every hope for high passenger revenues.

Changes in the fortune of domestic industry were accompanied by changes in the status of agriculture. Whilst some of the more remote parishes in the east and north-east

[1]See note, p. 22.

achieved their maximum populations early in the nineteenth century and were in decline by 1850, rural populations generally showed well-marked increases up to, and in some cases, beyond that date. Hence there would be good reason for including not insignificant wayside stations in the formulation of any viable railway plan.

The rapid growth of towns in the agriculturally less favoured west stimulated a demand for farm produce, which the 'New Statistical Account' describes as shipped particularly from the numerous small ports and harbours of the east. In the case of Dunfermline, it then had to be carted for as far as four miles inland. Direct access from loading sidings at inland rural stations to town distribution centres was another service which any potential railway could offer. When the railways were built, the carriage of farm produce by road fell immediately in all districts. So great was the fall that between 1846 and 1862 toll bar collections dropped by 40%.

Even before the turn of the century, there were indications of the potential reserves in what was to be one of Scotland's largest coalfields. Its limited exploitation could not, however, have been expanded much without an alternative form of transport far superior to the road system.

Coal from the Auchterderran coalfield, situated in the interior of Fife some eight miles from the Forth and fifteen from the Tay, was highly recommended by the Edinburgh Coal Committee to its city's inhabitants. Of the average annual output—upwards of 120,000 tons—it may be reckoned that no less than 110,000 tons had to be carted over very inferior roads to the nearest ports. Were a railway to be built, it was calculated that savings to Perth could amount to as much as 7 shillings per ton and to the Forth a probable reduction of 3 shillings. Indeed, it was reckoned that ten times the current output could be raised immediately if required as a consequence of railway conveyance.

Blackband ironstone had already been discovered throughout the coalfield, but the day when it would be extensively worked and furnaces established, with all the

21

associated increases in trade and population, also had to await the coming of better communications.

To the north of Markinch, the suggested main railway route would run for over five miles alongside an unbroken limestone outcrop at Forthar. Of a quality fully equal to that of Cults, its isolated situation had hitherto prevented it from being worked to any great extent.

Although these deposits were comparatively near the Forth, it is possible that practical reasons deterred the early nineteenth century coalmasters of the Dunfermline district from extending their wagonways north towards the lucrative interior.

The following chapter details the history and varied nature of these primitive railways, used almost exclusively to convey coals from the earliest workings down to the Forth.

* Strictly speaking, the division is between north-east and south-west. For geographical purposes the term 'east' has been taken to coincide with what is now the North East District of Fife Region. Both the former counties of Kinross and Clackmannan are included in the 'west'.

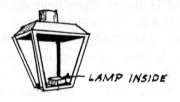

LAMP INSIDE

2

Early Colliery Wagonways

COLLIERY WAGONWAYS were built during the eighteenth century to supply ports on both sides of the Forth. As early as 1722 there existed a link from Tranent to Cockenzie in Haddingtonshire. Its example, with modifications, was soon copied north of the Firth.

The Bishop of Ossoray, when visiting Leven in 1760, remarked in his journal that he had encountered extensive coal pits in that town's vicinity and that wagon roads carried their coals some two miles downhill to the Firth. Whilst it is known that several such roads were being used about that time in Kirkland and other areas west of Leven, there is a regrettable lack of more detailed information.

Very much more detailed information is, however, available regarding two lengthy wagonway systems extending from Fordell and Halbeath, both near the village of Crossgates, down to St Davids Bay and the port of Inverkeithing. The Earl of Elgin, one of Fife's major landowners, was the proprietor of collieries situated to the north-west of Dunfermline and also owner of two harbours by the Forth at Charlestown and Limekilns. By the end of the eighteenth century a complexity of lines conveyed limestone from local quarries and coal a distance of over five miles to an impressive array of lime kilns at both ports.

In 1709 another noble colliery owner, John, the Earl of Mar, despatched the manager of his Alloa colliery to Newcastle where he inspected machinery for a potential wagonway. It was to be some sixty years later before this was laid.

The building of early Scottish wagonways was greatly influenced by earlier undertakings in the Tyneside and Shropshire coalfields. A most significant difference was reflected by the relative ease with which the Tyneside deposits could be reached using adits, whilst in Shropshire deeper workings were

23

necessary. On Tyneside, the colliery railways frequently ran straight out of the adits to staithes on the river banks and by comparison with Shropshire both gauge and wagon size were less restricted by the avoidance of deep underground running. Scottish colliery owners modelled their wagonways on one or other of these two English designs—or at least incorporated what was best in both. The large size wagons of up to 60 cwt. capacity used on the Fordell and Elgin lines early in the nineteenth century, together with track gauges of 4 feet 4 inches and 4 feet respectively, reflect Tyneside influence and contrast with the Alloa lines where a gauge of 3 feet 3 inches and 30 cwt. wagons were in contemporary use.

By far the most documented of the lines is that which eventually extended nearly six miles from St. Davids Harbour through the Fordell estate to the L.N.E.R. Dunfermline-Cowdenbeath line near the former Crossgates station. The extent of this documentation is due to the line's long history, no other early wagonway surviving in modified form until after the end of World War II. The development of the railway from its eighteenth century origins until closure in 1946 may be divided into three main stages.

The first stage, lasting to about 1833, is the history of a wooden wagonway. Coal from the earliest workings on the Fordell estate, having been laboriously mined, was carried by horse and pannier over a 'coalroad' to the road from Fordell Castle which led south to Hillend. Here the horses joined the highway between Aberdour and the port of Inverkeithing. When Sir Robert Henderson built a harbour at St. Davids in 1752, this route was changed and the 'coal-road' extended across the main highway and down to the new harbour—capable of taking vessels of up to 600 tons. St. Davids rapidly developed into a bustling harbour with houses built on the quay and South Pier and saltpans constructed on the west side. The harbour was enlarged and deepened in 1826 whilst in 1832 an extension of its South Pier by 150 feet made room for additional sidings, turntables and coal hoists.

The village of Fordell was built about 1800 on a site some

two miles north of the Castle. This self-contained village originally comprised two rows of cottages which survived until conversion into the railway's repair shops during the early 1860's.

Throughout the first half of the nineteenth century, all coal destined for export was carried down the railway to St. Davids, and the original wooden wagonway replaced by a new line laid with malleable iron rails. However, in 1853 a northward extension began, carrying coal over the short distance to the recently opened Edinburgh, Perth & Dundee Railway. This extension annually increased the output which it carried. Because more collieries were brought into operation, there was a continual increase in seaborne sales from St Davids. Here sales reached a peak between 1909 and 1913 with an annual average export of 81,761 tons. Shipments represented some 62% of total colliery output, compared with 95% of the total between 1835 and 1844. During World War II only 8.7% was shipped from St. Davids—the Admiralty being virtually the only customer. Immediately after the War, a plan was implemented whereby all coal from the more southern pits was taken north to the Alice Pit and from there despatched by L.N.E.R. standard wagons. On the 10 August 1946 a last shipment of coal, weighing 40 tons was brought down to St. Davids. Directly afterwards, the track and harbour fittings were removed, leaving only the section between Fordell workshops and the main railway at the Alice Pit.

An accompanying map illustrates the Fordell railway system. The wagonway was laid on the surface of the ground and single throughout. Gradients were severe—at Vantage it was 1 in 13 with the load, while at Hillend there were gradients against the load as steep as 1 in 90. It is estimated that at the end of the eighteenth century there were some 30 wagons in use. Each wagon required two horses and these were obtained under contract from neighbouring farms.

In 1833 operations commenced on the second stage of the railway's development. Whilst the northern part of the line from the pits to Fordell House remained unchanged, substantial

1 Map of the Fordell railway

MAP OF THE FORDELL RAILWAY

| FORDELL RAILWAY |
| WOODEN WAGGONWAY |
| L.C. LEVEL CROSSING |
| E.H. WHEEL INCLINE |

sections to the south were re-laid and re-aligned. The improved line incorporated two inclined planes at Colton and Fordell House. To assist wagons up from St. Davids and across the Inverkeithing road, an extra horse was stationed at Hillend. The Colton Incline was 332 yards long and had an overall gradient of 1 in 24. The Vantage Incline—1148 yards long—had a very similar gradient of 1 in 23.75. After inspection of the line by Robert Hawthorn of Newcastle in 1834 several modifications to the southern part were adopted. These included a cutting and tunnel under the Inverkeithing—Aberdour road at Hillend together with a third inclined plane, some 480 yards long with a gradient of 1 in 28. This incline extended almost to the South Pier at St. Davids. All three inclines were gravity operated—4 full wagons pulling up 4 empty ones. The new line adopted the same gauge as the original wagonway and throughout its 4.6 miles the gradient favoured the load. Sets of 4 wagons were hauled between inclines by two horses. Additionally, there were three horses at St. Davids and a similar number between the top of the Colton Incline and Lady Anne Pit. The new line coped with an annual average traffic of 50,000 tons—almost double the maximum capacity of the wooden wagonway. To carry this increased traffic, the workshops located first at St. Davids and then at Fordell, had by 1890 built no fewer than 180 wagons.

With the steady development of traffic, a decision on the use of steam locomotives could not be long delayed. The decision to obtain locomotives was made in 1867 and in preparation the line was re-laid with heavier rails and gradients considerably improved. The first engine, supplied by Messrs Hawthorn & Co. of Leith and aptly named *St David*, entered service on 2 April 1868. It is believed that this engine was an 0-4-0 tank with 11 inch outside cylinders and 3 feet 6 inch diameter wheels. A second locomotive—*St George*—was delivered from Henry Hughes & Co., Loughborough, in 1871. An 0-4-0 saddle tank with 12 inch diameter cylinders, this more powerful locomotive worked between the Fordell workshops, where new marshalling sidings had been installed, and St Davids, while the first engine was employed assembling wagons from the various pits. Both engines were scrapped about 1900.

When in 1880, the Alice Pit was sunk close to the main N.B.R. line plans were made to extend the wagonway from the William Pit across Moss Morran to the Alice Pit and thence round to the George Pit. Before the line could be completed in 1895, large quantities of brushwood had to be dumped on Moss Morran. The new line was laid with mixed gauge as were extensive sidings installed near the Alice Pit between 1900 and 1903.

Unlike the first two locomotives which were both delivered at St Davids, a third locomotive, the *Alice*, was delivered from its builders, Grant, Ritchie & Co. of Kilmarnock, to Crossgates. From here it was horse-drawn through the streets on a temporary track. The *Alice*, which was built in 1880, was also an 0-4-0 saddle tank and like its two companions was fitted only with a handbrake. All three engines had at both ends large wooden buffers suitable for both standard and Fordell wagons. Two more engines were later supplied by the Kilmarnock firm of Andrew Barclay & Sons Ltd. *Fordell* was purchased in 1901 and *Lord Hobart* in 1912. Both were equipped with steam brakes.

In 1946 there was a stock of some 190 wagons, all of a type designed by William Gofton in 1833. These springless, four-wheeled wagons, which opened at one end, were coupled by side chains placed level with the wooden buffers. Although the Fordell railway never carried fare-paying passengers, a private coach was used on the line by the Laird and his family. Built at the Fordell workshops about 1870, the coach was 11 feet long and 5 feet 6 inches wide. Two windows on either side were separated by a narrow centre door. Despite the use of four wagon wheels, the vehicle's bodywork was resplendently finished in polished mahogany with the family coat of arms on both sides. The coach was withdrawn about 1912 but remained in the workshops until 1945 when it was removed for use as a hut.

Less than two miles west of the Fordell railway, the Halbeath railway followed a parallel course from Halbeath, between Crossgates and Dunfermline down to Inverkeithing. The line was projected in 1781 by two English merchants in Amsterdam who became owners of Halbeath colliery. Opened in 1783 at a cost of £750 per mile including wagons, the railway comprised a single track with passing loops, known also as sidings or bye-stands, placed at intervals of 550 yards. Unlike the Fordell railway, which used sprags to brake the wagons, Halbeath wagons were equipped with beams of birch to pull behind as drags on gradients.

An indication of the comparative size and importance of these railways can be gained from the number of wagons operated. By the end of the eighteenth century the Fordell railway had about 30, while in 1795 the Halbeath railway had a mere 14. At the same time, it was common for colliery companies in north-eastern England to operate over 100 wagons.

In 1841 a junction was installed on the Halbeath railway at Guttergates giving what became known as the Townhill tramway access to the Townhill collieries just east of Dunfermline. In November 1848 the Edinburgh and Northern Railway was authorised to make a branch from near where it passed under the tramway to a point on the tramway some 300 yards to the north. It was also empowered to lay down an additional rail on the tramway from the junction of the branch to the Townhill Colliery and alter and improve the tramway so as to enable traffic to join the main railway. The same company also constructed a spur to connect with the Halbeath railway near Guttergates providing access to the Halbeath colliery. The Townhill tramway was extended westward to connect with the Elgin railway and Wellwood collieries probably in 1856 when the West of Fife Mineral Railway was built. Although by 1850 the Halbeath colliery had itself closed, the railway's branch to Townhill and Wellwood, with connections to various lime and freestone quarries, continued to operate. However in 1867 the Halbeath Company ceased coal shipments from Inverkeithing as better facilities were now provided at nearby Charlestown, served by the Elgin railway.

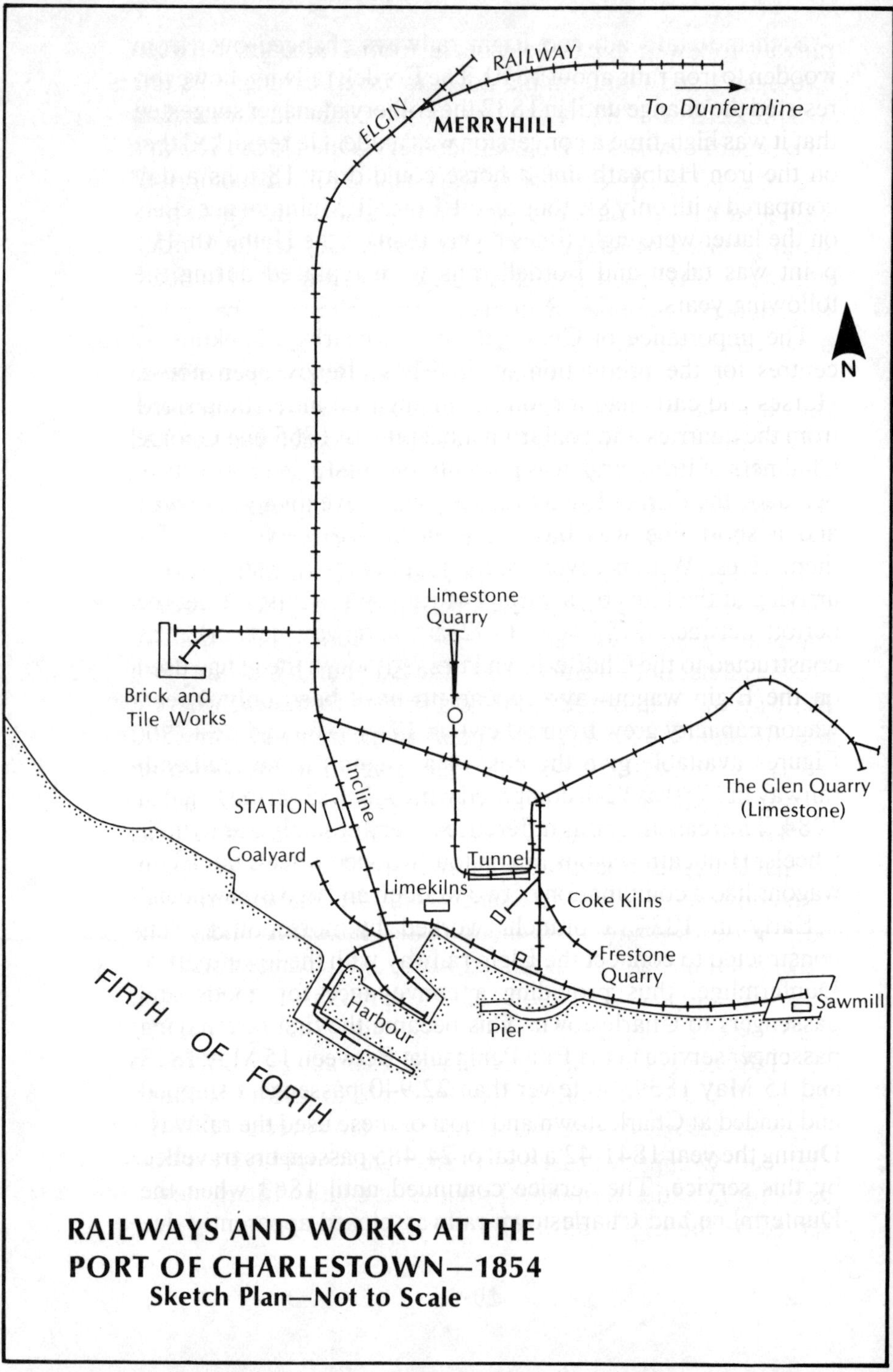

RAILWAY

ELGIN

MERRYHILL

To Dunfermline

N

Limestone
Quarry

Brick and
Tile Works

The Glen Quarry
(Limestone)

STATION

Incline

Coalyard

Tunnel

Limekilns

Coke Kilns

Frestone
Quarry

Sawmill

FIRTH OF FORTH

Harbour

Pier

**RAILWAYS AND WORKS AT THE
PORT OF CHARLESTOWN—1854
Sketch Plan—Not to Scale**

Both the Halbeath and Elgin railways changed over from wooden to iron rails about 1810. The Fordell railway, however, resisted the change until in 1832 the colliery manager suggested that it was high-time a conversion was made. He remarked that on the iron Halbeath line a horse could draw 18 tons a day compared with only 8½ tons on the Fordell. Maintenance costs on the latter were eight times higher than on the Halbeath. His point was taken and Fordell rails were replaced during the following years.

The importance of Charlestown and nearby Limekilns as centres for the production of lime has already been noted. Horses and carts had for long been engaged in fetching stone from the quarries and coal from local pits. In 1765 one George Chalmers of Edinburgh was partially successful in his efforts to persuade the Earl of Elgin to grant a wayleave for a wagonway and a short line was built at Limekilns to serve the kilns themselves. Within seven years supplies of limestone were arriving at the kilns by a variety of railways, whilst during the period between 1777 and 1792 a wagonway network was constructed to the Charlestown kilns. Although the gauge used on the Elgin wagonways appears to have been only 4 feet, wagon capacity grew from 50 cwt. in 1784 to 60 cwt. in 1796. Figures available give the cost of a wagon on the Halbeath railway in 1780 as £20, compared with only £13 on the Elgin in 1784. The reason for this difference is very possibly due to their wheels. Halbeath wagons ran on four wooden wheels but Elgin wagons had a combination of two wooden and two iron wheels!

Early in 1834 a branch, worked by horsepower, was constructed to connect the Elgin railway with the lower part of Dunfermline, thus providing a conveyance for goods and passengers to Charlestown. This became the first fare-paying passenger service in the Fife Peninsula. Between 15 May 1838 and 15 May 1839, no fewer than 22,940 passengers shipped and landed at Charlestown and most of these used the railway. During the year 1841-42 a total of 24,485 passengers travelled by this service. The service continued until 1863 when the Dunfermline and Charlestown railway closed apparently due

EARLY WOODEN WAGONWAYS
IN THE ALLOA AREA

TILLICOULTRY To Kinross

FURNACEBANK CLLY.

COLLYLAND ✕

DEVON CLLY.

SAUCHIE

FISHCROSS

Gartmore Dam.

NEW
SAUCHIE

Old Pit

PARKHEAD ✕

✕ JELLYHOLM

Old Pits

Old Pit

**CLACKMANNAN
ROAD**

ALLOA

Tunnel

GABERSTON

To Dunfermline

Harbour

Black Devon River

To Kincardine

Ferry

**CLACKMANNAN
(GOODS)**

L.M.S.R.

River Forth

Quarry

Old Pits

✕ PARK

Clackmannan Pier

KEY

—————— OLD COLLIERY WAGONWAYS	– – – – – L.N.E.R.
++++++++ OTHER MINERAL RAILWAYS	oo OLD COAL PITS

to diminished traffic. If the following account, which appeared in the *Fife Herald* during 1857, is unexaggerated then the closure must not have been entirely unexpected:—

> I went down to Charlestown in the omnibus by the Elgin Railway. We started at 2.25 pm. and after nearly three-quarters of an hour's hard riding by horse and partly by steam, we found ourselves about 300 yards from the Dunfermline station. It was a stand every other half minute, or a run back, or a shift of some kind, and when we made the brae head at Charlestown, there was the steamboat (from Edinburgh) and the little boat under full sail half way out of the port to meet it.

When John, Earl of Mar, opened a railway between his Alloa colliery and the harbour in 1768, it was a close copy of the Tranent and Shropshire lines with regard to gauge, wagon size and operating practices. The original track consisted of single rails of Scotch fir measuring 5 inches by 4 inches. By 1785 it was worn out and its renewal, using the double way, made it unique from other railways described in this chapter. Very broad sleepers having been laid, a rail of foreign fir measuring four inches square was pinned down to them. Then another rail of the same dimensions was laid over it and the whole well beat-up in good clay. On top of the upper rail was positioned a bar of malleable iron some 1¾ inches in breadth and ¾ inch thick. In a Report by Robert Bald, mining engineer to the Earl of Mar and later the Alloa Coal Company, it is stated that the original line enabled a horse to draw a 30 cwt wagon in place of a 6 cwt cart. The improved line allowed the horse to draw three 30 cwt wagons, whilst the substitution of cast iron rails in 1810 permitted trains of 8 or 10 one ton wagons.

With the opening of the Edinburgh and Northern Railway and the rapid development of vast coal deposits to its north, the important eighteenth century wagonways assumed a less significant role. Even had there been no major east-west railway to convey lengthy coal trains to the flourishing port of Burntisland, the early wagonways and small harbours would have been quite unsuited to accommodate the volume of traffic. Had circumstances warranted it, these lines might have been rebuilt and extended north, or alternatively, the deposits in Beath and Auchterderran could have lain undisturbed.

3

The Best of Schemes

AT a meeting of gentlemen held at Cupar on 13 October 1840, the following Motion was unanimously agreed to:—

> That the formation of a Railway from some point on the north shore of the Firth of Forth, by Cupar, to a point at or near to Ferry-Port-on-Craig on the Firth of Tay, on Levels to which Locomotive Steam Power could be advantageously applied, is not only a measure of great national importance but is also one which cannot fail to be productive of most important benefits to agriculture, and to proprietors of minerals upon the Line, but also to the commercial and manufacturing interests of Fifeshire and conterminous counties.

It is not, perhaps, altogether surprising that the Motion gave a special emphasis to agriculture, mineral working, and the general interests of the Fife Peninsula, since of the twenty-five gentlemen present no fewer than fifteen belonged to Cupar—the principal agricultural centre in Fife. Although the Provost and Town Clerk of Arbroath both attended together with two Directors of the Arbroath and Forfar Railway, there was no representation from either Edinburgh or Dundee. From its inception at this meeting, the Edinburgh and Northern Railway was to be chiefly financed by landed gentry residing near Cupar, who sought a better outlet for the produce of their estates. A close scrutiny of the Roll of Subscribers reveals an indifference to the railway amongst entrepreneurs in the two cities.

At the initial meeting it was resolved to appoint a Committee of nine, with power to add to their number, to expedite the raising of funds for obtaining all necessary Parliamentary Plans and to appoint engineers and agents.

The engineers, Messrs Grainger and Millar, carefully explored the country between the Forth and Tay to ascertain the best line which the railway should take, having regard to

34

both ease of construction and. proximity to local traffic potentials. The route, which under all circumstances they considered most suitable, is illustrated on the General Map. Before their appointment, it had been resolved to include a possible branch to Perth within the engineer's remit.

With reference to that part of the line by Kingskettle and Ladybank, it may be noted that an alternate route, passing to the south of Kingskettle and thence by way of Pitlessie, was also surveyed and Parliamentary Plans of it given.

From the terminus at Burntisland to the summit of the line near to the New Inn involved a rise of only 230 feet over a distance of 16¼ miles, and although not uniform, nowhere was the rate of climb to be steeper than 1 in 264. On that portion of line between the summit and the Tay—a distance of 20¾ miles, if the route by Ladybank were chosen, the steepest descent was to be at the rate of 30 feet per mile. The branch line to Perth would be about 16 miles in length and proceed by Collessie and Lindores Loch to Newburgh, and thence inland to Bridge of Earn.

The result of publishing the first Prospectus in April 1844 was that instead of deposits being paid on the whole 32,000 available shares, or even 24,000—the number corresponding to £600,000 or three-fourths of the capital of £800,000—there were actually paid deposits on not quite 12,000 shares. This was about half the sum required by the Standing Orders to be paid up before application could be made for an Act of Parliament. The Chairman, addressing a meeting held in Edinburgh on 26 July 1844, believed the opinion of all persons well-informed on the subject remained that the proposed scheme was one likely to be of the greatest utility to both its proprietors and the general public.

In these circumstances his own attention and that of others had been directed to a consideration of whether it was practicable, by modifications of the original plan, to secure the formation of the railway with substantially the same benefits but with a smaller capital.

The Chairman went on to recommend the issue of a new

Prospectus containing the following as the basis of a revised scheme:—

1. A line of railway from Burntisland to Kingskettle and thence by Newburgh to Perth, with one branch to Kirkcaldy Harbour and another, of about five miles length, diverging to Cupar.

2. That instead of crossing the Tay opposite to Dundee, communication with the north side of the river should be made at a point a little above Newburgh opposite the western end of Mugdrum Island. A swing or floating bridge would be formed over the navigable channel of the Tay, whilst a causeway on piles carried the line across the Island and that portion of the river lying to its north.

3. That communication with Dundee should be effected by means of an Agreement with the promoters of the Dundee and Perth Railway.

4. That the railway, except between Newburgh and Perth, should comprise only a single line of rails, although the company in their purchase of land would be able to have double tracks wherever the necessity arose.

The following is the Memorandum of the proposed Agreement with the Dundee and Perth Railway Company:—

1. As proposed by the promoters of the Dundee and Perth Railway, the expense of erecting and maintaining the bridge shall be defrayed equally by the two companies.

2. In like manner, the expense of forming the railway from the bridge at Mugdrum to Perth shall be defrayed by both companies in equal shares, each company using one of the line of rails for their own traffic from Perth to the bridge.

3. That the line from the point of crossing the Tay to Dundee shall be made by the Dundee and Perth Company and that the Edinburgh and Northern Company shall have permanent power to use the line to the Dundee terminus, at such rates of toll as shall be settled and agreed on before going to Parliament.

It was conceived that a sum of £500,000 would be sufficient capital, allowing £22,000 for contingencies, and as there was every reason to hope that subscribers to the original scheme would transfer their subscriptions, equalling £300,000, it followed that only a further £75,000 need be acquired before presentation of the Petition of the Bill. No difficulties were foreseen with regard to the raising of this sum, but it was agreed, that in the event of a second failure, the whole undertaking should be abandoned and all monies advanced returned. However, at a subsequent date, a Mr Hudson from York was prevailed upon to underwrite the issue if required.

Many of the subscribers living in the vicinity of Cupar considered that a railway from there to the Tay at Ferry-Port was so important to their locality as to warrant the organisation of a separate company for that part of the original line. The Edinburgh and Northern readily agreed to afford all reasonable facilities to the Cupar, Ferry-Port-on-Craig and Dundee Railway and gave assurances not to impose discriminatory charges upon any form of through traffic.

The Provisional Committee of the Edinburgh and Northern was most satisfied with the results of a searching investigation of the probable annual revenues which they might expect along the amended route viz:—

Through Passengers	£31,000
Local or Intermediate Distances	21,903
	52,903
Goods between the Ports of the Forth and Tay	6,250
Local Traffic, Farm Produce Etc.	4,687
Minerals	18,000
Carriages, Mails and Parcels	3,500
Livestock	2,000
	£87,340

In making the above estimate, the average rate allowed for passengers and all manner of goods was taken to be under 1½d per mile.

From the estimated revenue of £87,340 there would have to be deducted tolls payable to the Dundee and Perth Railway Co. and interest on money necessary for the purchase of rolling stock, in total say £7,000. If a further £30,000 was to be set aside for working expenses, this still left a sufficient sum to secure attractive dividends of 10% on capital.

Forced by opposition, both from the Admiralty and the Magistrates of Perth, into abandoning their plans for a bridge at Mugdrum, the Edinburgh and Northern's Provisional Committee now carefully reconsidered the expediency of extending the line from Cupar to Craighead or Ferryport. The Secretary was instructed to prepare immediately the draft of a report to be submitted to the shareholders recommending extensions of the line to Craighead and St Andrews, further north, and westward to Auchterderran and Dunfermline. New negotiations were to be commenced with the Dundee and Perth Company for a common junction in Perth at the mutual expense of the two companies.

The Edinburgh and Northern had also to work against time in proving that their plans were better than those of the Edinburgh and Perth Railway scheme—a very serious challenger. This opposing scheme was for a line from the Edinburgh and Glasgow Railway at Gogar to South Queensferry, and then from North Queensferry by Cowdenbeath, the east and (or) west side of Loch Leven to Glenfarg and Perth. Branches would diverge to Dunfermline and Kirkcaldy—the latter providing an alternative outlet for the Lochgelly coalfield, whose mineral wealth was intended to provide the mainstay of the Edinburgh and Northern's non-passenger revenue. When, in 1845, the Northern chose to apply to Parliament for its line to Perth and Cupar, leaving possible extensions to the Tay until some later Session, it did so in an endeavour to forestall the Queensferry company.

Passage of the Bill met with stormy opposition. Only after seventeen days of heated debate, involving thirty-three witnesses for the scheme and thirty-eight against, did the Bill pass through the Commons. In the House of Lords, further opposition gave rise to fears that the Bill might not be passed before the end of the Session intervened and necessitated a repetition of the whole procedure. So grave were these fears,

38

that the Edinburgh and Northern was prepared to accept a conditional offer by the Queensferry company to withdraw it's resistance, thereby allowing the Bill to get through. The conditions imposed, and accepted out of desperation, would have been extreme in their consequences for the Northern, who had undertaken not to fight the Bill for the Edinburgh and Perth's main line to Perth or its branch through the Lochgelly coalfield in the ensuing Session.

But for a stroke of good fortune, it is certain that the Edinburgh and Northern's scheme, now so mutilated as to be hardly a viable proposition, would have foundered completely as a result. The plans for the Queensferry scheme were, to that company's abhorrence, so badly prepared that they failed to pass Standing Orders and the Bill was rejected out of hand. It had been stipulated that the Edinburgh and Northern would be allowed to proceed with their plans for a branch from Thornton to Dunfermline, in the event of the Queensferry Bill failing, and for this they very quickly obtained Parliament's consent. There now remained only the question of how best to gain access to Dundee.

Eighteen forty-five was remarkable for the extraordinary wave of railway speculation throughout the British Isles. Hardly a week passed but newspapers throughout eastern Scotland carried lengthy public notices of proposed Bills to be laid before Parliament. Some of the schemes were to become highly successful undertakings, particularly the main line from Carlisle to Aberdeen. which initially involved the co-operation of no fewer than five companies. The majority of promotions, however, failed lamentably, although not always deservedly. Two such schemes offered Dundonians very suitable routes southwards to the Scottish central industrial belt and into England.

A Prospectus was issued by the Glasgow and Dundee Direct Railway, whose Provisional Committee was chaired by the Marquis of Breadalbane. Having secured a capital of £700,000, the railway was to be built from a station close to the docks at Dundee and cross over the Tay to Newport by

Rendell's steam or floating bridge for which an Act had already been passed. The railway would then follow 'the most direct line', meeting and joining, in its course, the Edinburgh and Perth line near to Kinross, from where it was planned to proceed by the Vale of Devon to a junction with the Scottish Central Railway at Stirling.

About the same time a Prospectus for a Glasgow and Dundee Junction Railway also appeared. Both companies, having planned almost identical routes, quickly combined into a single larger promotion, which included the following branches from the main line viz:—

1.   A branch from Tillicoultry to the pier at Alloa Ferry, from whose south side the line would continue to join the Scottish Central just north of Larbert.
2.   A branch diverging from the main line at Auchtermuchty and terminating in Newburgh.
3.   Branches from Luthrie and Letham to Cupar and a branch from Bogton, in the parish of Forgan, to St Andrews, with a connecting line from Guardbridge to Cupar.

Financial speculators might at the same time have considered the Scottish Direct Northern Junction Railway, planned to provide an alternative to the Edinburgh and Northern's Granton-Burntisland crossing. It was proposed to construct a branch from Linton, on the East Coast main line to North Berwick, from where there would be established a 'well-organised' steam ferry-boat service to Elie. A short line of about a mile from Elie harbour was to provide a connection with the projected East of Fife line, linking Leven with Anstruther and, by way of St Andrews, with Dundee. No problems were envisaged in the joint use of Rendell's steam bridge across the Tay. A comparison of distances showed that the route from the south via Elie would be twenty miles shorter than that via Granton. To quote from the Prospectus:—

> The great advantage of having the mail thus accelerated between the south and the whole north of Scotland cannot escape the vigilance of Her Majesty's Government, who it is believed some

years ago entertained the intention of establishing a mail packet ferry at this very station.

The Scottish Direct Northern Junction Railway was rivalled by the Fife Central Junction Railway, planned to leave the Cupar–Ferry-Port line about two miles east of Cupar and proceed directly south by way of Dura Den and Ceres to Largo, where it would form a junction with the East of Fife Railway. Assurances that through traffic from Dundee and the North East to London and the great English markets must pass along this line were expected to raise adequate capital to provide for construction of a lengthy tunnel under Largo Law.

Across in the north-west of the Peninsula, the Strathearn Junction Railway was being formed to construct a line from the Scottish Central, at or near Hilton, by way of Bridge of Earn, Abernethy and Newburgh to connect with the Glasgow and Dundee Junction Railway at the village of Luthrie. There would also be a branch to Newburgh harbour. This line was almost identical to that proposed by the Edinburgh and Northern, after it abandoned the original route near to the river planned to suit the low-level bridge at Mugdrum. Rather than enter a Parliamentary contest, which although it felt assured of winning would have entailed heavy expenditure, the Northern company entered into an agreement with the Strathearn Junction. By this agreement, the promoters were to abandon their proposed line upon receiving payment of their expenses and a number of shares in the former company.

In total, no fewer than sixteen schemes were lodged with the Sheriff Clerk of Fife during 1845!

Only the Edinburgh and Northern's Bill was to succeed in Parliament, although the provision of double-track throughout was stipulated. When it did succeed, the company was able to proceed rapidly with arrangements for access to Dundee. It purchased the Ferry-Port-on-Craig ferry and easily agreed terms with the Dundee and Arbroath Railway for accommodation of its traffic between Broughty Ferry and Dundee.

The price paid to obtain the right to convey traffic less than two miles from Hilton Junction through the tunnel under

Moncrieffe Hill and into Perth was far more exacting. As a pre-condition and gesture of their intention to confer harmoniously, the Scottish Central directors insisted that the Edinburgh and Northern must abandon an agreement with the promoters of the Perth and Crieff Railway, by which the latter was to be leased on a guarantee of four per cent with an equal division of profits, after deducting an allowance for working expenses. The line from Perth to Crieff was about twenty-three miles long and expected to secure an important Highland outlet for mineral traffic conveyed by through wagons from Fife. Furthermore, the Edinburgh and Northern were required to undertake never to establish a rail-connected ferry at Newport in opposition to that which had become the property of the Scottish Central Railway. These pre-conditions having been, of necessity, adhered to, it was agreed that the following terms should form the basis of the proposed agreement viz:—

1.   That the nominal distance charged upon the traffic of the Edinburgh and Northern Company should be limited to a minimum of four miles, subject to a right of the Board of Trade to increase the distance up to six miles.

2.   That the rate of tolls on such distance would not exceed the average of the Scottish Central company's charges.

Whilst the Edinburgh and Northern Railway had been fighting its battles in Fife, there had been serious rivalry between the larger companies to secure traffic between Edinburgh and the Forth. Despite opposition lines sponsored by the Edinburgh and Glasgow Company and the Caledonian Company, and the conflicting schemes of the Edinburgh and Leith Atmospheric and Edinburgh and Leith Direct lines to the east, it was the small independent Edinburgh, Leith and Granton Railway—a major portion of which had already been built—that was to emerge as victor.

Thereupon, the Edinburgh and Northern entered into an agreement with it. The leading points in the agreement were:—

1.   That there should be an amalgamation between the two companies at par.

2.   The cost of the line when completed was not to exceed the sum of £310,000.

3.   The Preference Stock holders of the Edinburgh, Leith and Granton Railway would still be entitled to five per cent—of which the amalgamated companies guaranteed four per cent and the postponed stock of the Edinburgh, Leith and Granton Railway the remaining one per cent.

The Edinburgh and Northern directors stressed that, although their line began on the opposite side of the Forth from Edinburgh, the city of Edinburgh must be considered as its starting point. It was therefore material that the possibility of being deprived of the full and uncontrolled command of a railway connection between the city and the Forth at Granton Pier should be guarded against.

The Edinburgh, Leith and Granton Railway had originated in 1836 as the Edinburgh, Leith and Newhaven Railway. However, time-wasting litigation and a shortage of funds forced alterations to the original plans. By an Act of 1 July 1839, the line to Leith was abandoned, whilst the main line took a more westerly course making straight for Trinity, where there was to be a terminus and a branch to Leith. The extension to Newhaven was dropped. During the course of prolonged preliminaries before construction commenced, the harbour at Granton was greatly improved and enlarged. Probably the greatest innovation was the substitution of irregular sailing ferries by regular steam ferries plying to Burntisland. Clearly these new Forth ferries would play a vital role in any East of Scotland railway system and a company monopolising a connection between Edinburgh and the ferry terminal could expect a most lucrative traffic. Without delay the Edinburgh, Leith and Newhaven Railway was restyled the Edinburgh, Leith and Granton Railway and by the same Act obtained an extension of the line to Granton Harbour.

The railway down to Granton had its chief station at the North Bridge in Edinburgh, where the Edinburgh and Glasgow and North British Railways also met. To have accommodation at such a station, where in all probability the Caledonian would also meet, and a connection with these important trunk routes, was clearly of the greatest importance to the success of the Edinburgh and Northern Railway. Had the line fallen into adverse hands, the latter company might never have succeeded in overcoming the inconvenience and loss which would certainly have been experienced.

Until an Act could be obtained authorising the agreed amalgamation, the line between Edinburgh and Granton was operated under the control of a Joint Committee.

Leith, which had for centuries been the southern terminus of the Broad Ferry, as distinct from Queensferry, had grown to become a thriving town by the early nineteenth century. In 1818 John Rennie submitted plans for docks at nearby Newhaven to accommodate 'overspill' shipping. Although his plans did not materialise, Newhaven did become the port for Forth sailings to such an extent that a new pier, the famous Chain Pier, was built. Described as a godsend, this pier became so popular that local people called it the 'baggage pier'. However, its prosperity was short-lived after the rise of Granton as a port.

An Act for the Duke of Buccleuch's Granton Harbour was obtained in 1837 and the first part of the pier was opened on Queen Victoria's Coronation Day, 28 June 1838. Edinburgh's worthy citizens were most impressed both with the Harbour and the road leading to it, and in particular with its eligible situation, the facilities it offered for accommodating passengers, goods, horses and carriages and the depth of water afforded vessels at all times. When work was finally completed in October 1844, the pier was 1,700 feet long and provided berths for no fewer than ten steamers, some of them as large as 1,000 tons.

Following lengthy negotiations by a Sub-Committee and the report of an independent engineer, the Edinburgh and Northern Railway bought the harbour of Burntisland together with the ferry between the two ports in June 1847—a month before the agreed amalgamation with the Edinburgh, Leith and Granton Railway received Parliamentary approval.

44

Even before acquisition of this final link, which gave an unimpeded right of way between three of Scotland's major cities, an attempt was made by the North British Railway to amalgamate with the Edinburgh and Northern, but met with rejection. The North British, confident that the Queensferry company would sooner rather than later get its line to Perth, insisted, against strong opposition on including that company in the amalgamation. Following the consequent resignation of John Learmonth, Chairman of the North British, Edinburgh and Northern and Edinburgh and Glasgow Railways, from the Board of the Northern company, the North British proceeded to back revived support for the Edinburgh and Perth Railway. Although the latter's Bill suffered a humiliating defeat when presented to Parliament in 1847, the Perth promoters reformed for another attempt in 1848, but by then the Northern had successfully consolidated its position.

Actual building of the railway north from Burntisland had commenced at Kinghorn in 1846. Construction of the double-track railway from Burntisland to Cupar and Lindores presented no major problems, save in the vicinities of Kinghorn and Lochmuir. Although only 242 yards long, Kinghorn Tunnel, with its reverse curves, still requires a permanent way slow, whilst the retaining wall next to the track leading up from Burntisland to the tunnel mouth frequently gave cause for concern during spells of heavy rain. Due to drainage problems at Lochmuir summit, the contractors were forced to lay almost a thousand yards of rail over several layers of turf and brushwood in order to provide a secure track bed.

Before the Edinburgh and Northern line could be extended to Perth, it was necessary for Scottish Central contractors to complete a 1,180 yard tunnel under Moncrieffe Hill and the General Terminus station, which with adjoining workshops covered 25-30 acres.

Towards the end of 1845 the Sub-Committee appointed to enter into Contracts for Engines and Carriages reported that they had contracted with Messrs R. & W. Hawthorn of

Newcastle for a supply of Locomotive Engines—16 in number, of the following descriptions and prices viz:—

3	Light Passenger Engines at the price of £1,750 each........	£5,250
7	Coupled Passenger Engines at the price of £1,750 each........	£12,250
6	Heavy Goods Engines at the price of £1,750 each........	£10,500
16		£28,000

The tenders for these at the following prices:—

3	Tenders at £375 each	£1,125
13	Tenders at £360 each	£4,680
16	Amount of Contract	£33,805

Eight of the engines and tenders were to be delivered at Pettycur Pier, connected to the main line by a short ascending branch west of Kinghorn, on or before 16 May 1847. An additional engine and tender was to be supplied every subsequent month.

The same Sub-Committee, having considered the quantity of carriages which it would be advisable to contract for, recommended the following:—

16	First Class Carriages at £400 each	£6,400
2	Coupe Carriages at £450 each	£900
24	Second Class Carriages at £225 each	£5,400
30	Third Class Carriages at £190 each.........	£5,700
72		£18,400

Prices were based on an Estimate obtained from Messrs Russell and Macnee, coach-builders, Edinburgh.

Each alternate carriage, except the coupees, was to have brakes. It was recommended that the Second Class carriages should have plate glass put into the quarter sides at an additional cost of £10 each and that the Third Class carriages, designed frequently with only one door on each side, should preferably have two on each side, despite an additional £5 to the estimated cost of each.

The carriages were to be built so as to accommodate the usual numbers:—

1st Class	18 Passengers
Coupe	18 Passengers
2nd Class	24 Passengers
3rd Class	36 Passengers

It was intended that the design and specification of the carriages would be the same as for those currently being built for the North British Railway—a reminder that the Chairman of this Sub-Committee was John Learmonth, then still Chairman of both the Edinburgh and Northern and North British Railways.

The first class carriages, consisting of three stage-coach bodies mounted on a single frame, were to seat six passengers in each of three compartments, whilst Second Class carriages would have box-shaped bodies accommodating eight passengers in each compartment. Third Class passengers were to be offered covered carriages with glass in the three side windows and two doors along each side. Seating was provided on wooden benches round the sides and ends thus affording standing space in the middle for the majority of the carriage's maximum capacity. All the carriages were to be four wheelers with an overall length of about nineteen feet.

Tenders for the following non-passenger vehicles were accepted at a meeting of the Directors held on 23 December 1846:—

40 Goods Vans at £80.50 each by Mr Landale, Kirkcaldy

15 Horse Boxes at £108.80 each by Mr W. McGillivray, Glasgow

16 Carriage Trucks at £79 each by Mr T. Barker, Perth

10 Passenger Luggage Vans at £83 each by J. Henderson & Son, Kinghorn

At the same meeting it was agreed to accept a tender for ten water cranes for various stations to be supplied by Messrs Blackie & Sons of Edinburgh at £65 each.

On 16 July 1847, the Sub-Committee on Appointment of Officers convened to consider applications in readiness for opening of the line. The style of the appointments, their remuneration and securities, where required, give some idea of relative responsibilities.

	Location	Annual Remuneration	Security Required
		£	£
I — *Goods Department*			
Manager	Edinburgh	250.00	500.00
Sub Goods Manager	Burntisland	120.00	
First Guard		54.60 +	
First Guard		54.60 +	
Second Guard		46.80 +	
Second Guard		46.80 +	
Goods Porter	Burntisland	46.80 +	
Goods Porter	Burntisland	46.80 +	
Goods Porter	Burntisland	41.60 +	
Goods Porter	Burntisland	41.60 +	
Goods Porter	Granton	46.80 +	
Goods Porter	Granton	41.60 +	
Goods Porter	Granton	36.40 +	
Weigher	Burntisland	46.80 +	
Weigher	Granton	46.80 +	
Clerk	Burntisland	60.00	
Clerk	Granton	60.00	
Collecting & Canvassing Clerk	Edinburgh	80.00	200.00
Delivering & Receiving Clerk	Edinburgh	80.00	
Book-Keeper	Edinburgh	100.00	200.00
Clerk	Edinburgh	60.00	

II — *Passenger Department*

Superintendent	Burntisland	120.00	300.00
1st Class Booking Clerk	Burntisland	20.00	50.00
2nd & 3rd Class Booking Clerk	Burntisland	70.00	100.00
1st Porter	Burntisland	46.80 +	
7 other Porters (to begin)	Burntisland each	41.60 +	
Pointsman	Burntisland	57.20 +	
4 First Guards	Burntisland each	62.40 +	
4 Second Guards	Burntisland each	57.20 +	
Station Keeper	Collessie	50.00	80.00
Porter	Collessie	41.60 +	

III — *Locomotive Department*

Superintendent	Edinburgh	170.00	
Assistant Superintendent	Edinburgh	100.00	
Assistant Superintendent	Ladybank	120.00	
Foreman	Burntisland	120.00	
Wrights & Coach Building Foreman	Burntisland	100.00	
8 Enginemen		each 106.00 +	
8 Firemen		each 52.00 +	
Storekeeper		60.00	80.00
Return Clerk		90.00	200.00

+ Denotes workers paid weekly.

The overall number employed was 103 and their total annual remuneration amounted to £6,556.

Having acquired its rolling stock, engaged recommendable employees and completed locomotive works at Burntisland and Ladybank, the railway was in a state of readiness for its grand opening day.

4

Running the Edinburgh, Perth & Dundee

BY THE MORNING of 17 September 1847, all but the remains of a slow moving depression, with an associated belt of heavy rain, had moved clear of east central Scotland and out into the North Sea. There were still a few heavy showers, interspersed by warm sunny periods, whilst two trains made preparations to depart from Burntisland. The first train[1] had journeyed down from Cupar, stopping on its way, to uplift those invited to the grand opening banquet. Waiting, already entrained, at Burntisland were a great number of guests, who had crossed by the Granton Ferry from Edinburgh. Both trains then left to run non-stop to Cupar.

As the trains, separated by only a short time interval, climbed away round the bay and uphill towards Kinghorn, puffs of white smoke floated up towards a clearing sky. From their carriages, the occupants might well have marvelled at the panoramic view across the Forth—Edinburgh Castle and Arthur's Seat the most prominent landmarks. North Berwick Law and the Bass Rock could also be discerned from the dark bank of cloud, which met the distant coastline on the horizon. Schooners, barques and many smaller vessels were plying the waters of the Firth or lying at anchor in Leith Roads.

At each village and town through which the trains were to pass, large crowds had gathered and flags were displayed in every quarter.[2] As they came into view, hearty cheers were raised by both young and old. Church bells rang out and with

[1] The first train, driven by Mr Grainger, the engineer of the line, consisted of twenty carriages and moved off at about twenty past twelve.

[2] On account of their great weight and a prudence connected with the multitude of spectators, the trains moved at a slow speed, requiring nearly one hour and 25 minutes to reach Cupar. . . .

the sound of music gave expression to the great joy felt by so many.

Immediately on arrival at Cupar, the guests, who numbered over 600, entered the banqueting pavilion, erected close to the station, and by all accounts fitted out in the most tasteful manner possible. After a sumptuous luncheon, with unlimited allowances of champagne, speeches expressing approval and gratitude were given. At four, the company broke up, returning southwards in two trains, one calling at all stations, whilst the other went non-stop to Burntisland.

With effect from Monday, 20 September, four daily trains each way between Burntisland and Cupar provided through connections between Edinburgh and Dundee. Departures from Edinburgh were at 7.00 and 10.30 in the forenoon and at 1.45 and 4.45 in the afternoon.

Leaving the gloom of Edinburgh's Canal Street Station, which stood at right angles to the North Bridge Station of the Edinburgh and Glasgow Railway, the passengers' engine-less train was let down a 1 in 27 gradient through the 1,052 yard long Scotland Street tunnel, its speed regulated by special brake trucks with brakemen seated on their roofs.

At the lower end of the tunnel, an engine was attached at Scotland Street Station to haul the train to Granton. Trains ascending to the terminus were hauled up the incline by a wire rope, operated by a stationary steam engine.

From Granton, the connecting ferry was due to sail for Burntisland 20 minutes after the Edinburgh departure time. Forty minutes were allowed for a favourable crossing and transfer to the Cupar train. The journey time by this train to Cupar was one and a quarter hours. Passengers, who had left Edinburgh on the 7.00 am. train and were continuing their journey by coach and ferry to Dundee, could expect to take a further one and a half hours. For those who travelled by later trains, an extra fifteen minutes were scheduled. From its outset, the Edinburgh and Northern had succeeded in bringing Dundee to within four hours travel from the Scottish capital. Leaving Edinburgh by the 7.00 am. train, a businessman could now have 5¼ hours in Dundee, before returning by the last connecting coach, which left that city as early as 4.00 pm. His Dundonian counterpart might prolong his business by an additional half hour.

There would appear to have been a certain degree of conflict between national and more familiar local views regarding the quality of passenger comforts. *The Railway and Shipping Journal*, in its October 1847 issue, made the following favourable observations:—

> The First Class carriages are of the most modern description; they are roomy and high roofed and from the smoothness with which they proceed we should say they are constructed on the best principles. The Third Class carriages are likewise comfortable; and being covered and well lit and ventilated put the passengers therein almost on a footing with the First Class, setting aside the mere gentility pertaining to the latter.
>
> What we were most delighted with, however, is the Second Class carriages. These are in every respect equal to the First Class ones, with the mere exception of side stuffing within. The seats are cushioned, the door windows are of plate-glass and there are panel windows of the same quality as well. The Directors are well entitled to commendation for this great improvement.
>
> Along with every train there is sent a luggage van of a new and improved description. It is half covered and half open, and on the latter part a porter stands and arranges luggage destined for the successive stations towards which the train is approaching.

An Editorial, published in the *Fife Herald* on 3 October 1850 and entitled 'Fake Economy on our Railway Line', gives a fascinating if somewhat sardonic glimpse of the times. It states:—

> The Directors evidently expect every Third Class passenger shall bring his own candle to light him on his way at night, for every train consists of two wise carriages that have their lamps trimmed and burning and two foolish carriages that have lamps with no oil in them. Forgetfulness or carelessness is not the cause, for the railway servants assure travellers the Company cannot afford the least illumination and that the pennyworth of oil needed would consume all the dividends so earnestly looked for. The only conceivable motive which the Directors can have is to force travellers into First or Second Class carriages.

This paragraph hints that all trains were of a standard composition.

For providing passengers on the new railway with the most comfortable ferry crossing possible, the E. & N. acquired improved passenger boats to be in readiness on both the Forth and Tay. When the railway opened, the Company possessed two wooden and five iron paddle steamers, built between 1834 and 1847 and varying in gross tonnage from 76 to 210 tons. One was disposed of in 1851, whilst the others had saloons fitted during the same decade. The following article appeared in the *Fife Herald* of 17 July 1851:—

> A very elegant and pleasant improvement has been made in one of the E.P. & D.'s steamers plying between Granton and Burntisland. The vessel, "The Express", has had an extension fitted to her former cabin accommodation below, and this serves all the purposes of an awning from the storm, while at the same time it grants a beautiful promenade above equal to what is obtainable on the poop of a man-of-war. This apartment is covered all around with plate glass. It is about 20 feet broad and 30 feet long and gives accommodation to many more passengers than the vessel formerly carried.

The railway from Ladybank to Perth had, as yet, to be completed and passengers transferred to coaches at a temporary station near Lindores Loch. Only the first and last of the four trains between Burntisland and Cupar had Perth connections. Journey times between Edinburgh, Lindores and Perth were the same as to Cupar and Dundee, so day return journeys with similar stop-over durations could be made.

Coaches ran to and from the towns of Auchtermuchty and Falkland to connect with trains at Falkland Road and from Leslie to Markinch. Although there was as yet no Sunday service on the railway, ferry-boats between Burntisland and Granton sailed according to their pre-railway timetable.

A revised timetable was published only a week after the railway opened. Whilst the four Dundee arrival and departure times remained unchanged, journey times on the Cupar-Dundee section were increased by fifteen minutes and Edinburgh departures and arrivals adjusted accordingly. The service to Perth was improved to provide connections with all Edinburgh trains and a new train introduced starting from

Dysart at 7.50 am. to connect with the 8.15 sailing from Burntisland. The number of ferry sailings remained ten in each direction.

Coach services between Cupar and the Tay ferry were abandoned as soon as the line to Ferry-Port-on-Craig was completed in May, 1848. A timetable which came into use on 23 May 1848, shows that five trains now ran daily between Burntisland and Ferry-Port, reducing the fastest Edinburgh-Dundee journey time to 2 hours 45 minutes and lowering the average time to a little over 3 hours. Whilst the last departure from Edinburgh to Dundee was brought forward from 4.30 to 4.15 pm., that from Dundee, originally at 4.00 pm. was deferred until 6.00 pm. The line from Ladybank to Perth had been extended as far as Abernethy Road and handled 6 passenger trains daily. One northbound and two southbound trains now ran independently to and from Burntisland. Although departure from Abernethy was 1¼ hours after the coach had left Perth, the through journey from Perth to Edinburgh could be accomplished in exactly 3 hours. It could even be made by an overnight service which, leaving Perth at 1.22 am., met the 4.07 am. crossing from Burntisland and arrived in Edinburgh an hour later.

The railway through Fife was not the first railway to reach Perth from the south. The Scottish Central Railway was opened throughout its entire length between Greenhill Junction and Perth on Monday, 22 May 1848. A temporary wooden station was used at Perth until the extensive stone built General Terminus, then under construction, was completed. The initial S.C.R. timetable shows two morning and two afternoon trains with carriages from Perth for both Edinburgh and Glasgow. By 8 June, arrangements were announced for conveying cattle, horses and carriages between Perth, Stirling and intermediate stations to Edinburgh and Glasgow *without* change of truck. Dealers were required to give one day's notice of their numbers. With effect from 1 July, an additional passenger train ran between Perth and Edinburgh/Glasgow in both directions.

Thus, when the Edinburgh and Northern Railway was

opened throughout by the completion of a single track from Abernethy to Hilton Junction on Tuesday, 18 July 1848, it was in the position of having to improve the service already established for through traffic to Edinburgh. Indeed, barely ten days after its opening, it was seen to be outdoing all former tempting inducements to travellers, by offering a return visit to Edinburgh on Saturday, 29 July, at half the usual fare, which charge included admission to the Zoological Gardens and Castle. The train was advertised to depart from Perth at 7.00 am. and arrive in the Capital at 9.30. The return journey commenced at 6.00 pm. For tickets taken out before 2.00 pm. on the previous day, the fares charged were:—

1st Class 8/6; 2nd Class 6/- and 3rd Class 4/-

After 2.00 pm. on Friday, fares were increased by 1/-, 9d, and 6d respectively.

Normal single fares between Perth or Dundee and Edinburgh were:—

1st Class	*2nd Class*	*3rd Class*	*4th Class*
8/6	6/-	4/-	3/9

First and Second Class passengers travelling a distance exceeding 12 miles could purchase return tickets for less than two single fares. The savings averaged 20% on First Class and 18% on Second Class rates. Third Class return tickets were also available between Edinburgh, Kirkcaldy, Dysart and Dundee only.

After 1 August, return fares between Edinburgh and Perth were reduced to 12/9 for First Class and 8/9 for Second Class. To help retain passengers, the Scottish Central, which offered no Fourth Class accommodation, was obliged to meet this reduction.

Table 1 shows the fares applicable at 10 August 1848:

TABLE 1

Perth-Edinburgh

Single Fares

	1st Class	*2nd Class*	*3rd Class*	*4th Class*
By E. & N.	8/6	6/-	4/-	3/9
By S.C.R.	10/6 (12/-)	7/6 (8/6)	5/- (5/9)	—

Fares in brackets were those charged by the S.C.R. on 1 July.

The S.C.R. maintained higher rates from intermediate stations, where passengers could not take advantage of the E. & N. The fare from Greenloaning to Edinburgh, for example, remained at 4/5, so Perth passengers were carried a distance of 22 miles to Greenloaning for 7d!

The Edinburgh and Northern also provided a more frequent service and faster journey times:—

TABLE 2

Comparitive Timetables—7 August 1848

By E. & N.		By S.C.R.	
Perth Dep.	*Edinburgh Arr.*	*Perth Dep.*	*Edinburgh Arr.*
2.10 am	*5.07 am*	*6.00 am*	*9.20 am*
6.30	*9.05*	*9.00*	*11.30*
9.40	*12.10 pm*	*11.30*	*2.20 pm*
11.15	*1.55*	*2.30 pm*	*6.00*
1.30 pm	*3.45*	*5.30*	*9.45*
3.30	*6.05*		
6.30	*8.50*		

Edinburgh Dep.	*Perth Arr.*	*Edinburgh Dep.*	*Perth Arr.*
7.00 am	9.15 am	7.00 am	11.00 am
8.17	11.10	10.00	12.50 pm
10.00	12.15 pm	11.00	2.35
11.45	2.00	2.00 pm	6.00
2.40 pm	4.55	5.30	9.00
4.15	6.55		
8.17	11.10		

Undoubtedly, many Perth-Edinburgh passengers would choose Scottish Central trains to avoid the six mile Burntisland-Granton sea passage and the discomfort of having to change into carriages with 'cold seats'.

Equally important in attracting passengers was the way in which the above two companies' trains provided connections at Perth. An examination of a contemporary Scottish Midland Junction Railway timetable shows that of three trains from Perth to Forfar, the E. & N. could provide connections for two trains and the S.C.R. for one. In the opposite direction, both companies could provide two connections, but by the S.C.R. there was over an hour to wait in both cases.

When the Dundee to Perth Railway was extended from its temporary terminus at Barnhill, Perth, over a newly completed viaduct across the River Tay, it became possible to dispense with a circuitous omnibus journey and inform Dundonians of the following attractive alternate route to Edinburgh:—

DUNDEE AND EDINBURGH

Additional Accommodation, Morning Train and Reduced Fares to Edinburgh via Perth and Stirling

---

NO FERRIES OR CHANGE OF CARRIAGE

Notice—Passengers are booked in Edinburgh for this route at the Edinburgh and Glasgow Railway Station, Waverley Bridge.

FARES BETWIXT DUNDEE AND EDINBURGH

First Class	Second Class	Third Class	Fourth Class
6/6	5/3	3/11	3/3

Trains leave the Dundee and Perth Railway Station, South Union Street, Dundee:—

	am.	am.	Noon.	pm.
At	6.00	8.15	12.00	5.53
Arrive Edinburgh	10.15	11.40	2.50	9.30

Trains leave the Edinburgh and Glasgow Railway Station, Waverley Bridge, Edinburgh:—

	am.	pm.	pm.
At	7.30	12.25	4.00
Arrive Dundee	10.30	4.08	7.30

Dundee and Perth Railway Office, Yeaman Shore, Dundee, 11th February, 1851

Although the distance by this route is an extra 20 miles, the above quoted fares are substantially lower than those charged by the S.C.R. between Perth and Edinburgh in August 1848. An internal report published in 1964 states:—

> In the course of our examination, we agreed to recommend the withdrawal of the through CK[1] for Edinburgh conveyed on the 7.45 am. and 12 noon trains Dundee to Glasow (Buchanan Street). Records show these are seldom used from either Dundee or Perth, passengers preferring to travel by the direct services via Fife. The two vehicles involved are received empty at Dundee from Perth.
>
> As from 22nd March 1964, the CK on the 12 noon train has been withdrawn. We recommend that consideration be given to the withdrawal of the CK on the 7.45 am train.

This withdrawal took place shortly afterwards and so ended the last trace of competition for Dundee-Edinburgh passenger traffic.

The Edinburgh and Northern's branch from Thornton to Dunfermline was opened as far as Crossgates early in September 1848. Passengers were conveyed to and from Dunfermline by coach. Of the four passenger trains arriving at Crossgates, two provided connections from Edinburgh and three connections from Dundee and Perth. Because Dunfermline is situated close to the Queensferry Passage and the new railway link with Burntisland was very circuitous, Edinburgh passenger traffic was inevitably minimal. Even passengers from Kinross preferred to travel throughout by coach, rather than use a special coach service connecting with trains at Cowdenbeath.

Two goods train services (one in the very early morning and the other at lunch-time) operated daily in both directions between Edinburgh and the northern terminals. This initial service was augmented from 13 September 1848 by an early morning service to and from Crossgates (later Dunfermline) and an evening departure from Dundee. On 28 February 1850, it was intimated that Fourth Class passengers would be conveyed to and from all the stations in Fife and the Northern

---

[1] CK denotes a carriage with first and second class accommodation.

Section of the line (except the Dunfermline branch) at a cheap rate:

By the Goods Trains leaving Burntisland at 11.30 a.m.
       arriving Perth about   4.30 p.m.
       and Dundee about   7.30 p.m.

And leaving Perth at   12.30 p.m.
  and Dundee at   9.05 a.m.
  to arrive at Burntisland about   3.30 p.m.

The first accidents involving personal injury to passengers occurred during October 1848. One resulted from neglect on the part of the crew of a train approaching the station at the Tay terminus. For some reason, the brakes were not applied in time and the train ran with great force against the end of the platform. Several passengers received wounds to the head and face. The second accident, after which two passengers later died, happened about a mile south of Bridge of Earn Station. It involved the 7.00 a.m. train from Edinburgh, which was particularly busy on account of the Perth cattle and sheep fair. Apparently, the flange of one of the engine's wheels gave way, causing it to derail and run down the embankment. Fortunately, the couplings of the engine snapped, so that its tender and carriages remained on the rails. Several passengers were hurt, especially four women and a man, who for want of accommodation in the carriages, were obliged to travel in an open truck immediately behind the tender. In addition to abrasions and concussion, these unfortunate individuals were very badly scalded by escaping steam.

By December 1848, the number of trains between Edinburgh, Perth and Dundee had been reduced from seven to five in both directions. Except for relatively minor adjustments to their timings, the service remained unaltered throughout 1849. For the first time, Sunday services were introduced, with a morning and afternoon train in each direction between Burntisland and the Tay.

The volume of freight handled at Fife ports had been steadily growing since the railway opened. Unfortunately, it had to be removed from trains at Burntisland and Ferry-Port and transferred to the conventional ferries. These transhipments were costly, timely, and frequently caused damage to goods. A schedule of ferry services between Burntisland and Granton, effective on and after 1 January 1849, shows four passengers only sailings and five passenger and goods boat sailings in each direction.

The construction of more adequate harbours at both Broughty Ferry and Tayport had been opposed by Dundee shipowners, who feared that smoke from the ferries might obscure the Tayport lights to inward bound ships or that there might be confusion with the ferry lights. At Broughty, no structure was permitted to project into the estuary from the high water mark at the Castle and this clause in the Harbour Act was very significant in determining the capacity of the railway harbour. In 1848, the Edinburgh and Northern acquired their first steamer for this passage—the 269 ton *'Express'*, an iron paddle ship which was to work the crossing for thirty one years. Although the Dundee and Arbroath Railway had been opened in 1838, most of the goods traffic was shipped by a privately operated service direct from Dundee to Ferry-Port, so saving extra transhipments.

With existing shortcomings in mind and aspirations of increased traffic, arising from the pending completion of the railway to Aberdeen, Thomas Bouch, the company's Manager and Engineer, placed orders for two train ferries—the first of their kind in Europe. Whilst awaiting their completion, successful negotiations enabled publication of the following announcement on 27 September 1849:—

'The Edinburgh, Perth and Dundee Railway give note that from the 28th current, they will DISCONTINUE their conveyance for goods to and from their various stations by the Forth and Clyde Canal, but to ensure greater despatch and to prevent change of trucks, all goods for Glasgow, Liverpool, Manchester, Birmingham and other west coast towns will be forwarded daily from Hilton Junction via the Scottish Central Railway.'

Simultaneously, The Forth and Clyde Canal Company

intimated an improved service by their tug packets between Glasgow and Kirkcaldy for the accommodation of the Glasgow and Fife trade.

The 'floating railway' between Burntisland and Granton was the concept of Thomas Bouch, who was later to be responsible for designing the ill-fated Tay Bridge. In order to load and unload wagons, masonry inclines or slips were constructed alongside both piers. Upon each incline was placed a heavy platform, some 61 feet long and 21 feet broad, with four malleable iron girders attached to the front. These girders, 35 feet long, spanned the distance from the platform to the vessel, and afforded an adequate depth of water for the keel of the vessel to clear the surface of the slip. They could be raised or lowered by means of winches—on either side of an 18 foot high staging erected across the platform. The entire platform rested on 16 wheels and could be moved up or down the slip to suit tide levels, by means of a small stationary steam engine, which was also used to move wagons on and off the ferries.

The first ferry, named *Leviathan*, was a double-ended vessel of 389 tons with a speed of 5 knots. Her train deck had three tracks, capable of accommodating up to 34 four-wheeled wagons. *Leviathan* entered service in February 1850 and made four or five return trips across the Forth every day. Average time for a single trip, including loading and unloading an average of 21 wagons, was 56 minutes. During her first ten years in service, over 75,000 wagons were carried every year.

A second ferry, also built on Clydeside by Robert Napier & Co., of Govan, commenced crossing the Tay estuary between Ferry-Port and Broughty Ferry on 28 March 1851. Named the *Robert Napier*, this single-ended ferry, with accommodation for 18 wagons on two tracks, made up to seven round trips each day, carrying approximately 56,000 wagons annually. Its inaugural sailing coincided with the opening of a new harbour at Tayport (as Ferry-Port had come to be known) and was the only occasion when occupied passenger carriages are known to have been ferried by either of these vessels.

Workmen were still completing installations when the

official party toured the harbour. This was because some three months earlier the principal part of the coffer dam had been breached by an unusually high tide, which swept away some 40 feet of the pier itself, including the rounded pierhead intended for a large turntable. The visitors were able to admire the spacious new basin—600 feet in length and 300 feet broad with an entrance lock 85 feet in width. A staith, similar to those on the Tyne, was in the course of erection and already in working order was a tipping cradle, by which a vessel could be loaded with coal in a very brief space of time. It was particularly hoped that boats, leaving Dundee in ballast, would ship coal at this new harbour.

After the harbour was declared open, the party of Directors and shareholders from the E.P.&D.[1], numbering over 300, together with Directors of the Dundee and Arbroath Railway, entered the six carriage train and crossed to Broughty. Here they were joined by Directors of the Aberdeen Railway, who had been late in arriving, and inspected the new branch being completed from the main railway to Broughty Castle Pier. The original D. & A. branch line to the ferry had been brought into use for passenger traffic at or about the same time as the Edinburgh and Northern line opened between Cupar and Ferry-Port. Its route diverged from the re-aligned Dundee and Arbroath line near Broughty Ferry station and the new junction, facing trains from Dundee, followed a sharp curve. Now that the new train ferry was in operation, the branch was almost rebuilt, with improved curvature and facing Arbroath instead of Dundee. The newly inspected branch was opened on 1 May 1851, and finally closed on 18 June 1887, when Fife services began using the present Tay Bridge. It was thereafter used as carriage sidings.

Satisfied with their inspection, the Edinburgh party re-crossed the Tay and travelled to Ladybank, where they were entertained to a cold colation in the station refreshment rooms.

The *Robert Napier* later served on the Forth as well, like

[1]The Edinburgh & Northern, feeling this title rather vague, was re-styled the Edinburgh, Perth & Dundee in April, 1849.

many of the other Tay ferry ships, according to circumstances and demand. In the following decade two other train ferries, the *Carrier* (1858) and *Balbirnie* (1861) were added to the company's fleet. None of these ferries had passenger accommodation and rail travellers from Dundee continued to use the steamer *Express*. Indeed, delays to the train ferry were common. Occasionally, wagons would run away on the loading ramp, or roll overboard when the ferry struck the pier. Probably the most dramatic accident occurred as the *Robert Napier*, whilst berthing, hit Broughty Pier with a full complement of wagons. Rebounding with great force, the wagons, containing mostly coal and flour, jumped the chocks and ran overboard in two long lines. For three days the harbour entrance was blocked.

Almost immediately after *Leviathan* entered service, the Aberdeen Railway Company opened to Portlethen, near Aberdeen, and the following advertisement appeared in the local papers:—

EDINBURGH, PERTH AND DUNDEE RAILWAY

Daily Conveyance of Livestock and Goods from Aberdeen and the North to London via the E.P. & D. and North British Railways

---

On and after 1 March, a DAILY EXPRESS CATTLE AND GOODS TRAIN will leave Portlethen Station at 6.00 a.m. for London and is intended to arrive there in 44 hours or about 2 o'clock morning of the second day. The loaded waggons are now conveyed across the Forth by the Floating Railway and a direct through conveyance is thereby secured.

Cattle and Goods leaving Perth at 12 o'clock noon reach London in 38 hours. From the various stations in Fifeshire in from 32 to 36 hours.

Existing arrangements between the Dundee and Arbroath and the E.P. & D. Railways, regarding working of the line from Dundee to Broughty Pier, were embodied in a Minute signed by respective Directors on 19 February 1859. It was provided that whilst the Dundee and Arbroath Co. should perform haulage of all Passenger, Goods, Mineral and Livestock traffic north of the Tay, the Edinburgh, Perth and Dundee Co. would determine passenger fares and the hours of such trains. Passenger receipts were to be divided according to the actual mileage passengers were carried over the respective railway lines. Mileage rates for Mineral class traffic were fixed at 6d per ton, for Special Class traffic 7½d per ton, and for all other classes 1/- per ton. It was agreed that for all traffic in the latter classes sent between Dundee and intermediate stations to Newburgh the rate would be 9d per ton, such rates being for haulage on the Dundee and Arbroath Railway—the Edinburgh, Perth and Dundee supplying all the wagons, covers and ropes necessary and arranging trains at Broughty Ferry Pier.

The goods station at Dundee was to be worked jointly under the superintendence of a Committee of four Directors—two appointed by each Board. The expenses of working the station, including a rent of £1,800 p.a. paid by the E.P. & D., were divided in proportion to the tonnage belonging to each company using the station. Sums required to pay wages and accounts would be contributed equally by each company, who would mutually arrange the hours of goods and mineral trains between Dundee and Broughty Pier.

Early financial rewards were hard to find. At an Extraordinary General Meeting of the company, held in the Hopetoun Rooms, Queen Street, Edinburgh, on 19 June 1850, the Chairman, Mr. John Balfour, accounted to the shareholders for their company's considerable deficiency. This was partly attributable to the extra work incurred on the different contracts. Despite the shareholders' consent, given eighteen months previously, to the creation of Preference Stock to meet these difficulties, and so place the company in a safe and secure position, such had been the difficulties, that the Directors now had to impress a portion of the unallocated stock amounting to £97,000, which had been offered to shareholders some time ago. It was also necessary to authorise the Directors to exercise the remaining borrowing powers of the company to such an extent as shareholders might think proper, in order to meet their

1 Horse drawn wagons being shunted at St Davids harbour

2 Fordell workshops converted from cottages in 1862. *J. C. and F. Inglis*

3 Despite a brake on one side only, these 30 cwt Fordell wagons could carry over two tons of coal. *J. C. and F. Inglis*

4   *Lord Hobart* seen at St Davids weighed 33 tons in working order and was the largest engine used on the Fordell railway. *J. C. and F. Inglis*

5   *Leviathan*, the first of Thomas Bouch's 'flying bridges' at Burntisland slipway. *British Rail*

6 Burntisland docks here seen in the nineteenth century at the height of its importance as a coal exporting facility. *British Rail*

7   Class D11 4-4-0 No. 2680 *Lucy Ashton* at Lundin Links station. *British Rail*

8 Thornton based Class B1 No. 61103 at Largo station. *British Rail*

9   Methil docks in 1912 just before the heyday of their prosperity. *British Rail*

10 Drumochie, near Methil, suffered decline with the completion of the Largo viaduct on the right. *British Rail*

11   The crew of the LNER No. 722 pose in front of their engine in Stirling. *British Rail*

12 Gresley designed No. 2756 *Selkirkshire* at Dunfermline not long after Class D49s were introduced in 1927. *British Rail*

13　Aftermath of the Wormit disaster. In the background the piers of the ill-fated Tay Bridge can be seen to the right of the present structure.
D. C. Thomson

14 An excursion train stops at Newburgh whilst a Class B1 4-6-0 shunts in the siding. *Real Photographs*

15   Ex LMS 2-6-4T No. 42690 departs from Dunfermline Upper station. *Real Photographs*

16 From inside the high girders, the narrowness and fragility of the first Tay Bridge are clearly shown. *British Rail*

outstanding liabilities and obligations. The Chairman stressed that the additional powers asked for were only to enable the settlement of obligations incurred in the formation and execution of works on the line.

Although, unquestionably, the company was then and had been for some time in an embarrassing financial position, the Directors had made every exertion in their power to meet the extraordinary difficulties of their situation and had refrained from calling upon shareholders for as long as had been possible.

The whole 67 miles of railway, embraced in the original Act of 1845 and subsequent Acts of 1846, were contracted for in 18 separate portions. The aggregate amount of the sums was £639,589, but now that accounts with all except two of the smaller contractors had been finally adjusted, the aggregate cost totalled £783,302—23½% in excess of the contract sums. The Directors admitted an insufficient justification for so large an excess, but added that it had arisen from causes entirely beyond their control. Separate expenditure under the head of rails, chairs, sleepers, girder bridges and fences had amounted to £320,276—a very large excess over the sum estimated. This sum had been inflated following extraordinary rises in the price of timber and an untimely high cost of the very large quantity of rails required. Rails which had cost the company £11 per ton, were now available for little more than half that sum. Regarding expenditure on property and the payment of compensation to lessees and occupiers of other lands, every practical mode of settlement was resorted to, and although extravagant prices had in most cases been obtained, the aggregate amount paid was less by £70,000 than the claims made by proprietors.

From the floor of the meeting, a Mr. Munro W.S. remarked that whilst shareholders heard at every meeting about the vitality of the line, they still remained without any dividend and in his opinion would remain so, for as long as the present system of management continued. In responding, the Chairman felt that although there had not been the increase in traffic, which they had been led to suppose and which might have been expected, yet there was a cheerful acquiescence on the part of officials and servants, sufficient to instill absolute confidence that the line would build up a position of security.

The writer is inclined to the opinion of Mr. Munro, who in his remarks had noted that traffic on the line was decreasing, although the carriage of coal had begun. Almost three years after the railway opened, the mineral fields were still in a comparatively undeveloped state and average weekly receipts for coal traffic were only £275 or 12% of average weekly total revenue.

At the company's half yearly Meeting in September 1848, the Chairman had stated:—

> 'With regard to the station at Perth, the company's goods traffic there has been exceedingly limited. In fact, although we have had an opportunity of carrying coal into Perth ever since the line was completed two months ago, trains have not as yet carried a single ton of coal into that district, simply because the station is not in a state to receive them'.

Over two years later, the following brief comment appeared in the *Fife Herald* of 26 December 1850:—

> 'We understand Messrs. John Henderson & Co. of the Lochgelly Coal and Iron Works have been shipping from Burntisland to various parts of the Continent for some time past, between 200 and 300 tons of coal each week and, we are informed, that could more accommodation be given by the railway company, a great increase might be made to this important branch of their traffic. This is surely a matter well worth the attention of the Directors.'

Even as late as 1858, representations were made for provision of bulk handling facilities at Lochgelly, so that heavy goods would no longer require collection from Cardenden or Cowdenbeath. Farmers could then cease conveying most of their produce in carts to Kirkcaldy or Burntisland.

So great was the financial embarrassment of the company, that before the close of 1851 it became necessary to negotiate with the several classes of creditors for the acceptance of preferential securities to satisfy their claims, together with a partial abatement in the rate of interest thereon for a definite period. The offer, having been accepted, was subsequently

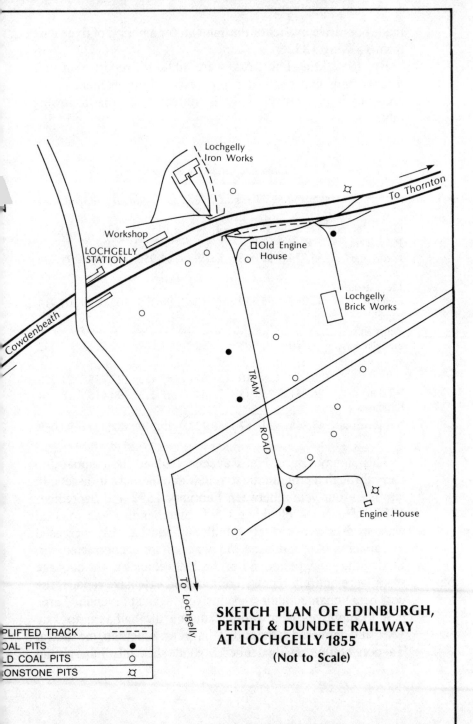

SKETCH PLAN OF EDINBURGH,
PERTH & DUNDEE RAILWAY
AT LOCHGELLY 1855
(Not to Scale)

made operative by Act of Parliament, for a period of five years from 15 May 1852.

By 1857, the Directors were able to report that this arrangement had enabled a progressive improvement in the company's prosperity. This is reflected in the following table:—

TABLE 3

Summarised Revenue Accounts

For years ending 31 January 1852 to 31 January 1857

Gross Revenue	1852 £	1853 £	1854 £	1855 £	1856 £	1857 £
Passengers, horses and carriages	55,774	60,363	61,597	62,956	68,054	71,476
Merchandise, minerals, parcels	62,205	65,339	75,126	90,310	103,069	107,914
Rents and miscellaneous	2,720	2,708	1,948	2,187	2,216	2,333
	120,699	128,410	138,671	155,453	173,339	181,723
Working Expenses	76,831	73,843	78,449	85,213	90,615	88,654
Net Revenue	43,868	54,567	60,222	70,240	82,724	93,069

This steady rise in Net Revenue enabled the company to carry through a programme to renew and increase its assets. In less than four years, between February 1852 and September 1855, of a stock of about 1,500 merchandise and mineral wagons, 509 were entirely rebuilt and considerably increased in capacity. An additional 55 wagons were contracted for. During the same period, 89 of the 189 vehicles in the carriage stock were entirely renewed or received extensive repairs, the cost being charged almost exclusively against revenue. Three new locomotives were ordered during the half-year to July 1855 and delivered at the end of that year. A new engine shed at Tayport, station at Cowdenbeath, goods shed at Edinburgh and an additional repairing shop at Burntisland were provided for, together with general improvements including increased accommodation at stations.

The improved financial position during this crucial five-year period was achieved as the relationship with its rival, Scottish Central steadily changed. The period began at a time when detrimental competition between the two companies was carried to great lengths and concluded one year after they had established a working arrangement aimed at far-reaching economies.

When, early in 1851, the Scottish Central Board discarded an agreement, assigning East Coast traffic exclusively to the E.P. & D., in return for a monopoly of all West Coast traffic, the Directors of the Edinburgh company had no alternative but to lower fares on their route, although still keeping them higher than at the opening of the line. Differential fares were adopted for travel by ordinary and express trains. Instead of 8/- First Class, 6/- Second Class and 4/- Third Class for all trains, as originally charged, the Edinburgh-Perth/Dundee rates for Ordinary trains became 8/-; 6/6 and 4/10 respectively. For Express train passengers, the corresponding tickets cost 9/-, 6/6 and 5/-. These fares were no sooner announced than the Central company matched them and a further reduction was followed by a similar move on their part. By April 1851, the two companies were both charging a minimum fare of 6/-, 5/- and 3/- for the three classes.

The E.P. & D. had the great advantage of a far more direct, although often more uncomfortable, route and this it sought to profit from by the increased provision of Express trains. Intending passengers were advised that with effect from 1 January 1851, the time by Express trains between Edinburgh and Perth, Dundee and Aberdeen would be 1 hour 50 minutes, 2 hours 15 minutes and 5 hours 43 minutes respectively. Return tickets for all the trains and classes would be available at greatly reduced fares.

The Edinburgh-Dundee journey time, less than 40 minutes longer than the average 1976 d.m.u. timings, involving seven intermediate stops, was a particularly remarkable feat, as no extra minutes were gained on those stages between Edinburgh and Burntisland and Tayport and Dundee. In order to run to their schedule, these Express trains were required to cover the 36¼ miles through Fife in no less than 75 minutes.

The four purpose built 2-2-2 express passenger engines, with 6 foot driving wheels, built by R. & W. Hawthorn in 1848 were rostered for this arduous task. Their rear axles, which were built behind the firebox so as to give greater stability at high speeds, had eliptic springs, enabling the driver to adjust the adhesion from the footplate in accordance with load and gradient.

When a substitute engine was called for, one (if not two) of the ten 0-4-2 passenger engines, ordered from Hawthorn in 1847 with which to open the line, would be coupled up front.

Having started upon their journey from Burntisland, the Express trains were expected to be able to tackle a continuous 5¾ mile climb, including one mile at 1 in 128 before Kinghorn tunnel, and depart from Kirkcaldy ten minutes later. For the following 5 miles to Thornton Junction a more liberal 13 minutes were allowed. After a climb out of Kirkcaldy against gradients of 1 in 143, 105, 100 and 114, there followed the steep downhill run from Dysart into Thornton. Leaving Thornton, drivers were faced with lengthy uphill gradients of 1 in 129 and 104 during their 2½ mile journey to Markinch. As far as Markinch, the Expresses were, by reason of not stopping at lesser stations, able to gain 10 minutes on the time of all-station trains. Moreover, the stations omitted each involved ordinary trains re-starting on an incline. Beyond Markinch the line climbs for more than 1½ miles at 1 in 102½ to Lochmuir summit, before descending for 1 mile at 1 in 105 to Falkland Road, then at 1 in 95 for a further 1¼ miles and passing Kingskettle at 1 in 111. The Express trains were scheduled to cover this 5¾ mile Markinch-Ladybank section in 8 minutes, but stopping services, which could not avail themselves of the downhill sprint, all required 18 minutes. Thus by Ladybank, the expresses were now 20 minutes ahead of all others. Between this latter station and Tayport there are no gradients of any significance and it required the full 17¼ miles for expresses, which did not stop at Springfield or Dairsie, to make an additional saving of 9 minutes. The service to Perth took 35 minutes from Ladybank with stops only at Newburgh and Bridge of Earn. Because railway companies had not yet titled any of their trains, some room has been left for romantic conjecture!

Problems With The Mail

Opening the E.P. & D. may have accelerated movement of passengers and goods, but in November 1849 Cupar Town Council felt it necessary to take aggressive action to improve the dilatory mail service from Edinburgh. They made it clear that since a perfectly adequate rail service now existed it was both slower and more expensive to continue using horsedrawn gigs to provide a twice daily service from the capital. The E.P. & D. had made an offer of £1,000 to convey mails to Fife. The GPO countered this figure with its own offer of a mere £500, though it was known that currently four times this amount was being spent. Moreover arbitration was refused. The Council heard with astonishment how the GPO had made arrangements very readily with their rivals the Scottish Central and Caledonian companies to convey mails through a district with half the population of Fife for £20,000 p.a. Prior to arrival of the railways mails had been routed through Fife twice daily and it had been supposed this would be retained, particularly since the terminus of the E.P. & D. was Perth now chosen as the grand central mail depot in favour of Edinburgh.

The following statement was issued by the GPO:

'In order that the public may have before them the whole question currently under discussion, between Post Office authorities and the Railway Co., we think it right to give the following extracts from various Acts of Parliament.'

'It shall be lawful for the P.M.G. by notice to require the mails to be carried by any railway company and they shall be conveyed either by ordinary or special trains and at such times as the Post-Master shall direct, together with guards appointed and employed by the

P.M.G. in charge thereof, and the company shall at their own expense provide such carriages and engines to the satisfaction of the P.M.G.'

'That every company of proprietors of every railway on which mails or post letter bags shall be required to pass shall be entitled to such reasonable remuneration to be paid by the P.M.G. and to be fixed and agreed on between the P.M.G. and such company, or in the event of disagreement, as shall be determined by arbitration.'

'The Act 7 & 8 Vict. Cap. 85 contains the enactment under which the Post Office authorities contend that they are entitled to send guards as passengers by all ordinary trains, where fixed mail trains are not considered warranted, while the Railway Company contend that no such privilege is conferred by the Act and that such guards are, like other passengers, not entitled to have luggage beside them in the carriage or to hand out the same in pieces at any of the stations.'

'In the Act the mail guard is put on the same footing as any other passenger. The Railway Company ask whether it would be tolerated that such a passenger should half fill the compartment of any carriage with a number of dirty mailbags, as until recently the guards on the Fife railway were apparently in the habit of doing. The Post Office wish to stress that they make a fair payment for their services.'

In December of that year Edinburgh Town Council took up the cudgels on behalf of the neighbouring county of Fife by writing to the P.M.G. to complain about the recent changes effected in mail handling.

Mail bags, before November 1849, had been sent in the charge of Mail Guards travelling twice daily between Edinburgh and Dundee whose duty it was to uplift and deposit bags at all stations en route. The guard travelled as a second class passenger, the bags were his luggage and excess was paid where necessary. £700 was paid by the Edinburgh and Northern for such an arrangement which did not in any way interfere with the company's service.

It occurred to the railway company that they would still be acting within the terms of their agreement with the GPO if they only allowed guards to uplift and exchange mail bags at the main stations of Cupar and Kirkcaldy giving them no power to do so at intermediate stations. It was intended that this measure would induce the GPO to accede to their terms for a regular contract and additional remuneration. Both were refused.

72

To meet this emergency measures were taken by the GPO to use gigs to provide a service outside the main stations and so it could be argued the postal service was almost as poor as before the introduction of the railways.

In January 1850, the E.P. & D. proposed to the GPO that the inconvenience to the public could be relieved by agreement with the following terms:

> 'The Directors are ready to resume the services of the Post Office as formerly, or in such other way as may be desired, on condition that the P.M.G. will consent to leave the amount of remuneration or compensation to be resolved by the award of arbiters to be mutually named in section 16 of the Statute 1 and 2 Victoria Cap 98.'
>
> 'Or alternatively the Directors offer to resume the services of the Post Office as formerly on the following conditions:—
>
> (1) That the P.M.G. shall forthwith raise an action or declarator against the Company, for establishing by the judgement of a court of law the rights of the Post Office authorities to send a Mail Guard as an ordinary passenger with the privilege of delivering and receiving mail bags at intermediate stations.
>
> (2) In the event of the P.M.G. failing in that action, the amount of remuneration or compensation shall be settled by arbiters, mutually named in terms of the above Act.'

The E.P. & D. were informed that the Commissioners of Railways, in the opinion of the Lord Advocate of Scotland, on the question of the Company's liability should instruct the Solicitor of the Treasury to institute legal proceedings against the E.P. & D. Railway to carry the Mail bags and Guards as required by the Post Office, and this they would do.

In March 1850 an interim agreement to alleviate so great an inconvenience was reached between the two interested parties and a year later action was at length raised in the Court of Session. The Lord Ordinary refused to interdict the railway company from charging the mail-bags delivered at intermediate stations as parcels, but His Lordship agreed to pass a note to the Inner House which subsequently decided unanimously in favour of the Post Office.

The Edinburgh, Perth & Dundee had lost its fight.

The Years of Expansion

The following table shows the progressive improvement which took place between the half-years ending 31 January 1852 and 31 January 1857:—

TABLE 4

Gross Revenue and Net Receipts

1852-1857

	Gross Revenue	Expenses	Net Receipts
Half-year to 31 January 1852	£120,699	£ 76,831	£ 43,868
Half-year to 31 January 1853	£128,410	£ 73,843	£ 54,567
Half-year to 31 January 1854	£138,671	£ 78,449	£ 60,222
Half-year to 31 January 1855	£155,453	£ 85,213	£ 70,240
Half-year to 31 January 1856	£173,339	£ 90,615	£ 82,724
Half-year to 31 January 1857	£181,723	£ 88,654	£ 93,069

At an Extraordinary General Meeting of the E.P. & D. on 29 January 1856, it was resolved that a working arrangement between the E.P. & D. and Scottish Central Railway should be ratified and approved. The Chairman stated that competition between rival railways had proved ruinous, to the lines concerned. He reminded those present that at one time competition between the two companies had been carried to a great length, and that although after 1854, they had worked under an agreement which more clearly defined traffic rights, competition had still not been properly extinguished. There could be no proper economies so long as the two companies were obliged to maintain separate and distinct establishments, though the two routes might be said to have common termini in Edinburgh and Perth. The agreement became effective on 1 February 1856.

It was destined to be shortlived and the joint working agreement was abandoned as of 30 April 1857, upon notice being given by the Scottish Central. During the entire fifteen months, the rolling stock of both companies was under the charge of the Locomotive Superintendent of the Scottish Central at Perth. Towards the conclusion of the original negotiations questions regarding the appointment to offices were considered and the principal managerial posts were all allotted to Scottish Central servants. E.P. & D. directors strongly remonstrated against this but the Scottish Central pleaded successfully that any other arrangement would contravene the terms of its agreement with another company.

Whilst wishing to adhere to their agreement, which was designed to give a greater financial benefit to the E.P. & D. than the Scottish Central, directors of the former company did not hesitate to make repeated concessions at the solicitation of the Scottish Central. However, a formal demand that they should provide part of the capital proposed for engines, rolling stock and other plant associated with new lines wholly connected with the Scottish Central could not be entertained. It was agreed, therefore, to terminate joint working forthwith.

Until 1859 the E.P. & D. had been entirely excluded from any share in through goods and mineral traffic between Dundee, Glasgow and north-west England. A combination amongst companies to the west prevented them obtaining the facilities granted to the Scottish Central, the through rates conceded to the latter company not having been given to the E.P. & D. The extension of the N.B.R. in 1859 from Hawick to Carlisle successfully circumvented this obstacle and gave a much needed boost to traffic crossing south from Fife.

In the same year, what had been termed the 'Stirling Agreement' was ended. Five companies were involved in this Agreement—the Scottish Central, Edinburgh and Glasgow, Dundee and Perth, the Scottish North Eastern and the E.P. & D. By the terms of the Agreement all goods and mineral traffic had been carried round by Perth and for five years wagons were not conveyed across the Tay.

Goods and mineral traffic on the line for the half-year ended July 1859 exceeded the corresponding period of 1857 by £20,000, whilst passengers carried numbered no less than 754,000. During the second half of 1859 traffic on the Forth ferry had outgrown the capabilities of the two boats in that service and the directors tendered for a boat similar to, but somewhat larger than those then in use. The following table shows a considerable increase in traffic on the railway in the short space of two years:—

TABLE 5

Tonnages of Goods and Mineral Traffic

1858-1860

	Tonnage
Half-year to January 1858	299,024
Half-year to January 1859	299,848
Half-year to January 1860	309,769

Although these figures represented a modest increase of 10,000 tons, certain short-haul traffic was entirely abstracted —such as the 17,000 tons carried over a distance of not more than three miles to the Lochgelly Ironworks. The natural increase was estimated at about 40,000 tons. Longer distance traffic crossing Fife to Burntisland accounted for the very large growth in locomotive running between 1859 and 1860—an increase of 11,179 miles. At Burntisland the number of wagons carried across the ferry increased by 30% during the second half of 1859—in some weeks as many as 1,600 wagons were taken across.

The new Forth ferry boat, with a capacity for 31 wagons—6 more than the *Leviathan*—was delivered in October 1860. Whilst it greatly helped alleviate congestion, the problem remained so long as standage at the slipways was not expanded nor further orders for wagons placed. In the six months to July 1860, 50 new goods wagons were placed on the line and, by arrangement with one of the coal proprietors, a firm order was placed for 60 new coal wagons. Whilst at the end of the period a similar order was being negotiated with a neighbouring proprietor, an even greater number were expected to be supplied during the following winter.

In its half-yearly Report prior to amalgamation, the

E.P. & D. set out passenger and goods traffic comparisons as follows:—

Passengers	Half Year to	31/1/62	31/1/61	31/1/60
	1st Class	86,071	81,297	84,083
	2nd Class	93,114	94,077	101,161
	3rd Class	352,679	326,765	332,685
	Parliamentary	303,650	303,271	306,999
	Total	835,514	805,410	824,928
Goods and Coal		368,905 tons	335,726 tons	309,769 tons

The number of wagons crossing the Forth showed a very substantial increase during the last half-year, 42,460 wagons being transferred as against 37,000 in the previous half-year. This was largely due to yet a further increase in coal wagons— by arrangement with coal owners 117 additional wagons were brought into use during the relevant six months.

In all there were 46 engines, which for a line only 78 miles in length was a very large number.

Rivalry and Amalgamation

In Dunfermline and its neighbouring district there had grown a considerable dissatisfaction with the E.P. & D. and ample local support for a more direct line via Queensferry. In 1860, an earlier scheme was revived and although called the Edinburgh and Dunfermline Railway, it was intended that it should run on to Perth. The plan was to link with the Edinburgh and Glasgow at Corstorphine and the E.P. & D. at Dunfermline. Its projectors approached the E.P. & D. to run the railway for them, but this they would only do on condition that the line entered Edinburgh by way of Granton and the Scotland Street tunnel. This stipulation was unacceptable to the promoters and the North British subsequently agreed not only to operate the railway but also to put up some of the capital.

There followed a period of fierce opposition. Both the Edinburgh and Glasgow and Scottish Central Railways sought to secure a monopoly of traffic to the north via Stirling by 'blocking' the southern end of the Queensferry Passage. South of the Firth, a branch was projected from the main Edinburgh and Glasgow Railway at Ratho, running northwards as far as South Queensferry. This scheme would complement a railway from Dunfermline to North Queensferry, which originally had the backing of the Edinburgh and Glasgow and Scottish Central, although these companies later disowned it.

The E.P. & D., aware of its own inadequacies, now entered into secret negotiations with the North British. A Bill which the former company had, of itself, presented to Parliament in 1861 was withdrawn and that, together with rejection of the opposition schemes, left the way clear for a real melee in the ensuing Session. In September 1861, the N.B.R. and E.P. & D. called their shareholders together at simultaneous meetings in Edinburgh and announced that they had decided to amalgamate.

The Chairman of the N.B.R. summarised the situation when he said:—

> '... the E.P.&D. shareholders may look down a long lane and see no prospect of a dividend, whereas under this arrangement they see a clear dividend in the immediate future.'

In the 1862 Session of Parliament the official union of the N.B.R. with the E.P. & D. and the West of Fife Railway was sought and these companies jointly promoted their own Queensferry scheme. Again they were opposed by the Edinburgh and Glasgow with its line from Ratho to the Ferry. When the Bill reached the Standing Orders Committee, it was discovered that notice had only been given to seek permissive powers to take the Ferry, whilst in their Bill the promoters asked for compulsory powers. Consequently the Bill was thrown out without a hearing. Strong appeals and local petitions failed to have it revived in the same Session.

Fortunately the Edinburgh and Glasgow's Bill also failed and so the challenge remained to be renewed in 1863. Twelve days after the defeat of the Edinburgh and Glasgow Bill, the Act of Amalgamation of the N.B.R., E.P. & D. and West of Fife Railways received the Royal Assent.

In 1863, the N.B.R. brought forward a Bill for a line from Piershill to Granton and along the Forth to Queensferry. The ferry was to be bought over and on the northern shore a railway would continue to Dunfermline. The opposition scheme from Ratho was also renewed. The result favoured the N.B.R. which was granted an Act for that section of the line through the Edinburgh suburbs from Piershill to Granton. Although the Edinburgh and Glasgow was also given permission to build its Ratho-Queensferry line, the N.B.R. was to have absolute running powers over it. The right to buy the ferry was given to the N.B.R., but purchase had to be within two years or it would fall to the Glasgow company. Possibly this arrangement might have led to further disputes but for a decision by the N.B.R. and Edinburgh and Glasgow to amalgamate in 1863.

5

Some Early Branch Railways

BY 1851, the E.P. & D. had become involved in agreements to operate, on behalf of independent companies, four such lines, all less or more feasible and all less or more in a state of progress. They were all to comprise a single track of rails and be constructed in keeping with the most economical methods. The main line looked for no financial reward, save for any additional traffic which they originated, until such times as the shareholders received a dividend of 4.5% upon their investments.

The St Andrews Railway

This short 4.5 mile line, laid over flat cheaply acquired ground presenting no engineering difficulties, was estimated to cost no more than £21,000. Scarcely 200 yards of retaining wall were required and the most difficult section—the bridges over the Motray Water and River Eden—were constructed of wood and calculated to last over thirty years without incurring repairs.

It was estimated that the St Andrews Railway Company's annual outlay for maintenance of way, employees and payment of taxes would not exceed £700, and that if annual revenue were only £3,000, there would still be a surplus, after payment of dividend, of £1,175—a sum comfortably expected to meet working expenses by the main line. These expenses were fixed at one shilling per mile for each passenger train not exceeding five carriages or for a mixed train not exceeding eight vehicles. The same rate applied to any mineral trains not exceeding ten wagons. For any additional number of trucks or carriages, a proportionately higher rate was to be paid. After these payments, any remaining surplus was to be divided equally between the two Companies. To carry out the 25 year agreement, a Joint Committee was set up, comprising the

Chairman and another two Directors of each company—the Chairman of the St Andrews Railway being Chairman of the Joint Committee.

In support of the company's bright future, the Prospectus stated:—

'It may be stated that the number of passengers who travelled between St Andrews and the Leuchars Station, during the year ending 26 October 1850, as can be shewn from the books of the Railway Station at Leuchars, amounted to 42,420. Instead of trebling this amount, as is usually done in contemplation of railway communication, it is only proposed to add one half, giving a total of 63,630, which of itself would yield a revenue of £1,843-6s-6d. The probable revenue may therefore be stated, thus—

1. Passenger Traffic	£1,843	6s	6d
2. The Mails	40	0s	0d
3. Coals, Merchandise, etc.	300	0s	0d
4. Parcels	75	0s	0d
5. Lime	40	0s	0d
6. Pavement and hard stones from Forfarshire	15	0s	0d
7. Free-stone to the Tay, etc.	175	0s	0d
8. Seggie Distillery Traffic	130	0s	0d
9. Guard Bridge Pier and Tilework Traffic	80	0s	0d
10. Kincaple Tilework Traffic	100	0s	0d
11. Farm Produce, Cattle and Manure	100	0s	0d
	£2,898	6s	6d

The *Fife Herald*, in an Editorial published on 21 August 1851, believed that this estimate was understated by at least £350:—

'There can be no doubt that the passenger traffic is under estimated, when we consider not only the general tendency of the public to avail themselves of railway facilities, but also the absolute certainty of many excursion trains to St Andrews. Again, the third item appears to be understated, as there can be little doubt of coals being largely carried to St Andrews and the East of Fife from the western coal-fields, and also that the main traffic in merchandise will then be by rail and not as now by packet, which is at once slow, hazardous, and, we may add, unprofitable to the packet company, who have not for several years paid one farthing of dividend. Further, the free-stone traffic is evidently under the mark, considering the vast fields of Strathkinness, Nydie, and Kincaple, and the demand for the stone not only in Dundee, but also in Perth, in various towns in Fife, and even in Leith and Edinburgh. Moreover, there is nothing set down for the carrying of fish to inland markets and nothing is reckoned upon the ironstone of Denhead, which may yet find its way to the foundries of the west of Fife, instead of as at present, to the furnaces of Newcastle.'

The company's Prospectus sets out the probable annual expenses as follows:—

1. Maintenance of Way, Buildings and Works 4.5 miles at £50 per mile	£225	0s 0d
2. Taxes	125	0s 0d
3. Station Clerks	140	0s 0d
4. Signal-man at Milton	40	0s 0d
5. Gate-keeper at Guard Bridge	31	4s 0d
6. Two Porters	54	12s 0d
7. Stationery	25	0s 0d
8. Sundries	30	0s 0d
	£670	16s 0d

The St Andrews Railway was opened in July 1852 and provided connections to meet all main line trains stopping at Leuchars. Throughout the 1850's and early 1860's, most timetables provided for seven passenger trains in each direction. Four of the trains were for Edinburgh and Perth travellers and three for those going to or coming from Dundee. In addition, two early morning coach services—one from Crail and the other from Pittenweem and Anstruther—gave the inhabitants of those towns an opportunity to make a day return journey to Dundee. The coaches departed from St Andrews upon the arrival of the mid-afternoon connection from Dundee.

The company's half-yearly accounts show that operations more than lived up to expectations, necessitating the provision of additional sidings at St Andrews and Seggie (near Guard Bridge) and permitting improvements at Guard Bridge Station.

Possibly in order to help maximize profits, the company appears to have neglected maintenance of its permanent way during early years. This contributed to an accident in May 1864, when the branch was worked by the N.B.R. A train, marshalled with tender in front, a six-wheeled engine, guard's van, one 2nd, one 1st and one 3rd class carriage, was proceeding from Leuchars down to St Andrews. There was no turntable at St Andrews and so the engine worked tender foremost in going down. About 300 yards beyond Guard Bridge, when the train was travelling at 10-12 m.p.h. on a rising gradient of 1 in 409, the tender left the rails on the outside of a 30 chain curve, followed by the engine and leading wheels of the guard's van. The passenger carriages remained on the rails and nobody was injured.

Apparently, the off leading wheel of the tender struck the end of a rail, where the key of the joint chair had dropped out. In his Official Report, the Inspecting Officer made the following comments:—

> 'It would be desirable that this line be worked with a light tank engine. The line itself is of very light and poor construction. The rails are single-headed in lengths of 16 feet and are considerably worn. Joint and intermediate chairs are weak, too narrow in the throat to admit a good key and reported to be continually breaking . . . .'

> 'I consider that the whole permanent way wants renewing. There are two wooden viaducts which have had considerable repairs, but the cross-beams on the Eden viaduct are too weak. The North British line, from the junction with the St Andrews Railway to Leuchars Station is also indifferent; the rails, points and crossings being very bad indeed. The company have got some new rails on the ground for relaying the line and the sooner it is done the better.'

A few months before the accident, a February issue of the *Dundee Courier* carried the following editorial criticism of Leuchars Station:—

> 'A more ill-provided junction does not exist on the line. The waiting room for First and Second Class passengers is a small circumscribed compartment or rather box, with three wooden chairs and a small fire, minus a poker, in a grate scarcely fit for a ploughman's bothy.'

> 'What we have said of the compartment for gentlemen applies equally for the room for ladies. Both rooms are simply despicable. The fact is that the station was never meant for a junction at all, being originally built for the village of Leuchars alone, and no additional accommodation has been provided after the construction of the St Andrews branch.'

Unfortunately, St Andrews passengers were frequently subjected to frustrating delays at Leuchars, due to the lack of a revised track lay-out, to enable a rapid exchange of traffic between the branch and the main line.

The line had, in effect, been designed as a light railway of a kind especially intended to meet the needs of small rural companies operating trains hauled by light locomotives at low speeds. In 1857, the overall journey time between Leuchars and St Andrews was exactly twenty minutes—the equivalent of 13.5 m.p.h.

Criticisms of the St Andrews Railway have, with hindsight, been levelled at its consulting engineer, Thomas Bouch, who accepted its construction as his first commission after resigning from his brief appointment as engineer and manager of the E.P. & D.

The Leven Railway

This short line from Thornton Junction was constructed in the same economical manner and worked by the E.P. & D. under a similar agreement as with the St Andrews Railway. It was regarded by many as providing a most beneficial extension of the through route from Stirling via Alloa and Dunfermline to one of the most important local ports, and the centre of a rich, populous, agricultural locality. Spinning mills, a distillery and bleachfields, on the lower portion of the River Leven, stood adjacent to the land traversed.

The company's Prospectus, advertised in October 1851, refers to the earlier abandonment of a far more grandiose East of Fife Railway scheme, and recognises that a railway could only be secured by pursuing a less adventurous course. It states:—

'The promoters therefore propose to limit their efforts to a short branch of six miles from Thornton Station to Leven, with a single line of rails, and to avoid expensive engineering, by adopting as far as possible the natural gradients of the Orr and Leven Water. They also intend to save entirely on the heavy outlay involved in the

84

purchase of locomotive power and other rolling stock. It is hoped to open the line at an outlay not exceeding £25,000 . . . . There will be branch railways terminating at or near Kirkland Works and the harbour of Leven.'

Addressing a public meeting held two months later, Sir Ralph Anstruther, who had been elected Deputy Chairman, stressed how cheaply the railway could be built and added that of eight offers for constructing the line the lowest barely exceeded £13,000. This view was affirmed by Mr Thomas Bouch, the company's consulting engineer, who, in a short speech, stated that the trouble with the railways constructed in 1845/46 and 1847 was excessive cost and wastage of capital in construction. Reflecting personal disillusionment with the E.P.&D. in this respect, he stated that many railways in the London area, although carrying vast traffic, paid no dividend, whilst many small railways, even in less populated areas, had much lower costs. The Dundee and Arbroath Railway, he instanced, paid a higher dividend than the E.P. & D., whilst the Arbroath to Forfar railway gave a better yield than any other in Scotland. The Leven Railway could also promise its shareholders high returns, because it was fulfilling a current need for inexpensive railways.

The railway, which received a gala opening on 10 August 1854, crossed the rivers Orr and Leven half-a-dozen times by 'substantial but not very elegant' bridges, built with stone pillars and having wooden flooring. Sleepers were laid 4 feet apart on the straight lengths and at 3 feet intervals on curved sections. Leven Station, although small, was considered commodious and situated in the immediate neighbourhood of the principal works, whilst the junction at Thornton was contrived with ingenuity so as to prevent any of the frequent delays encountered at Leuchars.

Trains ran in connection with those on the main line and also with Dunfermline branch services. Initially, departures from Leven were at 7.20 a.m., 10.45 a.m., 3.55 p.m. and 7.00 p.m.; returning from Thornton about 8.15 a.m., 11.25 a.m., 4.25 p.m. and 7.35 p.m. Journey time was 25 minutes.

At the half-yearly Ordinary General Meeting, held just over two months after the opening, the Chairman, John Haig, told how passenger traffic had exceeded the most optimistic expectations—the average number conveyed per week being 1,081, compared with 570 estimated in the Prospectus. Already it had been necessary to take steps to increase accommodation for shunting goods traffic at Thornton and additional goods facilities would soon be available at Cameron Bridge and Leven. Their availability was very timeous, for between February and July 1855, inclusive, no less than 14,293 tons of goods, 753 cattle and 1,318 sheep were carried along this line designed by Mr Bouch.

A year later, a meeting of the company was given a very full explanation of the circumstances whereby the E.P. & D. had ceased to work the line, as from Saturday, 31 July 1855—less than a year after it had opened.

Preparatory to the opening of the Leven Railway, a Joint Committee of the Directors of both companies was appointed to administer the working agreement. This agreement needed the ratification of both the Board of Trade and the E.P. & D. Directors, since the latter had contested every clause in the contract, and because they desired the Board's sanction to devolve upon the Leven directors alone.

On 17 July 1854, the Board of Trade intimated its sanction with certain modifications, the most important of which were to reduce the length of the agreement from 25 to 10 years and omit its 11th and 12th clauses, designed as a safeguard against the E.P.&D. favouring competing modes of conveyance and thereby reducing the volume of through traffic to the Leven Company.

At a meeting of the Joint Committee thereafter, it was agreed that a deputation of Leven directors go to London and there advise their company's London solicitors on the preparation of a statement setting out in full the essential character of the two clauses, without which, it was contended, the agreement would not be of any use to the Leven Company.

In support of their appeal, the deputation waited for a decision from the President of the Board of Trade. On the 4 August, he affirmed the decision regarding the length of the agreement, but admitted that the 11th and 12th clauses, when modified, as proposed by the deputation, would be quite reasonable. However, because his legal adviser considered that the clauses might exceed the powers given the company, he withheld his sanction to them until he should be satisfied, by the opinion of Scottish counsel, that they were within the statutory powers of the contracting parties.

A decision was not obtained until 5 January 1855, when the Board of Trade gave its approval, subject to a novel provision modifying clause 12, in a way which would reduce the Leven company's protection against any arbitrary exercise of the powers vested in the E.P. & D. Before finally reporting to the Joint Committee the result of their efforts, the Directors resolved to ascertain by personal application to the President, whether any concession might be granted by the Board to ameliorate this new and objectionable provision.

Meanwhile, the President had vacated his Office and the E.P. & D. Directors, apparently anxious about approval of the Agreement, allegedly took matters into their own hands, and succeeded in having the Board uplift the 10 year restriction. This placed the Leven directors in a dilemma. Either they totally abandon the agreement, or accept it with alterations, placing them entirely at the mercy of the E.P. & D. Apparently, that company, consciously masters of the situation, then called upon the Leven directors to give approval in an insolent and threatening manner. Before the Leven company could call a shareholders' meeting, the E.P. & D. announced that they would finish working the line as from their year end, 31 July 1855.

Not surprisingly the E.P. & D. directors made known in their subsequent Report, that, following protracted negotiations, their requests to the Leven directors to attend discussions were repeatedly ignored and this had prevented any resolve in the matter, resulting in their withdrawal.

To whomsoever the blame should be apportioned, the Leven

company found itself placed in a precarious position on 1 August 1855.

As the result of painstaking research for his fascinating book 'Scotland's Forgotten Railways', Mr John Thomas has been able to ascertain that the Leven company's directors, among whom were country gentlemen, were oblivious of their engineer's shortcomings both for his lengthy delays in producing plans, and because he succeeded in acquiring Board of Trade approval of a railway which had so little in common with its Parliamentary plans. An early disagreement with the E.P. & D. had dashed their prospective working agreement and left the company to seek its own engine and rolling stock. Amongst its acquisitions were Scottish Central Railway carriages. Having relented and agreed to work the line, the E.P. & D. demanded an immediate replacement of the totally inadequate engine which Mr Bouch had ordered from Hawthorn of Leith.

Before a new engine could be delivered in October 1855, the E.P. & D. had already ceased in attempting to maintain some kind of service using a really unsuitable temporary replacement, secured second-hand by their own locomotive superintendent from a firm in Chester. They had been unable or unwilling to lend an engine of their own and, from the relevant correspondence, appear not to have pressured Hawthorn into meeting the Leven company's requests for urgent delivery.

Now, acutely aware of their predicament, the Leven directors, who were nearly all proprietors of prosperous factories in that town's vicinity, cleverly managed to save their railway by a stratagem. With the port of Leven already so inadequate that vessels had been known to lie from two to five days without a berth, and frequently discharge their cargoes one over the other, the directors kept open this important supply route until delivery of their new engine and repairs to their original 30 defective wagons could be effected.

By the late autumn of 1855 the service was steadily gaining momentum, and at the half-yearly Meeting held in April 1856, the directors were able to report the complete success of the independent working of the line. The Chairman commented:—

> 'At the close of the half-year to 31 July 1855, when the line was worked by the E.P.&D., after all charges, there remained a surplus of £757 applicable to interest and dividends. But of this sum, £111 fell to the E.P.&D. as their share of profits, leaving a free balance of only £646.'
>
> 'During the last half-year, under independent management, the surplus, after paying all charges, is £1,204.'

A large proportion of this surplus was applied to correcting the insufficiency of rolling stock to meet traffic demands.

A joint working agreement with the new adjoining East of Fife Railway, effective as from 1 October 1857, fully realised the expectations of the Leven directors, who were now planning for the future of their line, no longer as a short branch, but as part of a trunk route serving the whole of East Fife.

During 1860 and 1861, the company declared dividends of 8%, while its Chairman believed it to be the most profitable of its kind in Britain. The line's original defective construction was found adequate to withstand the immediate post independence increase in traffic, until it could be largely renewed in 1859. Very probably it had been no more defective than the tracks to be seen at several of Scotland's surviving collieries, over which tremendous weights of coal are constantly being shunted.

The E.P. & D., who had forfeited a share in the now lucrative coastal traffic, but which never refused the Leven Railway access to Thornton, were apparently the only party not to benefit. Thomas Bouch, whose bad reputation could have, if indeed it did not, spread like a tinder fire, was able to develop a flourishing engineering consultancy in Edinburgh over the ensuing twenty years.

The Leslie Railway

In November 1856 proposals were published to lay a Bill before Parliament to make a railway running west from the south end of Markinch Station, on the E.P. & D. main line, to a terminus at Prinlaws, a part of Leslie. Three very short lines were to diverge along the 4 mile 17 chain route for the purpose of serving paper mills at Auchmuty, Leven Bank and Prinlaws.

The Leslie Railway Bill, incorporating a company with power to raise £35,000 by shares and borrow £11,500 was passed in 1857 and construction began immediately thereafter.

Of special interest to local residents was the viaduct across the river Leven at Cabbagehall comprising 14 extensive arches varying up to 80 feet in height. Although most of the trackbed has long been buried under the new town of Glenrothes, the rather splendid viaduct has been restored and is maintained as a public pathway. A comparison of the original plans with a post-Grouping description suggests that only minor changes were made to Leslie Station and its track lay-out during the line's seventy years of passenger service. The stone station building, although quite lengthy, was, despite its pointed roof, of low stature. The greater part of the platform, including that which fronted the building, comprised wooden planks set at right angles to the single running line. At the back of the station was a high wooden fence, whilst across from the platform were two sidings—the furthest of which was partly enclosed by a goods shed.

Passenger trains commenced running on 1 February 1861 in connection with the four daily main line trains which stopped at Markinch. Journey time was 20 minutes in both directions.

By April 1862, exactly a year after goods trains began to work the line, 15,000 passengers had already been conveyed together with 24,000 tons of goods and minerals. Traffic receipts rose from £1,324 for the half-year ended 31 July 1864, to £1,824 in the corresponding period of 1872, whilst dividends paid to Ordinary Shareholders remained a constant 4 per cent. Following growing recognition that the line was too small to exist as an independent concern, it was formally amalgamated with the N.B.R. as from 1 August 1872.

Branches to Kinross

The Fife & Kinross Railway, which received the Royal Assent on 16 July 1855, was to run initially over a distance of

14 miles from Ladybank to Kinross, with provision for a possible future extension to Tillicoultry, where a connection could be made with the line to Alloa.

At the first General Meeting of the company, held in Auchtermuchty Town Hall in September 1855, the vast benefits which the line would bestow upon Kinross-shire were repeatedly stressed. The splendid scenery of that county would draw numerous tourists to the railway, whilst on agricultural and commercial grounds it was impossible to speak too highly of the advantages to be reaped. During the Meeting, reference was made to their great good fortune in securing the services of Sir G. Graham Montgomery, as Chairman of the new line. The amazing success of the Peebles Railway, of which the baronet was also Chairman, was outlined to the Meeting as the best testimonial of that gentleman's fitness for the office to which he had been chosen.

The Directors reported to the Meeting how very considerable opposition had been encountered by them in Parliament to the passage of the Bill. They were opposed in the House of Commons first on Standing Orders, and thereafter on the merits, by several landowners and road trusts in the county of Fife, and also by the E.P. & D. and Scottish Central Railways, under the pretence, in so far as these two companies were concerned, that the proposed undertaking was to be a through or competing line of communication, rather than an important feeder to their own lines. That Sir Graham Montgomery of Stanhope, through whose lands the railway would run for a considerable distance, had been an original promoter of the expired Glasgow and Dundee Junction Railway added strength to this contention.

Upon the Bill thereafter reaching the House of Lords, the Trustees for the Great North Road for the first time intimated their intention of opposing it on the ground of injury to the tolls under their charge. Because continuance of such opposition might have endangered the safety of the Bill, it was deemed advisable to formulate an agreement with the Trustees.

A contract having been entered into with Mr William Scott

of Kilmarnock for construction of the line and works at a sum of £47,818-16s-7d, there followed a ceremonial cutting of the first turf near Auchtermuchty on Monday, 12 January 1856. Construction of the line was in itself relatively simple, there being no obstacles to necessitate any major engineering works.

An application was made to Parliament in November 1856 to authorise the Company to relinquish that portion of its railway situated between a point in the parish of Orwell and the terminus to be sited on the eastern side of the Turnpike Road near to the Black Bridge, and in lieu:—

1.   To make a deviation line which would commence at the said point and, passing near the town of Milnathort, terminate at a point west of Kinross on the Gallow Hill Road near a field called Hopefield.

2.   To make a new railway commencing by a junction with the deviation line and terminating at a junction with the Dunfermline branch of the E.P.&D. Railway at or about South Lumphinnans.

3.   And also to make a branch railway or tramway from near where 2 above would cross Kelty Burn as far as Kelty Colliery.

At the same time, the Kinross-shire Railway Bill was laid before Parliament. This Bill, promoted chiefly by shareholders of the E.P. & D., sought to establish a seven mile line running northwards from the Dunfermline branch near South Lumphinnans to a terminus near the south extremity of Kinross, upon the east side of the Great North Road. There was also to be a branch line or tramway diverging west, at a point south of where the proposed line crossed the Orr Water. This would serve Roscobie Lime Works and mines in the vicinity of Kingseat before joining the West of Fife Mineral Railway. According to the estimates of Mr Bouch, construction of the main line and its associated branch, both of which were intended to be single track, would cost £53,579. If the application to Parliament were successful, there would be a working agreement with the E.P. & D. for 25 years, the latter having power to name three Directors of the Kinross-shire Company.

Parliament approved the Kinross-shire Railway Bill in 1857 and refused to sanction the application of the Fife & Kinross

Railway in so far as it would compete with the Kinross-shire. By the next Parliamentary Session, the Fife & Kinross and the Kinross-shire had agreed jointly to present a Bill to connect their two lines at Kinross and to make a joint station. The Fife & Kinross Railway was opened as far as Milnathort on 15 March 1858 and to Kinross five months later on 26 August. The Kinross-shire Railway was opened to the public on Wednesday 20 June 1860—the junction with the Fife & Kinross being effected shortly afterwards.

Whilst the Kinross-shire Railway was, from its opening, worked on generous terms by the E.P. & D., Fife & Kinross Directors were, even in October 1860, still negotiating with the Kinross-shire and E.P. & D. Railways to obtain a 'proper and satisfactory' traffic arrangement. One question still to be resolved was the Fife and Kinross Railway's entitled proportion of the traffic coming from the west. At that time, coal from Kingseat was not allowed to come to Auchtermuchty by Kinross but had to be sent via Thornton and Ladybank! It was not until 5 April, 1861 that the working of the line passed to the E.P. & D. Railway. In the next Session of Parliament, application was made for an Act to enable an amalgamation between this small thriving line and the E.P. & D. Amalgamation of these two railways took place a year after that between the Kinross-shire and its working partner.

At the same time as the Stirling & Dunfermline Railway was projected in 1845, proposals were afoot for a branch from Cambus to Kinross, where passengers would be able to join trains on the Edinburgh and Perth Direct Railway. Plans for the latter railway having failed, the Stirling & Dunfermline decided to proceed only to Tillicoultry, where a temporary terminus was opened in 1851. Powers to extend the railway from Tillicoultry to Kinross were obtained by the Devon Valley Railway Company on 23 July, 1858, but financial difficulties resulted in slow progress and it was not until 1 May, 1863 that the 6½ miles from Kinross to Rumbling Bridge were opened and worked by the N.B.R.

TABLE 6
Kinross as a Railway Centre in 1866
Rumbling Bridge and Kinross to Cowdenbeath, Dunfermline, &c.

STATIONS	Classes	1 Pass.	2 Coal	3 Pass. 1 2 4 am	4 Coal	5 Pass. 1 2 3 pm	6 Coal	7 Pass.
Rumbling Bridge	dep			9.40		3.35		
Crook of Devon	"			9.44		3.39		
Cleish Road	"			9.52		3.47		
Hopefield	arr			9.58		3.53		
	dep			9.59		3.55		
Kinross	arr			10.01		3.57	Sats only	

	Class	1 2 4 am	am	1 2 3 am	pm	1 2 3 pm	pm	1 2 3 pm
Kinross	dep	6.40		10.05		4.10		7.15
Blairadam	"	6.50		10.15		4.20		7.23
Kelty	arr	—		—		—		—
	dep	6.57	9.00	10.22	12.50	4.27	5.00	7.30
Lumphinnans	arr	—	9.10	—	1.00	—	5.15	—
	dep	—		—		—		—
Cowdenbeath	arr	7.10		10.38		4.43		7.43
	dep	8.31		10.43		4.48		7.50
Crossgates	"	8.39		10.50		4.55		7.57
Halbeath	"	8.45		10.55		5.00		8.02
Dunfermline	arr	8.50		11.00		5.05		8.07

Dunfermline, Cowdenbeath &c., to Kinross and Rumbling Bridge

STATIONS	Classes	1 Pass. 1 2 4 am	2 Coal am	3 Coal am	4 Pass. 1 2 3 am	5 Coal pm	6 Pass. 1 2 3 pm	7 Sat only pm
Dunfermline	dep	7.00			11.40		6.00	8.35
Halbeath	"	7.05			11.45		6.05	8.40
Crossgates	"	7.10			11.50		6.10	8.45
Cowdenbeath	arr	7.15			11.55		6.15	8.50
	dep	8.33			12.03		6.28	8.58
Lumphinnans	arr	—			—		—	—
	dep	—	8.00	11.35	—	3.45	—	—
Kelty	arr	—	8.15	11.50	—	4.00	—	—
Blairadam	dep	8.49			12.28		6.45	9.18
Kinross	arr	8.57			12.38		6.55	9.28

	Class	1 2 4			1 2 3
Kinross	dep	9.05			12.47
Hopefield	arr	9.08			12.50
	dep	9.10			12.53
Cleish Road	"	9.15			12.58
Crook of Devon	"	9.25			1.08
Rumbling Bridge	arr	9.29			1.12

Trains for Ladybank depart Kinross at 6.20 a.m., 10.02 a.m. and 3.50 p.m., returning from Ladybank at 8.30 a.m., 11.45 a.m. and 6.25 p.m. Journey time was approximately an hour.

The Cults Lime Works Railway

This was a privately-owned standard-gauge mineral railway which formerly connected the E.P. & D. main line with the lime works at Cults in Fife. The lime works are situated on a hillside some 250 feet above the main line and in order to gain height the railway adopted a somewhat circuitous route incorporating a spectacular horse-shoe curve, with both high embankment and a very deep cutting. Although both the East and West Lime Works are, as the crow flies, about 1¾ miles from the main line, the mineral branch was 3¼ miles long. There was also a trailing connection off this branch, approximately ¾ mile long, which ran parallel to and on the south side of the main Kirkcaldy road as far as the Malt Barns at Pitlessie.

The branch up to the lime works, which opened in 1856 and closed in 1948 was severely graded for most of its length, the gradient on the main ascent reaching 1 in 60. At the junction with the main line, near Hospital Mill level crossing, a short distance south of Springfield station, there were two exchange sidings with a trailing connection to the up Edinburgh line. The points on the up main line were controlled from a lever ground frame and operated by the main line train crews.

Turning abruptly away from the main line in a southward direction on a falling gradient, the branch passed under a road on the Crawford Priory Estate and, after emerging from a shallow cutting, crossed the river Eden by a single span girder bridge where the river is about seventy feet wide.

From the south bank of the river the line traversed open fields on a gently rising gradient, passing a siding which served Cults Mill Farm, to reach the main Cupar-Kirkcaldy road. This road crossed the railway by a substantial stone bridge constructed to extremely tight clearances. The bridge still exists, even though it is not readily noticeable. During the branch's latter years, there were occasions when the lime works private locomotive was out of service and the L.N.E.R. supplied the motive power. The latter's locomotives could get through the bridge—but only just!

Immediately beyond was the divergence of the branch to Pitlessie. From this point to the East Lime Works the ascent was continuous. From here the line continued on the level for a further half mile to the West Works where it terminated. Both the East and West Works possessed sidings and in addition the West Works had a run-round loop and small locomotive shed.

Traffic conveyed up the branch to the works was mainly coal. In the line's heyday, three or four trains would make return journeys daily, the normal complement of workers engaged being four—a driver, fireman-shunter and two permanent-way men.

6

Around the East Neuk

THE very early years of the Leven Railway, which ran for a distance of six miles from Thornton Junction to Leven, were described in a previous chapter. Because of the great traffic potential which lay further east, plans for an East of Fife Railway were being enthusiastically welcomed only a few months after the Leven Railway opened on 3 July, 1854.

At a public meeting of gentlemen favourable to an extension of the railway from Leven to Anstruther, held at Colinsburgh in September, 1854, Sir Ralph A. Anstruther of Balcaskie, who had been unanimously called to the chair, observed that during an earlier meeting proposing the construction of the Leven Railway he had predicted its ultimate extension to Anstruther. Unforeseen delays and difficulties combined to hinder attention to a parallel project and it was felt prudent to concentrate on completing the Leven Railway first.

Sir Ralph went on to note that Thomas Bouch had been consulted for an estimate there being no time to advertise for tenders. He commented wryly that knowing Bouch he could be relied upon to estimate 'on the safe side' and was duly informed the twelve mile stretch could cost in the region of £58,000. In wishing to substantiate that there would be sufficient traffic to generate a dividend of 7% he called on certain gentlemen present to give some statistics on the agricultural and fish traffic of the district.

Mr John Wood, Banker, Colinsburgh, then presented the meeting with a number of interesting statistics in connection with agricultural traffic. From the statistics which he had collected it could be concluded that whatever might be the traffic from grain, there could be no doubt of a large amount of traffic from potatoes and cattle and that the expense of transit would be greatly reduced. Mr Wood also made reference to a species of traffic which was of great importance to the economy of East Fife. He referred to coals, the difficulty of procuring which was often very great.

Then Mr Mackintosh, joint-agent with Mr Conolly for the National Bank at Anstruther addressed the meeting. He said that he need not remind the meeting that the East Coast of Fife was all sprinkled over with towns and villages which derived their existence mainly from the sea; and the configuration of the coast was such as to almost isolate them from the inland world. The coast towns alone, at the last census (1851), had a population of 8,435. They owned 27 vessels of 1427 tons, exclusive of 226 boats engaged in herring fishing and 74 in the white fishing. The total annual average value for five years of landings was £63,000 and the weight between 8,000 and 9,000 tons. The coasting trade from Elie to Crail for the year ending 4 January, 1854 was—vessels outwards and inwards with cargo—inwards, 157 vessels of 6,115 tons; outwards, 275 vessels of 11,521 tons. He wished, further, to allude to the effect which steam to Leith, and the opening of the English railways had created. Fourteen years earlier fish could be purchased at prices from 70 to 100 per cent lower than those currently being asked. Not only were there in Anstruther numbers of English buyers during the winter herring fishing, but English fishmongers found it to their advantage to open permanent curing establishments there. And the advantage arising to the fishermen of more steady facilities for transit than even the steamer afforded, was proved by the frequent fact that the price of fish, more especially winter herrings, rose and fell with the despatch of the steamer, which could only be at certain stages of the tide.

Despite widespread public support, a meeting of subscribers held at the same venue on 9 November was told that there appeared to be no prospect of obtaining sufficient subscriptions to enable a Bill to be laid before Parliament that Session. Rather than abandon the scheme or postpone application to Parliament, it was resolved to build the line from a junction with the Leven Railway, at or near Leven Station, to a temporary terminus at or near the Minister's Glebe in the town of Kilconquhar. The estimated cost from Leven to Kilconquhar would, it was claimed, be cheaper per mile than the cost from Kilconquhar to Anstruther, on which section considerable engineering expense was to be incurred. Furthermore, delays were envisaged because Sir John Bethune had raised objections to the line travelling through his grounds east of Kilconquhar. Statutory Notices of intention to apply to Parliament appeared in the Press towards the end of November.

The line was opened for goods traffic as far as Largo (2m 54ch) on 1 February, 1857. Although steamers started almost from the very doors of the fishcurers, the traffic in fish was, from the outset, very extensive. Clearly the steamers had not been able to provide a punctual service, essential if the fish was to arrive at the southern markets in a satisfactory condition.

Construction of the line to Kilconquhar was comparatively easy. For a considerable part of the way the track crossed over the 'benty' links by the sea shore. The only difficult and expensive part was immediately west of Largo station, where the line was carried across the Boghall Burn by a four arch viaduct. Its central arches were 60 feet high and had a 60 foot span.

The following timetable came into effect when the entire line opened to Kilconquhar—6m. 46 ch. from Leven—on 11 August, 1857:—

Class		1 2 4	1 2 3	1 2 3	1 2 3
		Mail		Mail	
Kilconquhar & Elie	dep	6.45 am	10.15	4.20 pm	6.40
Largo	"	6.57	10.27	4.32	6.52
Lundin Links	"	7.00	10.30	4.35	6.55
Leven	"	7.15	10.45	4.50	7.10
Cameron Bridge	"	7.23	10.53	4.58	7.18
Thornton	arr	7.43	11.13	5.20	7.33
Thornton	dep	8.13 am	11.38	5.43 pm	7.58
Cameron Bridge	"	8.32	11.55	6.00	8.15
Leven	"	8.40	12.03 pm	6.08	8.23
Lundin Links	"	8.47	12.10	6.15	8.30
Largo	"	8.50	12.13	6.18	8.33
Kilconquhar & Elie	arr	9.10	12.28	6.30	8.53

An agreement had been made with the Leven Railway by which all trains worked through from Kilconquhar to Thornton. A Coach left Anstruther at 5.35 a.m. and 3.00 p.m. to connect with the 6.45 a.m. and 4.20 p.m. trains from Kilconquhar. It returned eastwards shortly after 9.10 a.m. and 6.30 p.m.

In 1861 two important Bills were presented to Parliament. By the first, the Leven and East of Fife Railway Companies (Amalgamation &c) Bill, it was proposed to dissolve the Leven and East of Fife Railway Companies and to incorporate their shareholders as 'The Leven and East of Fife Railway Company'. "The united share capital of the company will be made up of 'Leven capital stock', which will consist of the Leven Company's present share capital of £23,000 together with a further £14,000 to be authorised by this Bill and of 'East of Fife capital stock' comprising the present share capital of £32,000 and a further £3,000 to be authorised by the Bill. The united Loan Capitals of £5,000 and £10,600 were the authorised Loan Capitals of the two companies respectively. The clear revenue of the undertaking is to be appropriated, as to two-thirds, to the proprietors of the 'Leven capital stock', and as to one-third, to the proprietors of the 'East of Fife capital stock'".

The second Bill, the Leven and East of Fife Railways (Extension &c) Bill, proposed to enable the two companies to appoint a joint committee for making, maintaining, and managing an extension railway, length 6 miles 45 chains, from a junction with the East of Fife Railway at Kilconquhar station to a terminus in the parish of Anstruther Wester, to be completed within 5 years and to be vested equally in the two companies. For the purposes of the Bill each of the two companies sought to raise additional sums of £20,000 by preferential shares and £6,600 by borrowing.

The extension was not dependent on the outcome of the amalgamation Bill, but if this were successful the powers of the second Bill would be vested in the amalgamated company.

The two railways were amalgamated on 22 July, 1861. On the same day powers were obtained to continue the line eastwards to Anstruther and this extension was brought into use on 1 September, 1863.

From Leven to Anstruther the line was single track throughout with passing loops at all stations except Lundin Links, Kilconquhar and Pittenweem. At Kilconquhar there was a small goods yard, whilst about a mile to the west was a passing loop used only during the summer season when traffic was frequently extremely heavy.

Traffic at all stations on the new extension increased steadily and by November, 1863, was such as to require a special luggage train to be run daily. However, regular passenger services east of Leven were not increased beyond four trains each way per day until the summer of 1870. Trains stopped at every station on the line and took 50 minutes to complete the 12½ mile route.

The declaration of large annual dividends during the 1870s reflects a continuing prosperity during those years immediately prior to absorption by the North British Railway in 1877. For the half-year to 31 January, 1872, the directors recommended a dividend of 10½% to shareholders of the Leven stock and 4½% to East of Fife holders. Two and a half years later the corresponding percentages were 10 and 5.

It was not until August 1880 that powers were obtained to link Anstruther with St Andrews. The Anstruther & St Andrews Railway commenced by a junction 257 yards from the western end of the passenger station at Anstruther and immediately crossed the Dreel Burn on a skew bridge comprising two 35 ft. span arches. The bridge was so broad that only one side of it was required for rails, the other side providing a roadway by which officials from the new station beyond could communicate with the goods station, of which the original terminus became a part. This survived, complete with its platforms and buildings, until the 1960s.

Opened to passenger traffic as far as Boarhills on 1 September, 1883, the 8½ mile line from Anstruther surmounted several steep gradients. The first, an ascent at 1 in 60, began almost at Anstruther station and extended for nearly three-quarters of a mile. Following three miles of easier gradients, the final half-mile to Crail was on a rising 1 in 85. At

Crail, the railway turned abruptly inland and started climbing at 1 in 66 for nearly a mile before encountering about 3½ miles of easier undulations to Boarhills. The final 6 miles 49 chains between Boarhills and St Andrews—the final link in the loop joining Leuchars with Thornton—was not completed for a further four years. Having left Boarhills, trains climbed gradients continually varying between 1 in 50 and 1 in 59 to the summit of the line at Stravithie, 1¾ miles to the north-west. Once across the summit, the descent to St Andrews began with over a half a mile at 1 in 50, steepening to 1 in 49 for nearly 1½ miles beyond Mount Melville station. This steep descent, which was not without several sharp curves, became less severe as St Andrews was approached on short stretches of 1 in 63 and 1 in 60.

A single track throughout, there were passing loops at Crail, Kingsbarns and Stravithie.

So great was the demand by local farmers for railway services that the N.B.R., who were to work the line, consented to open it for local goods traffic as far as Crail early in May, 1883. The first train to depart from Crail comprised four wagons, three each containing seven prime oxen and the fourth a quantity of malt. It was hauled by the Directors' traction engine to Anstruther Junction, where it was attached to the ordinary 'Special' for transit across the Forth. A month later a powerful N.B.R. six-wheel locomotive was steamed to Anstruther to assist in this goods traffic, which was reported to have 'developed encouragingly'. The truckage of corn, manure and general merchandise was computed at 30 tons per day, even although the service was only operated in the morning or evening, so as not to interfere with the regular duties of 'that useful little engine belonging to the Directors'.

When the railway did open for passenger traffic, work on the new station at Anstruther had not been completed and for some three months trains to and from Boarhills had to reverse in and out of the original terminus.

By May of the next year trains were operating according to the following timetable:—

102

Boarhills	dep.	5.55 am	8.45	12.10 pm	3.30	6.40	
Kingsbarns	"	6.00	8.50	12.15	3.37	6.45	
Crail	"	6.08	8.58	12.23	3.48	6.53	
Anstruther	arr	6.20	9.10	12.35	4.05	7.05	
	dep	6.30	9.45	1.10	4.25	7.20 SO[1]	
Thornton	arr	7.40	10.42	2.20	5.35	8.25	

Thornton	dep		8.00	11.20	2.50	5.52	9.00 SO
Anstruther	arr		9.03	12.23 pm	3.53	6.55	10.05
	dep	7.55 am	9.25	12.50	4.20	7.20	
Crail	arr	8.06	9.36	1.01	4.31	7.31	
Kingsbarns	"	8.14	9.44	1.09	4.39	7.39	
Boarhills	"	8.20	9.50	1.15	4.45	7.45	

[1]Saturdays only

A coach, operated by Mr Rusack, proprietor of the Star Hotel, St Andrews, departed from that town at 7.40 a.m. and 2.20 p.m. It arrived at Boarhills an hour later where connection could be made with the 8.45 a.m. and 3.30 p.m. trains; the return journey to St Andrews commencing at 9.55 a.m. and 4.50 p.m.

Defying competition from the railway, the St Andrews and Crail Omnibus continued to attract custom. It set out from the Royal Hotel, St Andrews, 'every lawful morning' at 10.00 a.m. and departed from Crail at 4.35 p.m., returning about 6.00 p.m. The homeward journey was only marginally longer than that undertaken by train and connecting coach.

On 31 October, 1885, the *Fife News* contained the following:—

A most important improvement is in course at Anstruther railway station in connection with utilising the old station for fish traffic. With the double rails on either side of the spacious esplanade, there will be accommodation for 40 wagons in connection with the fast trains that will run during the season.

English buyers were formerly particularly exposed to annoyance and loss by limited facilities at the station, where it was not unusual on the first day of a heavy fishing to lock the gates in face of the traffic.

Herrings were carted from pier to station at 3d per barrel which led to bickering and delay but now the railway has arranged to convey them in lorries at a charge of 1/- a ton, to be included in the through rate.

Early in February of the following year the same newspaper reported that:—

> The herring fishing harvest has been immense this week. On Tuesday, no fewer than 190 railway wagons left the East Neuk laden with fish. On Wednesday, traffic was only 16 wagons less. It was higher on the Thursday and the large sum thus accruing to the railway will be apparent if it is borne in mind that the English traffic is valued at over 10/- a cran. We may observe that the change from the old to the new platform has proved a notable convenience, as it leaves the first free for just such a pressure as occurred this week.

Completion of the final seven miles from Boarhills to St. Andrews on 1 June, 1887 almost coincided with the opening of the second Tay Bridge on 13 July of that year.

St Andrews (New) Station was closer to the city centre than the old one at the Links, being located at the west end of Market Street in a park off City Road. The station, however, was badly situated in a deep cutting, although an improvement on the shed which formerly served the purpose. Two footbridges gave access to an island platform, one side of which was rather sharply curved.

When the railway was opened to St Andrews, freestone quarries at Stravithie and Nether Kenly were advertised to let. Stone from these quarries had been extensively used in the railway's construction.

Within three years of reaching St Andrews, communications with Edinburgh and the South were improved by the opening of the Forth Bridge on 4 March, 1890. This considerably enhanced the line's importance, both as an outlet for agricultural and fishery products, and as a means of access to the many attractive holiday resorts and weekend residences along its route.

The years just before World War 1 have been recognised by many writers as belonging to the golden age of railway travel. This was equally true for the East of Fife line, where services were building up towards their zenith:—

Departures from Thornton:—

7.40 a.m.	All stations to St Andrews (arr. 9.39)
9.52	All stations to Anstruther (arr. 10.52), except Cameron Bridge. Stops at Kilconquhar on Tuesdays only and on other days when requested.
10.45	All stations to St Andrews (arr 12.29)
1.15 p.m.	Cameron Bridge and Leven (arr. 1.31)
3.05	All stations to St Andrews (arr 4.48)
5.05	Cameron Bridge and Leven (arr. 5.21)
6.05	All stations to St Andrews (arr. 7.43)
9.10	All stations to Anstruther (arr. 10.08)

An additional train left Anstruther at 7.55 a.m. for St Andrews. This, together with the 7.40 and 10.45 a.m. trains from Thornton worked forward to Dundee.

Departures from St Andrews:—

6.26 a.m.	All stations to Thornton (arr. 8.07)
8.38	All stations to Thornton (arr. 10.13)
11.02	All stations to Thornton (arr. 12.58)
2.38 p.m.	All stations to Thornton (arr. 4.28)
6.36	All stations to Thornton (arr. 8.22)

There were, in addition, some intermediate workings. Trains left Leven at 2.15 p.m. and Anstruther at 4.04 p.m. for all stations to Thornton, whilst on Mondays only, a stopping train departed Crail at 5.45 a.m. for Thornton.

Every summer during 'fair' holidays regular services were strengthened and many special private excursion trains frequented the line.

Later in 1910, shortly after doubling of the line between Thornton and Leven had been completed, an express service was introduced between Glasgow and Crail. Named the *Fifeshire Coast Express,* it initially ran to Fife on Friday afternoons only, returning to the commercial capital on Monday mornings. In the following year, the train ran daily throughout the summer, covering the 66½ miles between Glasgow and Leven non-stop in 92 minutes. Calls were then made at Elie and Anstruther before the train terminated at Crail.

During the inter-war years the service was considerably modified. Eastbound, through carriages were detached from a Glasgow-Dundee train at Dalmeny and transferred to the 4.50

p.m. *Fifeshire Coast Express* from Edinburgh-Dundee, which was following six minutes later. The train from Glasgow ran on via Thornton Junction and Cupar to Dundee; whilst that from Edinburgh did call at Kirkcaldy, but passing Thornton, made Leven its next stop. When Crail was reached at 6.42 p.m., the Glasgow coaches were disconnected, before the train continued via St Andrews to arrive in Dundee at 8.06 p.m.—97 minutes after the Glasgow express. The next morning the Glasgow coaches, having been stabled at Crail overnight, formed a single *Fifeshire Coast Express*, which left at 7.05 a.m. and called at all stations to Thornton. After a stop at Kirkcaldy, the train divided at Dalmeny, the Glasgow section completing its journey at 9.46 a.m.—43 minutes later than the Edinburgh portion.

Following the Second World War the train was revived in summer months as a Glasgow-St Andrews express only. Departing from Queen Street at 4.07 p.m., and latterly Buchanan Street at 3.50 p.m., the restyled *Fife Coast Express* called at Burntisland, Kirkcaldy, Leven, Elie, Anstruther and Crail, before reaching St Andrews at 6.53 p.m. Westbound, an early 7.15 a.m. departure and elimination of the Burntisland stop enabled Glasgow to be reached by 9.50 a.m. For some time passengers could travel in the comfort of five pre-war articulated *Silver Jubilee* streamline coaches, although catering facilities were withdrawn early in 1952. By 1959, the through service to St Andrews ran only during July and August and called at all stations between Inverkeithing and Thornton. For the remainder of the year, a nameless Down express ran from Glasgow as far as Leven at the same times, but there was no corresponding return service. This train was withdrawn at the start of the 1960 Summer Timetable, in which St Andrews' prestige express no longer featured.

The *Fife Coast Express* was always steam hauled, usually by "Bl" 4-6-0s, but local trains, frequently composed of non-corridor stock in the hands of ex-N.B.R. 4-4-0s, were largely replaced by Gloucester built twin d.m.u. sets, before services on the line were withdrawn on 4 September, 1965.

When public notice was given to close the East of Fife line, the passenger timetable had already been pruned in response to a dwindling demand:—

Number of Westbound Trains
(July and August)

	1959			1965		
Section	*Mon-Fri*	*Sat*	*Sun*	*Mon-Fri*	*Sat*	*Sun*
St Andrews—Crail	4	5	—	4	5	—
Crail—Anstruther	8	10	2	5	8	1
Anstruther—Leven	9	12	3	5	10	3

The 1959 timetable shows some interesting through Saturday workings. The 8.30 a.m. Glasgow (Buchanan Street) to St Andrews train took the direct line to Alloa, from where it ran non-stop to Burntisland and Kirkcaldy. At Thornton Junction, passengers who did not change into a following Glasgow-Dundee via Crail service could continue to Leuchars, from where, after a 15 minute delay, the train worked south to St Andrews. The return working to Queen Street (Low Level), via the Forth Bridge, passed the 11.10 a.m. from Queen Street to St Andrews near Markinch. This latter train conveyed through carriages to Elie, which were detached at Thornton, and uplifted on the return journey to Glasgow via Crail.

The East Fife Central Railway, which commenced from a junction at a point about a mile west from Leven station and extended for 14 miles 47 chains north-east to Lochty, was opened for merchandise traffic on Sunday, 21 August, 1898. Authorised by the East Fife Central Railway Act, 1893, the line was of single track with intermediate stations at Kennoway, Montrave, and Largoward. Passenger services were limited to workmens' trains which travelled as far as Largobeath at a speed not in excess of 25 m.p.h.—the maximum permitted on any part of the line.

Competition from motor transport, especially advantageous where the traffic to be forwarded and received is scattered over a wide distance from railheads, significantly reduced the volume of goods handled at many stations, as the following figures, extracted from Traffic Statement Books, record:—

107

	Goods Tons	Minerals Tons	Coal Tons	Cattle Head	Sheep Head	Pigs Head
Anstruther						
Half year ending Jan. 1920	11,512	705	11,218	244	509	—
Half year ending Jan. 1930	8,439	619	14,004	192	556	3
Crail						
Half year ending Jan. 1920	8,019	684	2,941	167	202	—
Half year ending Jan. 1930	5,632	727	2,797	173	195	—
Kingsbarns						
Half year ending Jan. 1920	1,113	314	305	42	109	—
Half year ending Jan. 1930	263	102	94	27	57	1
Boarhills						
Half year ending Jan. 1920	948	187	211	50	182	2
Half year ending Jan. 1930	275	113	109	32	79	1
Stravithie						
Half year ending Jan. 1920	902	114	257	39	163	4
Half year ending Jan. 1930	297	151	155	19	104	1
Mount Melville						
Half year ending Jan. 1920	696	98	300	29	74	2
Half year ending Jan. 1930	210	66	197	14	36	—
St Andrews						
Half year ending Jan. 1920	14,919	667	14,743	142	88	—
Half year ending Jan. 1930	10,114	635	15,121	207	83	—
Kennoway						
Half year ending Jan. 1920	1,577	172	1,385	11	187	—
Half year ending Jan. 1930						
Montrave						
Half year ending Jan. 1920	3,661	245	874	85	75	4
Half year ending Jan. 1930	344	333	495	1	216	—
Largoward						
Half year ending Jan. 1920	1,197	105	867	53	77	—
Half year ending Jan. 1930	524	269	642	4	954	—
Lochty						
Half year ending Jan. 1920	744	159	403	45	207	2
Half year ending Jan. 1930	244	29	222	33	168	—

Kingsbarns, Boarhills, Stravithie and Mount Melville stations were all closed to passenger traffic on 20 September, 1930. The crossing loop at Kingsbarns was retained but that at Stravithie removed. A few years earlier, the newly formed L.N.E.R. closed Anstruther East signal box and shortened the crossing loop so as to terminate at buffer stops near the eastern end of the platform. Thereafter, all through trains used the station's southern platform, whilst that on the north side only accommodated trains from the west terminating at the station.

For many years scheduled services for fish traffic from Anstruther to Edinburgh were at 3.00 p.m. and 5.00 p.m. The first departure connected at Edinburgh with the 5.45 p.m. fish train to King's Cross, where booked arrival was at 3.35 a.m., but fish despatched by the second service travelled south by ordinary train—unless there were sufficient vans to justify a second special.

Following World War II, railway goods traffic in East Fife declined to an insignificant level. Even ten years before the line was completely closed east of Leven, the following two services only operated:—

		Daily				*MWFO*
Thornton Jct.	dep.	6.05 a.m.	Thornton Jct.	dep.	9.05 a.m.
Anstruther	arr.	9.12	Largo	arr.	9.58
	dep.	11.10		dep.	10.15
St Andrews	arr.	1.48 p.m.	Cameron Bridge	arr.	10.58
	dep.	2.10		dep.	11.25
Anstruther	arr.	4.25	Leven	arr.	11.35
	dep.	6.25		dep.	11.50
Thornton Jct.	arr.	9.58	Lochty	arr.	1.50 p.m.
				dep.	2.05
			Thornton Jct.	arr.	4.32

(extracted from 1955 WTT)

West of Leven, both trains worked through Kirkland Yard, in its time the main assembling point from which wagons were taken to Methil Docks.

The writer recollects only once having seen an engine working on the East Fife Central Line. It was a Holmes

109

NBR J 36 0-6-0 climbing eastwards up the 1 in 70 grade to the summit of the line near Montrave. Although during the summer, a snowplough was fitted to No. 65345 to remove mud from farm tracks crossing the line. The load—one van, one brake van!

Of Largoward station, Mr J.M. Bennett, a former station-master has written:—

> Living conditions at the station house were primitive, with a dry toilet at the bottom of the garden. For drinking water, we had to rely on two small barrels, which made alternate journeys from Cameron Bridge by the goods train running three days a week from Thornton.
>
> Seed potato traffic and grain were the main source of revenue. Once a year we loaded a big consignment of flax from the Earl of Crawford's farms destined for a mill at Blairgowrie. For a long time we had coal from (nearby) Radernie Colliery loaded to Methil Docks. Strange to think of it now, but the colliery transport man preferred small 6 ton wagons, as they made for easy tipping of his lorry load.

After withdrawal of passenger train services in 1969, the line was closed between East Fife Central Junction and Leven and singled from Thornton station to that junction. The track was downgraded to Goods Standard only and a ground frame installed at Cameron Bridge for Scottish Grain Distillers private siding. In May, 1975, the single goods line was slued to the Down (eastbound) side of the former island platform at Cameron Bridge, while that portion of the line on the Up side, although retained, was designated Platform siding and terminated by a buffer stop erected at the Kirkland Yard end of the platform.

7

The Rise and Fall of
Burntisland and Methil

LONG before the end of the last century, the vast network of railways which snaked its way deep inland to remote colliery workings became so busy that a rapid growth of port facilities was needed. In Fife, good co-ordination between train movements and shipping space was more an ambition than an achievement.

In every Half-Yearly Report to its shareholders the E.P. & D. was able to detail increased traffic. As early as September 1855, Sir William Dunbar, the Company's Deputy Chairman, remarked:—

> On mineral traffic the increase in revenue is considerable. The difference in favour of the past over the corresponding half year is about 33,000 tons and due largely to increased activity in coal districts.
>
> Rolling stock generally could not be maintained in a better condition. Since February 1852, of a stock of about 1500 wagons, 509 have been entirely rebuilt, whilst a considerable additional number have been reconstructed and charged to Revenue Account. We have also within the last year or two added a considerable number of new wagons to stock.

Both the new wagons and those rebuilt in an additional workshop at Burntisland were all of a greater capacity than those acquired earlier.

The following year the Chairman expressed to shareholders his belief that, because of soaring mineral traffic along the Dunfermline branch, Thornton Junction was becoming a more and more important part of their line. He felt it very fortunate that no works had been executed there at the same time as other works on the railway, as in all probability they would have required considerable alterations to accommodate extra track, by then necessary for handling coal trains destined for the

111

harbours of Tayport and Burntisland. At these harbours were constantly to be seen a number of vessels queueing to load coal.

Goods and mineral traffic on the Forth ferry had by the start of 1860 outgrown the capabilities of the two boats in that service and the Directors tendered for a third boat of larger capacity than the *Leviathan*. That same year, 50 additional goods wagons were placed on the line, whilst, shortly afterwards arrangements were concluded with two of the colliery proprietors for a further 121 new coal wagons to be supplied. Coal production did not, however, keep pace, and notwithstanding their delivery in 1861, the wagon stock still proved inadequate especially at certain seasons. Delays in coal handling were made more serious because the demand for wagons for this traffic was greatest, just at the time when traffic in the agricultural produce of the district was at its peak. To minimise delays, the Company had, of necessity, to incur considerable expenditure on the provision of greatly enlarged coal storage areas at all the larger stations throughout the mining district.

The final Half-Yearly Report of the E.P. & D., before its amalgamation with the North British Railway, shows that during the six months ended 31 January, 1862, no less than 369,000 tons of goods and coal were carried over the 78 miles of line. As many as 42,460 wagons were ferried across the Forth to or from Burntisland and then hauled to their destinations by any of the Company's 46 available engines. It is very creditable that operating staff were also able to provide sufficient passenger trains for some 835,000 travellers.

In the years following amalgamation the latent potential of the Fife coalfield was rapidly discovered and exploited. At Burntisland chronic delays, possibly tantamount to utter confusion, had been temporarily allayed with the commissioning of a new outer harbour at the end of 1860. For an estimated cost of £10,000, the contractors provided a sheltered dock, extending to over 20 acres, immediately to the south of the old harbour. Here as many as 15 or 20 foreign vessels, mainly Danish or German, were now rapidly loaded with coal or iron. Trains could be emptied more speedily and their wagons freed for immediate return inland.

112

After only a few years, expansion to eliminate delays became essential, as output from the collieries continued to reach new records. The *Fife Herald*, in its issue dated 5 September, 1872, reported that there were no less than 62 vessels lying in Burntisland harbour, some of them having spent 5, 6 or even 7 weeks waiting for coal. During the previous month 50 vessels had sailed, all with coal, chiefly for the Baltic ports, whilst arrivals numbered 66, of which 18 were direct from foreign ports in ballast. Such pressures forced the coal-masters to join with the railway and other interested branches of trade in making an application to Parliament to carry out an extensive harbour and railway scheme at Burntisland. This scheme was opened in December, 1876 with a show of much public rejoicing. A new dock, which had been incorporated in the plans, brought about a great transformation in the port facilities.

The tidal basin was reduced by practically half, the graving dock obliterated, a cattle pen done away with and adjoining ground merged into the dock area. Introduction of three hydraulic hoists enabled shipment of coal, previously carried out using hand-wrought cranes in the outer harbour, to be executed at an unprecedented rate of 1,000 tons per hour.

Within the next ten years trade figures were to rise beyond even the most optimistic predictions. Railway wagons, which in 1877 had trundled along the coast from Kirkcaldy with 287,000 tons of coal, helped to carry just over 773,000 tons only eight years later. Sometimes the coal trains would pass lengthy rakes of wagons being worked arduously up towards Kinghorn with imports of esparto grass, flax, sleepers, pitwood, linseed and straw. No fewer than 102 of the 639 steamers and 505 sailing vessels which called at Burntisland in 1885, arrived with cargoes of straw for widespread distribution throughout the Peninsula.

These figures are exclusive of all traffic handled by the railway's own train ferry sailings. Four wagon ferries, the largest being capable of carrying 40 wagons, were kept at full capacity day and night until the opening of the Forth Railway Bridge in 1890. During the month of March, 1887, the number of wagons transported to both sides of the Forth totalled 15,693. After making allowances for seasonal fluctuations, contemporary statisticians were able to calculate an annual transhipment of 188,300 wagons—considerably over 100,000 more than in 1862.

As work on construction of the Forth Bridge and connecting line from Burntisland to Inverkeithing rapidly progressed, plans were being formulated for yet another new dock at Burntisland. These plans were designed to amply accommodate the output estimated by the developers of an enlarged West Fife coalfield, which would very soon have a direct railway link with the port. Because of this link, the ferry harbour would become superfluous and enable a substantial saving in construction costs to be made.

The new harbour and dock area, extending to about 43¼ acres and served by over 9 miles of railway, was opened in 1901 with the immediate effect of practically doubling coal exports. Its wider entrance, by which vessels of up to 7,000 tons could be admitted, enabled a much larger class of vessel to call for cargoes. By 1905, cargo totals amounted to 1,817, 000 tons, growing in the following year to 2,013,000 tons. Shipments in 1911 were 2,431,000 tons and would most certainly have continued to increase if it were not that strong competition had arisen.

Prior to 1888 Burntisland had been the only major coal port on the north side of the Forth estuary, but in that year Captain Randolph Wemyss of Wemyss Castle completed his first dock at Methil.

The future prospects of Methil as an ideal outlet for Fife coal had become increasingly realised during the 1860s and '70s, especially because of the port's closer proximity to the then expanding East Fife coalfields. A railway, which had been opened from Thornton Junction down to the coast at Buckhaven in 1881 was extended north-eastwards to Methil in 1884, upon Captain Wemyss concluding satisfactory guarantees with his tenants as to annual shipments of coal from the port.

A new dock at Methil was built at a cost of about

114

£100,000, mostly on land reclaimed from the sea and from which it was protected by an imposing quarter-mile long sea wall, some 25 feet high with an average thickness of 12 feet. Three hydraulic powered coal hoists were installed and electricity used for illumination. Work was completed in time for a ceremonial opening held on 5 May, 1887, before a crowd of over 15,000 enjoying a local public holiday. A single platform station at Methil, together with the railway from Buckhaven one and a quarter miles distant, was opened to passengers on the same day.

Only two years later the line down from Thornton, together with the docks at both Methil and Leven, were bought by the North British Railway. A most significant clause in this sale agreement was a concession by the purchaser giving Captain Wemyss the right to build a private mineral railway to carry his tenants' traffic directly to Methil docks. Accommodation at the dock rapidly became inadequate for the volume of traffic arriving and on 11 June, 1891, the N.B.R. obtained an Act authorising construction of a second, or outer dock, covering an area of 6½ acres. Work commenced in 1894, when 725 steamers and 318 sailing vessels exported 823,000 tons of coal and was completed in January 1900, during which year 1,184 steamers and 320 sailing vessels loaded 1,681,000 tons.

Within another ten years coal exports grew to very nearly 3 million tons, while within the same period of time that at Burntisland increased by a mere 364,000 tons. For a brief period the two ports had kept on level terms, but in 1892 the east took the lead and continued to forge ahead.

Because of the greatly increased berthage provided by the opening of the second dock at Methil, annual tonnages of coal shipped from the port continued to rise, so that it was not long before traffic again outgrew all available capacity. Constant yearly increases in tonnage handled were helped in no small way by co-operation from the N.B.R., who, in September 1899, fully concurred with the terms of a lease and agreement giving the Wemyss Coal Company power to construct and operate the Wemyss Private Railway on behalf of Captain Wemyss. In

1894, some 140,000 tons of coal were lifted in the parish of Wemyss, but by 1913, when coal exports reached a peak of 3,224,000 tons, the private railway network, operating within a radius of four miles from the port, handled no less than two-thirds of this total. Many of the W.P.R. engines have been preserved in working order by Scottish enthusiasts.

Although by the Burntisland Harbour Act of 1896, Burntisland Docks had come under North British control, the railway decided to concentrate expansion at Methil, which was far nearer to both the Wemyss estate and the central districts of Fife from whence came the greater part of the county's coal output.

In 1907 Parliamentary powers were obtained for the making of yet a third dock, immediately to the east of the existing docks at Methil. The work, which commenced in 1908, involved reclamation from the sea of no less than 44 acres of foreshore and construction of a wet dock with an area of 16¾ acres. The contractors, Messrs. Blyth and Blyth, of Edinburgh, were required to make an immense sea wall to enclose the reclaimed land. This wall, about a mile in length, was subjected, during construction, to two very severe storms causing extensive damage which greatly delayed completion. However, within five years of work commencing, 22 January, 1913 was determined for the formal opening of the new dock complex by the Countess of Dalkeith.

The following table shows the total extent of the docks and facilities available at Methil in 1923, a year during which 2,934 vessels called to export 3,368,000 tons of coal:—

TABLE 7
The Facilities and Extent of Methil Docks—1923

		No. 1 Dock	No. 2 Dock	No. 3 Dock
Water Area	Acres	4¾	6½	16¼
Length of quay walls	Feet	1900	2340	5980
Width of Entrance Gate	"	50	50	80
No. of coal hoists	—	1	3	6
No. of coal cranes	—	—	1	—
No. of ordinary cranes	—	8	5	1
Shed and warehouse accommodation	Sq. Ft.	7780	8400	Nil

1979

(Sketch plan—not to scale)

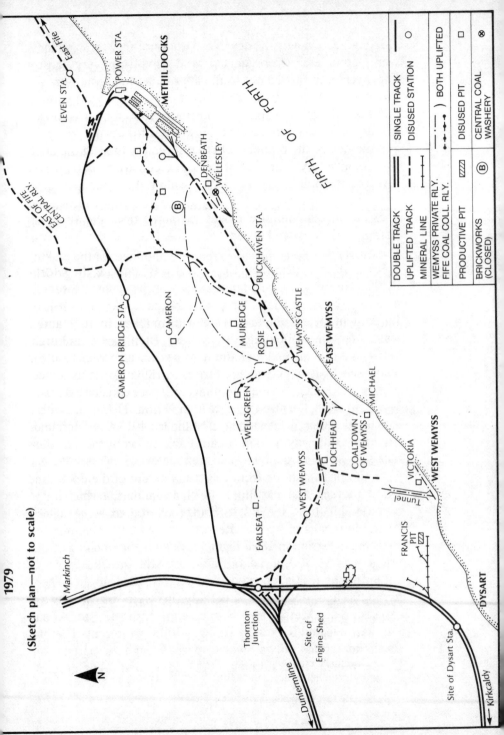

Legend:

DOUBLE TRACK		SINGLE TRACK	○
UPLIFTED TRACK		DISUSED STATION	
MINERAL LINE		BOTH UPLIFTED	
WEMYSS PRIVATE RLY.		DISUSED PIT	□
FIFE COAL COLL. RLY.			
PRODUCTIVE PIT	▨	CENTRAL COAL WASHERY	⊗
BRICKWORKS (CLOSED)	Ⓑ		

N

Markinch

East Fife

LEVEN STA.

POWER STA.

METHIL DOCKS

DENBEATH

WELLESLEY

EAST OF FIFE
CENTRAL RLY.

Ⓑ

CAMERON BRIDGE STA.

CAMERON

BUCKHAVEN STA.

MUIREDGE

ROSIE

WEMYSS CASTLE

EAST WEMYSS

WELLSGREEN

MICHAEL

LOCHHEAD

COALTOWN
OF WEMYSS

WEST WEMYSS

WEST WEMYSS

EARLSEAT

VICTORIA

Tunnel

FRANCIS
PIT

DYSART

Thornton Junction

Site of
Engine Shed

Site of Dysart Sta.

Dunfermline

Kirkcaldy

FIRTH OF FORTH

5   Railways in the Wemyss district, 1979

In connection with the new No. 3 dock, railway arrangements were completely reorganised and involved very costly improvements carried out to the approaches, especially at the Leven end. At Kirkland, to the west of Leven, a yard with 12 miles of sidings and capable of storing 30,000 tons of coal was laid down. To facilitate the working of traffic between this yard and the docks, the branch from the Leven Railway to the dock was replaced by four sets of rails, the construction of which involved the building of a retaining wall in the River Leven, as well as several bridges. The majority of the coal entering the docks from the Methil end was extracted from the Wemyss Estate and conveyed direct over the lines of the Wemyss Private Railway.

Regardless of the new Forth Railway Bridge, the North British Railway, however unwilling they may have been to continue the Burntisland ferry were bound to do so by Act of Parliament. The Company, which was required to maintain at least three steam-boats, crossing daily eight times each way between April and October and six times during winter months, dispensed with its goods only ferries in 1890. Although by no means antiquated, as may be imagined, problems could arise. When, in 1898, the passenger steamer *William Muir* was being over-hauled, her place was taken by the *Wemyss Castle* on loan from the Galloway Saloon Steam Packet Company. Unfortunately, this vessel could only accommodate passengers and great were the protestations from the many wishing to ship cattle, sheep, horses and carriages—a clear indication that for a considerable time the Forth Bridge offered to some a less desirable means of access. Records show that the number of passengers ferried in 1898 eight years after the opening of the bridge was 84,500, a rise of 5,000 over the previous year.

During the 1880s repeated attempts were made to set up new harbours and docks at Kirkcaldy in an effort to thwart expansion at Methil and Burntisland. In 1883, an Alloa, Dunfermline and Kirkcaldy Railway Bill was presented before Parliament. This railway was to pass through the parishes of Dunfermline, Inverkeithing, Aberdour and Auchtertool, emerging by the valley of the Tiel at West Bridge, Kirkcaldy and thence running along the Sands Road, terminate adjacent to the present harbour. Had the Bill, which was supported by the Caledonian Railway, been successful, the development of coal export traffic might well have been very different. The same session of Parliament did, however, approve the Seafield Dock and Railway Bill, drafted for the following two purposes:—

1. The provision of an oblong dock with two piers approximately at the site of the present Seafield Colliery. The basin would be 12½ acres in extent and incorporate a wet dock of about 5 acres, whilst the quayage would have sufficient space for at least 6 hoists capable of shipping 1½ million tons of coal every year.
2. A railway line, 8 miles in length, commencing at the north-west corner of the intended dock and terminating in the parish of Auchterderran very close to the bridge known as Bow Bridge, which carries the road from Auchterderran to Lochgelly over the River Ore. This railway would pass under that of the North British immediately west of Cardenden station.

The Capital asked for was £300,000, £66,000 for allocation to the railway and £175,000 for dock construction. It was calculated that receipts from coal traffic alone would yield a return of 5% and emphasis was placed on the expectation that trains might carry a fair proportion of the limestone and ironstone mined in that district.

As no advantage was taken of the Act during its three year probation, it was generally supposed that, following the failure of the Alloa, Dunfermline and Kirkcaldy Railway scheme, sufficient funds could not be raised and that the project had fallen through. But the promoters were quietly working away and had successfully raised the necessary funds and guarantees.

In November, 1887, the Company gave public notice of its intention to apply to Parliament to revive the powers granted by the original Act for the purpose of having time extended. The application was sanctioned in January, 1888, and three months later a contract for construction of the dock and railway was signed.

Work on the railway, which was to have precedence in construction, began in February 1889, when a number of workmen were employed at Seafield erecting sheds for holding tools and implements. This task, having been completed by the summer, it was announced that active operations on the railway would await the harvesting of crops. Meanwhile, wood had been driven to the site in large quantities from a sawmill in Kirkcaldy and many navvies had arrived in the town expecting employment. On 25 September, 1889, work was suspended, despite a large quantity of plant having arrived only the previous day, when there were estimated to be 100 men employed.

For reasons which have not come to light, the project was entirely abandoned. There may well have been growing apprehension as plans to revive the Alloa, Dunfermline and Kirkcaldy Railway scheme of 1883 materialised and were incorporated in a Kirkcaldy and District Railway Bill, laid before Parliament in the 1890-91 session. The Caledonian Railway intimated its intention to promote a Bill in the same session to extend their railway to form a connection with the Kirkcaldy and District near Cowdenbeath, so enabling Fife coal to be shipped from the Caledonian Company's docks at Grangemouth. To reach Grangemouth, engineers favoured the idea of tunnelling under the Forth in the vicinity of Kincardine. However, after a meeting in Glasgow with interested parties, the Caledonian Directors resolved upon an independent examination of the Fife coalfield's western discovery (made in 1890) and subsequently decided to support the Kirkcaldy and District Railway in extending its line to Alloa, if the latter decided to do so. This change in mind virtually assured the Kirkcaldy and District Bill of defeat. After only a half hour deliberation, the Select Committee of the House of Lords decided that the preamble to the Bill had not been proved.

It was not until 1912 that the N.B.R. brought into operation a freight only line linking Kirkcaldy with Cowdenbeath via Invertiel Junction and Auchtertool. Both the junctions at Cowdenbeath and Invertiel faced south to facilitate trains working through from the Dunfermline area or intermediate collieries to Burntisland. The line was never built for the purpose of fulfilling the original concept of developing Kirkcaldy as a major coal exporting port.

During the inter-war years the average annual shipments of coal from Methil and Burntisland were 2,654 and 1,128 thousand tons respectively.

No coal was shipped from Burntisland for the duration of World War II and when this traffic recommenced in 1946, the annual tonnages fell in some years to below 5,000 tons. Representations seeking future guarantees were made by the port's dockers to several government bodies including the Ministry of Transport, who in reply stated that shipments, whilst they remained at their present low level, were being concentrated on Methil. This, the reply continued, was mainly because Wemyss coal, which accounted for most of the export, had to be shipped from Methil as it was carried there over a private railway in wagons which could not be used on the main line. Moreover, it was contended that the approach to Methil was easier than to Burntisland, to which access could only be made by the heavily occupied main line.

One month before a conference convened at Dunfermline in November 1955 to discuss fears that Burntisland might close, a German ship docked there with 4,200 tons of coal from the Polish port of Gydnia. Part of the cargo was for household use and the remainder for British Railways. After discharging, the ship sailed for Blyth in Northumberland to take on a shipment of coal for Denmark, from whence she was due to return to Poland to collect a second cargo of coal for Burntisland. Occasional imports of coal, mainly from Poland, were handled during 1956 and 1957.

At the Dunfermline conference the Provost of Burntisland outlined measures already taken and proposed by the British Transport Commission which were giving rise to an uneasy feeling in his town. In September 1951, the B.T.C. had advised the Town Council of a proposed lease of the West Dock to the adjacent shipbuilding company for fitting-out purposes. Hoists

6 Layout of sidings at Burntisland harbour, 1956

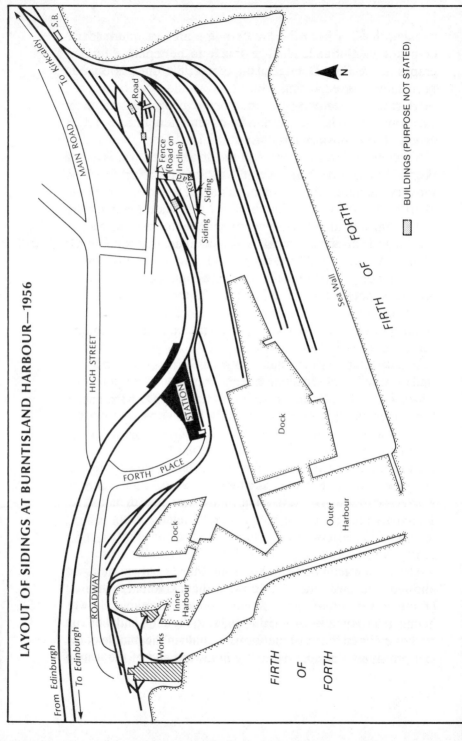

LAYOUT OF SIDINGS AT BURNTISLAND HARBOUR—1956

N

BUILDINGS (PURPOSE NOT STATED)

To Kirkcaldy
S.B.
MAIN ROAD
Road
Fence (Road on Incline)
Road
Siding
Siding

FIRTH OF FORTH

Sea Wall

FIRTH OF FORTH

From Edinburgh
To Edinburgh
ROADWAY

HIGH STREET

FORTH PLACE
STATION

Dock

Outer Harbour

Dock

Inner Harbour
Works

FIRTH OF FORTH

1, 2 and 3 at the West Dock were to be removed, while the two cranes there—of 1882 vintage—were to be replaced by new cranes at the East Dock. By June 1952, the three hoists had been duly removed, but no new cranes installed. No. 6 hoist had more recently been dismantled, it being recognised that there was now no reasonable demand for its retention. If the B.T.C.'s proposal to remove No. 4 hoist at the East Dock, which they claimed would cost £7,000 to put in good order, were carried out, then in the Provost's opinion No. 5 hoist would not remain for very much longer. His fears were well founded and before 1960 coal shipments could no longer be handled at the port.

The railway does, however, continue to play a role in handling the dock's principal cargo—bauxite, imported for the British Aluminium Company's works sited on the town's western periphery. On average there are 10 or 12 ships unloading each year. In 1974, 255,000 tons were landed, of which approximately 204,000 tons were despatched in trains comprising 16 ton coal wagons, whilst the remainder was conveyed through the town by road.

In only ten post-war years, of which the last was 1963, has coal exported from Methil exceeded one million tons. Shipments which by 1972 had fallen to as low as 385,000 tons were terminated in 1976. Coal trains now head west to cross the Forth Bridge and discharge their loads at a new handling plant in Leith docks.

In 1973, there were only three loading hoists still functional. They were collectively operated by one squad of eight men who worked on the day shift only. They have now been demolished. Ten years previously there had been 8 squads, each of eight men, working on a two shift system. The coal tower in use at the time was a structure approximately 60 feet high. When a signal was given, a wagon was released from a newly arrived train and allowed in its own time to run down a slight gradient to the foot of the tower. Here, on a small wooden turntable, it was manhandled round until at right-angles to the ship, and then run by gravity on to the hoist platform. A chain in the middle of the platform floor was secured to the landward end of the wagon before it was raised level with an adjustable shute above the ship's hold. Whilst the operator tilted the platform towards the ship, the emptying wagon was prevented from running forward because the rails at the seaward end were bent over into a loop. The wagon, once empty, was ready to be lowered to an intermediate level. Upon its descent the platform was inclined landwards. Here, the chain having been unhooked, the wagon rolled off on to a second small turntable, where it was turned by workers before trundling down an embankment to join other wagons waiting to form an empty train. The entire operation took an average two minutes.

The port of Methil still handles a considerable volume of assorted imports but none of these is now forwarded by rail.

8

Travels in Clackmannan and West Fife

THIS chapter contains personal experiences of a journey from Falkirk through Clackmannanshire and western Fife to Thornton and outlines some railway history.

It was on a Monday morning in late May, 1964 that we collected our 'Freedom of Scotland' ticket from the booking office at Falkirk's Grahamston station and walked on to a very crowded 7.53 d.m.u. waiting to leave for Larbert and Alloa. Despite the early hour, the unit had already made one crossing from Larbert to Alloa and was now on the return leg of a journey which had started from Alloa at 6.56 ending in Grangemouth 38 minutes later. Probably it had carried some passengers from Alloa who changed at Larbert into a following Stirling-Glasgow working only 9 minutes later. Their through journey of 30½ miles should have been completed as our train was preparing to stop at Camelon. Excepting Saturdays, no other connections or through train gave a quicker service by this, the most direct route. In two cases, passengers changing at Larbert were obliged to linger for no less than 55 minutes before proceeding forward!

Our own access to Larbert was considerably delayed by the late running of the 7.15 stopping train from Glasgow (Buchanan Street) to Dundee, from which there was an advertised connection with our train. Once away from Larbert, we covered the 8½ miles to Alloa in 16 minutes, including a stop at Throsk platform and adherence to a 25 m.p.h. speed restriction across a less well-known, but perhaps equally fascinating, Forth Bridge. Although we had gained three minutes on our advertised time for the journey, it was, nevertheless, impossible for the train to make its second departure for Grangemouth on time.

This journey was to afford the writer his only crossing of the bridge at Alloa. The bridge had been built when the Scottish Central Railway constructed a branch to the ferry terminal at

South Alloa from the main Stirling line at Alloa junction. It had been intended that this line would form a part of the proposed Glasgow and Dundee Junction Railway described in an earlier chapter. On 12 September, 1850, only fifteen days after the Stirling and Dunfermline Railway opened between Alloa and Dunfermline, a twice daily service commenced to and from South Alloa. Following the simultaneous opening, on 3 June, 1851, of the Tillicoultry branch, as far as Glenfoot, and a short spur from Alloa station down to the ferry, considerable additional traffic resulted in the Scottish Central providing no fewer than five trains in both directions. The service was not, however, without criticism. Why, it was asked, were there no through tickets available to beyond Alloa and why did those arriving from destinations in Fife with Third or Fourth Class tickets frequently find, on crossing the river, none but First and Second Class carriages waiting. When, on 1 July, 1852, the link through to Stirling was completed, the S & D station at Alloa Ferry closed and traffic on the South Alloa branch declined very rapidly.

In 1865 the Scottish Central Railway was absorbed into the Caledonian network and consideration given as to how an already improved branch service, now running through to Larbert, might be carried across the Forth. No positive measures were, however, taken and during the 1870's two independently promoted schemes were put forward but never authorised. Although the earlier Alloa Union Railway was to have pioneered an entirely new route from a short distance west of Grahamston, while the less lengthy Alloa Junction Railway would have diverged from the main line just north of Alloa Junction, both railways planned to cross the Forth, using a swing bridge, at a point about one mile west of the existing ferry ending at the junction of the Stirling and Dunfermline line. It was in August, 1879, that the Alloa Railway Company was authorised to construct a railway from the South Alloa branch at Dunmore Junction to cross the Forth at the already favoured site, but terminating at a quite separate station in Alloa. By prior agreement the Caledonian Railway was to

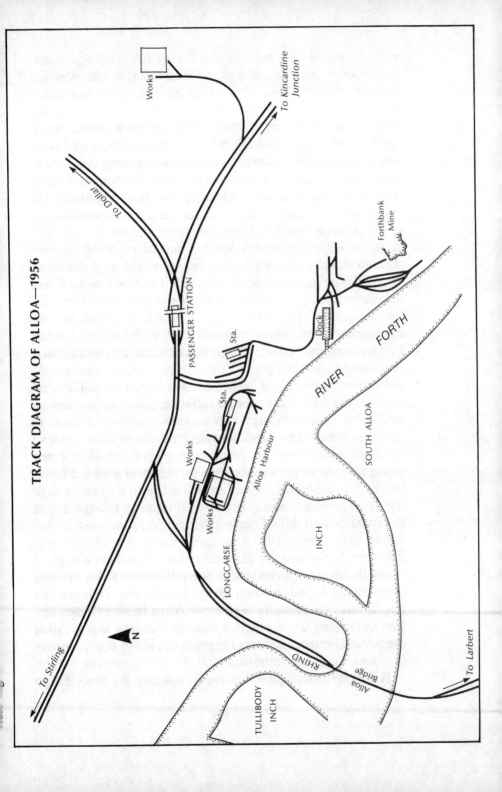

TRACK DIAGRAM OF ALLOA—1956

Works

To Kincardine Junction

To Dollar

Forthbank Mine

PASSENGER STATION

Sta.

Dock

Sta.

RIVER FORTH

Works

SOUTH ALLOA

Works

Alloa Harbour

INCH

To Stirling

N

LONGCARSE

RHIND

TULLIBODY INCH

Alloa Bridge

To Larbert

work the line. Following successful Parliamentary opposition to a rival scheme sponsored by the North British Railway in 1883, it was agreed that the latter company would have running powers over the new line from Alloa to Alloa Junction, and on the main line as far as Greenhill Junction, upon payment of a minimum £3,000 per annum. The Caledonian and Alloa companies undertook to double the line throughout, except across Alloa Bridge, whilst the North British were to provide a double connecting line between Alloa West and Longcarse Junctions along which coaching traffic would travel to the existing N.B.R. station.

Passenger services to South Alloa, but not the ferry boat, were withdrawn upon opening of the bridge route on 1 October, 1885. The bridge itself comprised nineteen fixed girder spans resting on twenty stone piers 24 feet above high water level. Its opening span, 150 feet in length, swung on a central pier comprising six cylindrical columns, and was surmounted by an octagonal engine house built above the railway on cross girders. Although ships had priority over trains, they caused little disruption to the railway timetable, for, as a result of several mishaps during construction, regular pleasure steamers sailing to Stirling were, probably at the expense of the Caledonian Railway, fitted with hinged masts and telescopic funnels to allow them to pass under the closed bridge. Post World War I traffic up river from Alloa was rather sparse and after the pier buildings at Stirling were demolished in 1935, the bridge remained manned essentially for the passage of shipping to Banbeath Admiralty Depot at Throsk.

Passenger services between Larbert and Alloa were withdrawn on 29 January, 1968, whilst through freight workings, of which there were a considerable number, ceased in May of that same year. An occasional train did, however, traverse the bridge until the official closure of Throsk, Forth Bridge and Longcarse Junction signal boxes in May, 1970. Demolition of the bridge commenced nine months later and only its piers can now be seen as a reminder.

During the short period between opening the second Tay

Bridge and completion of the Forth Bridge, the North British, as the following table of goods trains shows, took maximum advantage of their running powers across Alloa Bridge:—

TABLE 8

Goods Trains Crossing Alloa Bridge 1 August, 1889
Until Further Notice

Time due at Longcarse	From	To
17.38	1st. Dundee	Carlisle
18.57	Dunfermline	Carlisle
21.36	Sighthill (Glasgow)	Perth
22.14	1st. Carlisle	Dundee
22.56	Glasgow	Aberdeen
23.11	Leith Walk (Edinburgh)	Aberdeen
23.11	2nd. Dundee	Carlisle
23.33	Bothwell Junction	Montrose
00.46	Berwick	Dundee
01.07	Dundee	College (Glasgow)
02.01	2nd. Carlisle	Dundee
02.37	3rd. Dundee	Carlisle
02.43	College (Glasgow)	Dundee
02.57	Dundee	Berwick
03.21	Aberdeen	Leith Walk (Edinburgh)
03.37	Perth	Sighthill (Glasgow)
03.52	Montrose	Bothwell Junction
05.37	Aberdeen	Glasgow

The 3rd Carlisle-Dundee and Carlisle-Dunfermline trains both ran from Edinburgh via Stirling.

It was important that both the 02.37 and 05.37 trains, which were classified as Express Goods, should get a clear road and in order to ease identification the engine carried two green head lights. Although considered to be Express Goods, these trains had already completed the first 3 hrs 17 mins. and 2 hrs 47 mins. of their journeys south from Dundee before they passed Longcarse.

The Dunfermline-Carlisle train took only 27 through wagons from Alloa West to enable it to lift 18 English wagons at Falkirk Grahamston, from where it was assisted by Pilot to Polmont.

129

The 1st Dundee-Carlisle was restricted to 30 loaded wagons and Van throughout. It was also an Express Goods. Alloa's *Second Night Pilot* would assist trains as far as Polmont, Greenhill and Cowdenbeath when whistled upon to do so.

If the bridge had a 'finest hour' it was perhaps on the evening of 27 October, 1959. A Trip Working at Polmaise, just south of Stirling, became derailed across the main line, necessitating diversions for two hours until one line could be restored. The 5.15 p.m. Glasgow-Oban and Down *Saint Mungo* to Aberdeen had to travel from Alloa Junction across to Alloa, where their Class 5 4-6-0s ran round. They then worked on, tender first, to Stirling, where the engines were able to resume their position at the front of the trains. The Up *Postal* and 5.30 p.m. Perth-Glasgow made the same detour but in the reverse direction.

Due to the late running of our train, we had little opportunity to investigate the 'nooks and crannies' of what appeared to be a busy junction station, before our diesel connection from Perth to Stirling drew into the Up through platform. A small number of passengers from Perth, Kinross or possibly intermediate stations in the Devon Valley alighted, whilst we obtained a panoramic seat at the front of the foremost three carriages. Alloa station had some similarity to a maritime oil-tanker in that all the platform superstructure was congregated at one end—the eastern end, where stairs led down from a booking office and general circulating area at road level. Gone, however, were the refreshment room facilities. At the west end there were two bay platforms, used by ex-L.N.E.R. and L.M.S. terminal services, while on the north side of the island's outer face were engine sidings and towards the east a few carriage sidings.

Leaving Alloa at 9.19 a.m., we ran non-stop through Cambus station and passed the site of that at Causewayhead, before arriving in Stirling, 6¾ miles to the west, at 9.30. Until 1 November, 1954, Cambus had been the juncture of a 3½ mile branch to Alva, set in the Ochil hillfoots.

The Stirling and Dunfermline Railway was opened from Dunfermline to Oakley (4m 33ch.) in 1849, reached Alloa (a

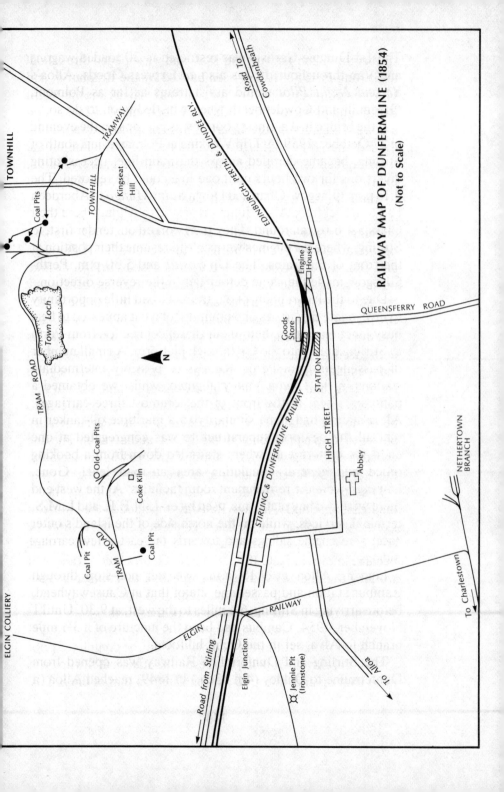

RAILWAY MAP OF DUNFERMLINE (1854)
(Not to Scale)

TOWNHILL

Coal Pits

TRAMWAY

Kingseat Hill

TOWNHILL

EDINBURGH, PERTH & DUNDEE RLY.

Road To
Cowdenbeath

Engine
House

Town Loch

TRAM ROAD

N

Goods
Store

QUEENSFERRY ROAD

STATION

Old Coal Pits

Coke Kiln

STIRLING & DUNFERMLINE RAILWAY

HIGH STREET

Abbey

NETHERTOWN
BRANCH

Coal Pit

TRAM ROAD

Coal Pit

To Charlestown

ELGIN COLLIERY

RAILWAY

ELGIN

Road from Stirling

Elgin Junction

Jennie Pit
(Ironstone)

To Alloa

further 9m. 22ch.) in August, 1850 and was opened throughout to Stirling in 1852. It had been backed by the Edinburgh and Glasgow Railway, who foresaw a means of encircling the North British and preventing the future development of a Caledonian empire. Litigation in the Court of Session followed refusal by the Edinburgh and Glasgow Railway to work the line on the terms agreed until the line was finished in its entirety. In the interim, what proved to be an inadequate service was maintained by the E.P. & D. and Scottish Central railways.

It was not, however, until exactly a year after the formal opening ceremony on 2 July, 1852, that the S & D line was opened across the Forth in Stirling's town centre. The Edinburgh and Glasgow directors insisted upon a second bridge, despite powers given to the S & D by Parliament to cross the river by the Scottish Central's bridge and come into the station on the S.C.R. line. Because the Edinburgh & Glasgow stipulated that the works to be leased by them should be the whole works as authorised by Parliament, it was necessary to construct an independent passenger terminus and continue the line beyond for no less than half a mile. This extension, which ran parallel with and at the back of the main line station, was considered to be of no use whatsoever, since there was no Parliamentary power to form a junction with the S.C.R. at that point. The line ended in nothing and even for storing carriages was unnecessary, there being sufficient space within the station for them.

Dissatisfied with the ruling by the Court of Session against it, the Edinburgh and Glasgow Railway appealed to the House of Lords, who upheld the decision given in Scotland's supreme civil court. Almost immediately the House of Lords ruling became known in July, 1853, the E. & G. arranged to take over working the line and within three weeks of assuming responsibility planned with the Scottish Central to establish a junction with that railway on the north side of the Forth.

Incredibly, this was done despite E. & G. insistance throughout litigation that the entire line into Stirling be completed prior to their liability to work it. As a result the station at Stirling was to be shut up and all traffic concentrated on that of the S.C.R.

The lessees did not appear deterred by the extra £1,000 per annum rent and liability for the upkeep of the bridge and lines south which they still incurred. Subsequent litigation between the S. & D. and Scottish Central, as a result of the E. & G. agreement with the latter to form a junction north of the Forth, determined that the S. & D. did have powers within its Act to form a junction south of the river. This was duly effected, but the independent station and continuing line were closed. Both railway bridges are generally similar in design, though differing in detail, and each has two intermediate piers with an arch span over the public roads on either side. They are of girder type with the girder structures below rail level.

The following timetable, which operated from 2 August, 1855, is typical of the passenger service provided between Stirling and Dunfermline during the 1850's:—

Stirling to Dunfermline

	Classes	1 3	1	1	1 2	1 2	1 3
Trains do not leave		a.m.	a.m.	a.m.	p.m.	p.m.	p.m.
Stirling before		8.30	9.30	11.50	2.30	5.35	7.36
Causewayhead		8.35	—	11.55	2.35	5.40	7.41
Cambus		8.44	—	12.05	2.45	5.50	7.51
Alloa		8.50	9.45	12.10	2.50	5.55	8.01
Clackmannan		8.57	—	—	2.57	—	8.08
Kincardine		9.03	—	—	3.03	—	8.14
Bogside+		9.10	—	—	3.10	—	8.21
Eastgrange for Culross & Torryburn+		9.17	—	—	3.17	—	8.28
Oakley		9.23	—	—	3.23	—	8.34
Or arrive at							
Dunfermline before		9.40	—	—	3.40	—	8.50

Trains do not leave	Classes	1 3 a.m.	1 3 a.m.	1 3 p.m.	1 3 '.m.	1 3 p.m.
Dunfermline before		6.45	—	12.15	—	6.00
Oakley		6.55	—	12.25	—	6.11
Eastgrange for Culross & Torryburn+		7.00	—	12.30	—	6.17
Bogside+		7.06	—	12.36	—	6.24
Kincardine		7.13	—	12.43	—	6.31
Clackmannan		7.17	—	12.47	—	6.36
Alloa		7.24	10.15	12.54	4.50	6.43
Cambus		7.30	10.21	1.00	4.55	6.49
Causewayhead		7.40	10.31	1.10	5.05	6.59

Or arrive at

Stirling before		7.50	10.42	1.15	5.10	7.10

+Trains will only stop at Eastgrange and Bogside Stations when there are Passengers to take up or set down, due notice of which must be given to the Station Agents or Guard, as the case may be.

To a great extent the frequency of services remained similar throughout most of the 19th century, although differently applied from time to time, but after the Forth Bridge opened in 1890 the N.B.R. were able to run services to Edinburgh via Dunfermline. From a scrutiny of sample timetables, it would appear that traffic on the Clackmannanshire lines reached a 'peak' during the seventeen inter-war years when services were operated by the L.N.E.R. For example, in 1926 trains arrived at Stirling from Edinburgh at 7.35, 9.42 and 10.26 a.m. and at 12.29, 2.52, 5.49, 7.19, 8.13 and 9.39 p.m. Several of these trains might have been classified semi-fast, while the 9.15 a.m. ex Waverley hauled carriages to be worked along the Forth and Clyde line from Stirling to Aberfoyle and Balloch, as part of the L.N.E.R. "Trossachs Tour". Return workings to Edinburgh left at 7.53 (to Dunfermline), 8.15, and 10.05 a.m. and at 12.10, 1.40, 4.00, 5.48, and 8.27 p.m.— the latter with through coaches returning from the west. In addition, there were five daily trains in both directions between Glasgow (Queen Street), Alloa and Perth, local Stirling-Alloa services and miners' trains to and from Manor Powis colliery.

Before the line between Stirling and Dunfermline closed to passengers on 7 October, 1968, the service had been pruned to eight eastbound and seven westbound trains on weekdays only. Three of the Stirling departures finally worked through to Edinburgh, whilst the others terminated at Dunfermline (Lower) where good onward connections could be made. There were also two local workings out to Alloa, one of which returned to Stirling.

Until 1954 it was possible to connect at Cambus with a service to Alva. A line from Cambus to Tillicoultry and Kinross, proposed in 1845, was never built in its entirety, but on 22 July, 1861, the Alva Railway Company was authorised to connect Alva and Menstrie with Cambus. The branch opened on 3 June, 1863, and prospered throughout the nineteenth and early twentieth centuries. As Bradshaw's timetable for April, 1910 shows, no fewer than eight trains made daily return journeys between Alloa and Alva.

Even on 1 November, 1948, exactly six years before services were withdrawn, as many as nine single class trains traversed the branch every weekday except Saturdays, when there were two supplementary workings. Freight workings, which continued as far as Menstrie (1 mile 73 chains from Cambus), are undertaken by a Trip Train working from Townhill Depot (Dunfermline) normally hauled by a Class 20 locomotive. On Mondays only, if required by the Area Freight Centre, this train also works empty Pozzolan presflos[1] from Larbert to Alloa.

On our Monday morning arrival at Stirling, there was more than adequate time to purchase light refreshments from the station buffet before entering the 10.08 d.m.u. for Dunfermline and Edinburgh. In spacious surroundings, created by poor patronage, we made several timetable calculations.

Our train left promptly and crossing flat rather featureless country, with a view to the hills in the north, reached Alloa at 10.22 a.m. W.D. 2-8-0 No. 90114 passed us on a freight train at Manor Powis, where two Barclays were visible in the open. Since our visit, the line has been singled and three level

[1]Tank wagons designed to carry cement.

crossings on the outskirts of Stirling modified to enable trains to pass in excess of 10 m.p.h.

At Alloa m.p.d.[1], where a carriage body was being used as the shedmaster's office, were assembled four Class N7 0-6-2 tank engines—all in steam. When consultations between Management and Staff concerning the proposed closure of Alloa m.p.d. took place in September, 1966, the depot operated eight diagrammed turns and six steam locomotives together with two diesel shunters were supplied from Dunfermline. The 45-strong staff, of whom 21 were drivers and 17 firemen, were shortly afterwards transferred to Alloa Yard which became a 'signing on and off point'.

Immediately east of Alloa station, whose overgrown platforms were demolished in 1978, could be seen the elaborate junctions where the branch to Dollar and Kinross curved away sharply to the left. Its passenger services which had, as the following table shows, with one exception already been terminated at Dollar, were withdrawn entirely from the 13th of October, 1964.

The branch remained in use until early summer 1973 when Dollar Mine ceased production. In August, 1976, the main line crossover was secured out of use pending removal and the relative signals dismantled. For the Scottish Railway Preservation Society, who had so desperately sought financial backing to preserve the branch with a view to operating their own steam-hauled passenger trains, this represented a final defeat.

Oakley was the only one of four intermediate stations between Alloa and Dunfermline to survive until the diesel era and only the sites of Clackmannan Road, Bogside and East Grange remained to be detected. Of Kincardine station, closed towards the end of the last century, there is no trace. A modicum of passengers emerged from the platform shelter to board our triple d.m.u. when it entered Oakley station but nobody alighted. All stations on this stretch of line had facing Up and Down platforms—those at Oakley surviving until May, 1975, shortly after the entire line was singled and some sections

[1]Motive power depot.

TABLE 9

Final Dollar-Alloa Passenger Service

Note:—	AD(2)	BD	D(2)	CD		ED(2)	FD(2)	GS	
	a.m.	a.m.	a.m.	p.m.	p.m.	p.m.	p.m.		
Dollar	d. 7.20	9.02	9.55	1.40		4.00	6.28	8.56	
Tillicoultry	d. 7.26	9.08	10.01	1.46		4.06	6.34	9.02	
Alloa	a 7.34	9.16	10.09	1.54		4.14	6.42	9.10	

Note:—	HD(2)	JD(2)	KDX		LDS	MD(2)	ND	PD(2)	QS
	a.m.	a.m.	p.m.		p.m.	p.m.	p.m.	p.m.	p.m.
Alloa	d. 6.56	8.36	12.45		1.17	2.47	3.20	5.50	8.35
Tillicoultry	d. 7.05	8.45	12.45		1.26	2.56	3.29	5.59	8.44
Dollar	a. 7.10	8.50	12.59		1.31	3.01	3.34	6.04	8.49

Notes:—

A Through train to Stirling arr. 7.50 a.m.
B Through train from Perth dep. 7.43 a.m. to Alloa arr. 9.16 a.m.
C Through train to Stirling arr. 2.09 p.m.
D Diesel Service
E Through train to Stirling arr. 4.33 p.m.
F Through train to Stirling arr. 6.58 p.m.
G Through steam train to Stirling arr. 9.22 p.m.
H Through train from Stirling dep. 6.40 a.m.
J Through train from Stirling dep. 8.17 a.m.
K Through train from Stirling dep. 12.25 p.m.
L Through train from Stirling dep. 1.02 p.m.
M Through train from Stirling dep. 2.30 p.m.
N Through train from Stirling dep. 3.05 p.m. to Perth arr. 4.52 p.m.
P Through train from Stirling dep. 5.18 p.m.
Q Through steam train from Stirling dep. 8.20 p.m.
S Saturdays only
X Except Saturdays
(2) Second Class Only

re-aligned. Whilst we waited for perhaps three minutes before the driver received his starting signal from the guard, Class B1 4-6-0 No. 61147 (ex-works) passed by on a lengthy coal train. The Yard at Oakley, now largely lifted, was, even in 1964, noticeably empty. We could see no evidence of the colliery branch which once left the main line at Whitemyre Junction, just west of Dunfermline. The branch had several offshoots and was extended all the way to Kelty where it joined the main line north.

At Kincardine Junction, 1½ miles east of Alloa, the coastal line to Dunfermline was seen to swing away sharply to the right. Prior to withdrawal of passenger services on 7 July, 1930, stations on the Kincardine branch, which opened for traffic west of Kincardine in 1893 and eastwards in 1906, normally had only two daily passenger workings each way between Alloa and Dunfermline (Lower), with two additional trips—one on Saturdays only—from Alloa as far as Kincardine. Kincardine and Longannet generating stations have given this single-track line a new life. Leaving the level and direct route at Kincardine Junction, heavy coal trains climb steadily past Clackmannan to a summit in a narrow cutting at the village of Kilbagie, before dropping sharply to the shores of the Forth. Engines appear to 'nose-dive' straight towards the water until, just east of the power station, they take an unexpected left-handed bend and travel along a regularly maintained sea-wall at the edge of the salt-flats. There is no trace of Sands siding nor the neat little station at Culross, one of whose two platforms was never used, as before opening one track was taken up, it being considered that a passing loop at Valleyfield colliery would meet all crossing requirements on this section. Valleyfield, a substantial colliery, had several sidings located on a neck of land between the railway proper and a jetty which they served. Having for 6 or 7 miles afforded magnificent day and night views across the spacious Firth, the route curves inland and uphill past Torryburn and Cairneyhill station sites towards Elbowend Junction and the main line into Dunfermline.

Dunfermline (Upper) was reached at 10.44 a.m., twenty-one minutes after departing Alloa—13¾ miles to the west. Five minutes later we alighted at the Lower station. Still very much in use at the time of writing, there is an island platform on the Up side, the outer face of which was often used by local trains, while a bay was provided at the north end of the Down platform. Both platforms, which were rather sharply curved and had

138

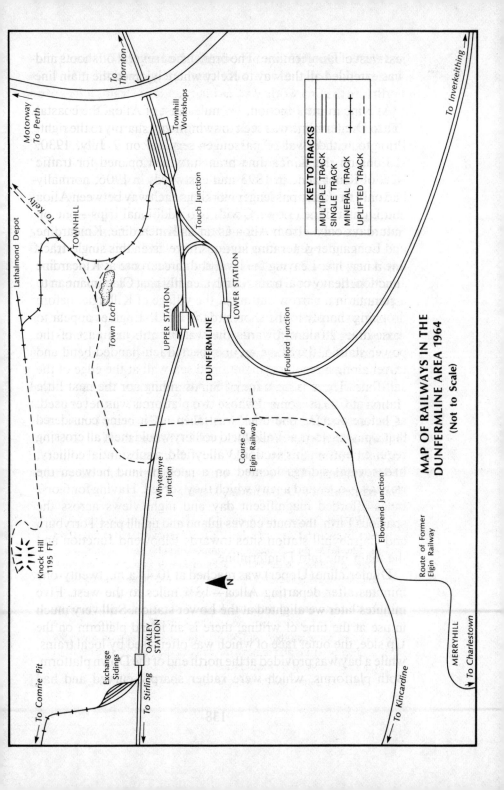

MAP OF RAILWAYS IN THE
DUNFERMLINE AREA 1964
(Not to Scale)

KEY TO TRACKS

MULTIPLE TRACK
SINGLE TRACK
MINERAL TRACK
UPLIFTED TRACK

To Thornton
To Inverkeithing
Motorway
To Perth
Townhill Workshops
To Kelly
Lathalmond Depot
Knock Hill 1195 FT.
TOWNHILL
Town Loch
Touch Junction
UPPER STATION
DUNFERMLINE
LOWER STATION
Foulford Junction
Whytemyre Junction
Course of Elgin Railway
Elbowend Junction
Route of Former Elgin Railway
MERRYHILL
To Charlestown
To Kincardine
To Stirling
OAKLEY STATION
Exchange Sidings
To Comrie Pit

N

extensive canopies, were modernised during 1971 when buildings on the Up platform were completely replaced.

Before the first world war, as many as seven trains left here on weekdays to work down the picturesque branch to Charlestown. This fascinating little single-line branch, only four miles long, has gradients of 1 in 50, 60 and 64 besides curves of 10, 12 and 15 chains radius. There was a station with one platform at Charlestown and four intermediate siding connections viz:— Elbowend Junction, Merryhill Siding, Charlestown Foundry Siding and Charlestown Goods Station. Signalling was carried out at the following boxes—Charlestown Junction, containing 18 working and 1 spare levers; Elbowend Junction, with 10 working levers, 2 spare levers and 4 unused spaces in the frame; and Charlestown Goods Station, containing 28 working and 2 spare levers.

Early booking office records show that of a population exceeding 2,000 in Charlestown and neighbouring Limekilns, upwards of 120 factory workers used the railway daily to reach Dunfermline.

Following a request from the Admiralty for the use of coal hoists to load some 80,000 tons of redd into barges at Charlestown Harbour, the North British General Manager was informed in a letter dated 11 April, 1918, that to ship 1,200 tons of redd traffic per day would mean discharging approximately 160 wagons. The letter, emanating from the Operating Superintendent's Department, stated:—

> We are of opinion that it would be quite practicable to deal with a turn-over of 160 wagons a day at Charlestown without laying down additional sidings. Storage accommodation for 160 wagons at one time, in addition to the traffic meantime dealt with, could be found, and the working forward of the traffic would be so arranged as to allow space for 80 loads and for 80 empties. A train could be put on in the night-time to work two loads of 40 wagons each from the Collieries to Charlestown and take back lifts of empties to the same number, while another train could be put on in the day-time to make another two runs and remove the empties that had been made from the loads worked forward during the night.
>
> In order to provide the wagons necessary, we would suggest that

400 of the Mineral type be selected from amongst those now standing waiting repair.

There is meantime a Pug engine working at Charlestown and Crombie from 10.00 a.m. till about 3.00 p.m. daily, but its time is fully occupied and it could not be spared to undertake the placing of the loaded wagons and the removal of the empty wagons from the lines serving the two hoists. It would therefore be necessary to provide a Pug engine and shunter at Charlestown continuously day and night . . .

During recent years Elbowend Junction has featured in several photographic books published on Scottish Railways. Seeing a Reid Class J35 0-6-0, perhaps fitted with a buffer beam snowplough, travelling with a light daily goods through the tranquil silvine setting, it is hard to appreciate what a very busy history the branch has had, even after passenger services ceased on 1 November, 1926.

Dunfermline's engine shed had been passed on the journey through the town's eastern suburbs between the Upper and Lower stations. The 30 or so engines still shedded there were mainly used to haul heavy freight and coal traffic. Exhibited outside were 2-8-0's Nos. 90306 and 90489; 4-6-0's Nos. 61262 and 61407; and 0-6-0 No. 65288.

Throughout the 1950's this shed had been thoroughly modernised. The first phase, completed in 1952, included installation of an electrically powered ash elevator, replacement of an obsolete manual coaling stage and provision of an articulated tractor turntable. Built of re-inforced concrete, the new locomotive coaling plant had two bunkers, one able to hold 100 tons of coal suitable for passenger and express freight trains and the other an equal quantity for shunting and trip workings. The ash handling installation comprised a 210 ft. long pit with steel tubes into which locomotive ash was discharged. Ash from the tubes fell down a chute into a skip which was electrically elevated and emptied into a bunker straddling a siding. In 1956 the shed's timber slated roof was replaced by a concrete unit construction—the first of its kind to be used in the Scottish Region. It was particularly designed to improve working conditions by the provision of a continuous smoke vent over every track and the use of glass for roofing. Floor space was increased as the 27 existing cast-iron columns were replaced by 5 concrete ones.

Thornton engine shed, at the eastern end of a rather uninspiring stretch of line, was built between 1930 and 1933. Measuring 360 ft. in length and 106 ft. in width, it could accommodate 36 engines on 6 running lines. Some of the engines had been displaced from the old roundhouse at Burntisland, which dated back to Edinburgh and Northern days.

By 1970 both Thornton and Dunfermline sheds had been closed, the latter having had all trackage removed. Subsequent to the closure of Dunfermline, the stabling point at Townhill Wagon Shops received the shed code 62C and an allocation of locomotives.

The late running of our train from Dunfermline did, at least, considerably shorten the wait we would otherwise have had at a rainswept Thornton Station.

Shortly after the above chapter was drafted, British Rail announced its intention to close, as from 6 August, 1979, a four mile section of the Direct Alloa-Dunfermline route and divert any through trains via Kincardine. The track between Bogside and Kincardine Junction has now been lifted and sidings at Bogside and Oakley are worked only from Dunfermline.

The last passenger train to journey over the line was on 12 May, 1979, when a locomotive hauled S.R.P.S. special with vintage stock ran from Falkirk via Stirling and Fife to Fraserburgh.

9

Lines in the North

I—THE NEWBURGH & NORTH OF FIFE RAILWAY

This railway, 13¼ miles long, when opened on 22 January, 1909, provided a useful link between Glenburnie Junction on the Perth to Ladybank route and St Fort on the main east coast line.

There were three stations, those at Kilmany and Luthrie having double platforms with a connecting footbridge, but that at Lindores having only one platform served by trains travelling in both directions. The platform at Lindores was situated on the south side of the line and had access to the main Cupar-Newburgh road. In each case the platforms were 450 feet long, sufficient to accommodate lengthy excursion trains, which it was believed the district would most certainly attract. All the stations had small but neat and comfortable offices and waiting rooms built of "Brandem" bricks so as to present a pleasing appearance.

Besides the stations, two goods sidings were provided, one at Ayton Smithy, half-way between Lindores and Luthrie, and at Rathillet, a short distance west of Kilmany.

The railway was single track, but double bridges were constructed throughout and there were long passing loops at various points. With rails weighing 84 lbs to the yard, the heaviest N.B.R. rolling stock could easily be carried.

Owing to the proximity of the railway to the road and the winding nature of the Fernie Burn and Motray Water, it was necessary to construct a large number of bridges—in all 22 steel bridges and 9 masonry bridges of 6 feet span and over. Of the underbridges, the lattice girder structures at Lindores and Luthrie might be mentioned. Both were very much on the skew, having girders 78 ft. 6 ins. and 97 ft. 3 ins. long respectively. Three overbridges, carrying the main roads to Lindifferon, Cupar and Newport were believed to be the first of a new design in Scotland. Each of these roads crossed the railway on the skew and would normally have required long deep girders. However in the design adopted a central pier was built and both it and the abutments were extended sufficiently to enable joints at right angles to the centre line of the railway to support the whole of the roadway.

The cost of earthworks was also heavy; a total of nearly 500,000 cubic yards, including about 35,000 yards of rock, being excavated. The largest cuttings were at Glenburnie, Mountquhanie and Kilmany, whilst most of the rock was taken from a long cutting east of Lindores station.

Signalling arrangements were as follows:—

Block Telegraph Signal Boxes

How Worked	Name of Box	Distance between Boxes		Hours of Attendance
		M.	Ch.	
	Glenburnie Jct.	—	—	
				Mon. 7.30 am-7.40 pm
				Tues. 6.45 am-7.40 pm
	Luthrie	5	70	Wed. 8.00 am-7.40 pm
Converted	Kilmany	4	17	Thur. 8.00 am-7.40 pm
Tablet.				Fri. 6.00 am-7.40 pm
				Sat. 8.00 am-7.40 pm
	St Fort West	2	14	Always
	St Fort North	—	43	Always
	St Fort South	—	34	Always

The railway had been open to traffic for less than three years when the Railway and Canal Commissioners met in Parliament House, Edinburgh, to hear evidence of an application by the Newburgh & North of Fife Railway Co., owners of the line, with regard to certain differences between them and the N.B.R. under an arrangement for working, maintaining and managing the railway. The N. & N.F.R. sought to have the N.B.R. restrained from continuing, in violation of the agreement, to divert from the railway to their own railway and routes traffic for which the applicant's railway formed the shortest route.

In evidence, Mr Walter Beer C.E., who had constructed the line on behalf of the Engineering, Electric and Construction Syndicate Ltd., was of the opinion that there was ground for complaint against the N.B.R. He alleged that they had failed to advertise the railway and to issue instructions to their staff in regard to it and to make arrangements for through bookings. The number of trains was insufficient and they did not give proper connections beyond Perth, Dundee or to the Fife coast. The only reason he could suggest as to why the N.B.R. had not given the line a greater share of traffic was because of their arrangements with the Caledonian Railway.

No lesser person than the Lord Provost of Dundee travelled to Edinburgh to complain that the North of Fife route was practically useless as a through route and that it was absolutely unknown to the great majority of the people whom he represented.

Mr W.F. Jackson, General Manager of the N.B.R. did not believe there was much wrong with the service, which was given at a heavy loss:—

	Total Receipts	N.B.R. Share	Cost of Working Line
1st Year	£2,473	£1,236	£3.946
2nd Year	£2,799	£1.399	£4,122
3rd Year (1st half)	£1,962	£ 981	£2,161

The gross receipts for the first year for local traffic were only £21-13-3d, which he considered an extraordinarily poor result. On the Invergarry & Fort Augustus Railway, which had had to be closed, the receipt for passenger trains per mile had been 1/3, compared with 7d for the Newburgh line.

Except for a short period during World War I, when services were completely withdrawn due to a shortage of staff, passenger timetables normally provided three trains daily in each direction between Perth and Dundee with additional ones on Saturdays. The mid-morning train from Perth, consisting of four coaches, was split into two portions at St Fort West signal box. The front section, comprising three coaches, went on to Dundee leaving a six wheeler composite coach to be picked up, usually by an 0-6-0 goods engine, and run via St Fort South through to St Andrews. A similar through service in the reverse direction operated during the afternoon. The poorly patronised Perth to St Andrews facility ceased soon after the 1914-18 War commenced.

A daily goods service worked from Dundee to Glenburnie Junction besides a livestock special to Perth on Monday mornings, and one back from Perth on Friday nights. Luthrie and Kilmany were both busy stations, especially during the winter months, with loading of seed and ware potatoes, grain, baled hay and straw. The sidings at Rathillet and Ayton Smithy also contributed their fair share. Mr J.M. Bennett, a former clerk at Luthrie station, can recollect as many as 61 loaded wagons being forwarded from the whole branch in one day.

Prior to the erection of an aerial railway by Bell Bros. from Marescraig Quarry near Newburgh direct to Glenburnie Siding, Lindores station assisted Newburgh in loading and despatching road metals.

Passenger revenue never seems to have represented more than a very small fraction of the total earned by the North of Fife Railway. In 1933, an application by the General Motor Carrying Company Limited to run a bus service from Newburgh to Wormit via Rathillet, Kilmany and Gauldry was refused by the Road Traffic Commissioners. For the L.N.E.R., the principal objector, it was stated that in 1932 gross receipts from local passenger traffic amounted to only £355, whilst for through passengers the amount was £296. Roughly, passenger receipts on the line equalled £2 per day and it was contended that were the application for a bus service granted, the railway would have to seriously consider withdrawal of passenger services.

The last regular passenger train, one of two trains daily in each direction, ran on 10 February, 1951. It comprised four ex N.B.R. coaches hauled by ex Caledonian McIntosh 4-4-0 No. 14447.

However, the railway continued to play an important role for a number of years. For eight weeks in early 1955 the Tay viaduct at Perth was closed every night for repairs and freight trains were diverted via the North of Fife line. Locomotives

146

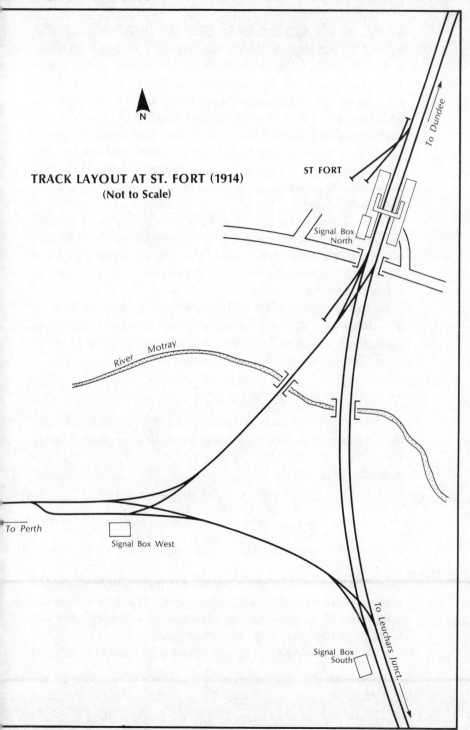

TRACK LAYOUT AT ST. FORT (1914)
(Not to Scale)

used on these trains included a *Clan* class 4-6-2, a compound 4-4-0 No. 40939 and class "K2" No. 61789 *Loch Laidon.*

The B.T.C. "Official Handbook of Stations" published in 1956 shows that all three stations continued to offer facilities for Goods Traffic, Parcels, Livestock and Horseboxes. In addition, Luthrie was equipped to handle Furniture Vans, Carriages and Motor Cars. Consignments were uplifted by the 10.20 a.m. MWFO train from Dundee, scheduled to terminate at Newburgh at 12.48 p.m. The return working departed Newburgh at 1.00 p.m. and arrived back in Dundee 2 hours and 40 minutes later.

Even eleven years after regular passenger services ceased, the line still attracted excursionists. During a four day rail tour entitled "The Scottish Rambler", held during April, 1962, the five coach train was hauled from Dundee as far as Lindores by Gresley J39 No. 64786.

By then goods services had been withdrawn and the junction at Glenburnie removed. During 1963 and 1964 the track extending east from Lindores was used for a lengthy static exhibition of condemned mineral wagons.

II—THE NEWPORT RAILWAY

The Newport Railway is described by William McGonagall, the Dundee poet and tragedian, when in one of his works, penned shortly after the opening of the line, he writes of the current traffic:—

> The thrifty housewives of Newport
> To Dundee will often resort
> Which will be to them profit and sport,
> By bringing cheap tea, bread and jam
> And also some of Lipton's ham.

In November, 1856, quite some years before the formation of the Newport Railway Company, an Act was unsuccessfully applied for to construct a line to be known as the Tayport and Craighead Railway. Powers were sought:—

Firstly, to make a railway commencing by a junction with the

E.P. & D. Railway at Tayport passenger station and terminating upon a pier in the river Tay at Craighead.

Secondly to enable the Company to acquire from the Scottish Central Railway—Trustees of the Ferries and Passages across the Tay—all the rights and interests they might possess to operate the Ferry.

The urgency of improved communication between Newport and Dundee is apparent from a Memorial to the Trustees of the Tay Ferries, signed by influential business people in the same month as the above Bill was introduced to Parliament:—

> The Tay Ferry is a most difficult one to work—rapid currents and tides have to be studied, dangerous banks avoided, heavy fogs encountered and difficult landings made.
>
> Along with the ship's master, there used to be a mate but now there is none should the master fall ill. The number of hands is insufficient to manage the steamer and when the steamer cannot get landed in Dundee, which happens fortnightly, passengers are landed in small boats in the charge of two men. Generally the boats are overcrowded, with 30 to 35 passengers. Low tides are invariably from 7-11 a.m., so businessmen are most affected.
>
> In the fore and aft cabins of the "Newport" the smell of bilge water is so noxious as to render them intolerable.

Nine years were to pass before the Newport Railway Company gave notice of its intention to apply for an Act to construct the following railways:—

A Railway (Number 1) commencing the parish of Ferryport-on-Craig by a junction with the North British Railway at the terminus thereof at Tayport and terminating in the parish of Forgan at a point 247 yards north east from the north east corner of Tayfield House and 373 yards south east of the principal entrance door of the Newport Inn.

A Railway (Number 2) commencing 247 yards north east of the north east corner of Tayfield House and terminating at a point 190 yards south from the south east corner of Wormit Steading.

A Railway (Number 3) commencing at a point 300 yards south of the seaward end of the pier at Woodhaven and terminating by a junction with the above Railway Number 2.

733 yards north west for the south east corner of Wormit Steading.

Although the Act was passed in July 1866, there was a marked lack of enthusiasm—no shareholders turned up for a meeting in the Newport Hotel on 5 November and another meeting called for the following day had the same result! As a consequence, the original Act was modified during the current Parliamentary session and Royal Assent received shortly before the North British Railway confessed to having encountered financial difficulties. Construction of all three railways was to be virtually abandoned as they would be rendered unnecessary by a Deviation Railway commencing at a junction only two furlongs from the start of railway Number 1. The Act would also have enabled an agreement to be made with the N.B.R. for the latter Company to work the line and if necessary share in the expenses of construction.

By 1873 the capital, amounting to £46,000 had been fully subscribed and all lands needed for construction of the railway were acquired in readiness for work on the line to begin. During the same year, the North British Railway obtained powers to work the line in perpetuity. In return, Newport Railway shareholders were guaranteed a dividend of 5½% p.a. and when the N.B. chose to take the line over, they would get a bonus of 10% on their holding. Unlike the Newburgh & North of Fife Railway, which retained its independence until the 1923 Grouping, the Newport Railway was taken over in 1888.

Only six months after the railway had been opened throughout, the Tay Bridge disaster on Sunday, 28 December, 1879, ended temporarily railway/ferry-boat rivalry.

Two years after the opening of the second Tay Bridge in 1887, there were four through trains from Leuchars Junction to Dundee via Tayport in addition to a total of 13 weekday trains between Tayport and Dundee. A similar number of trains ran in the reverse direction, whilst a further five trains from Dundee, including an empty carriage working, went out only as far as East Newport before returning across the bridge. Passengers using Wormit station were not served by 10 of the 22 trains,

150

several of which, by also not stopping at Dundee Esplanade, could reach West Newport in exactly 10 minutes. East Newport and Tayport were a further 4 and 9 minutes journey time away. On weekdays, two carriage sets, one based at Tayport and the other at Dundee worked the service. This arrangement involved an engine running light across to Tayport at 4.20 a.m. on Monday mornings and returning at 1.32 a.m. on Sunday mornings. Sunday services consisted of two return workings between Dundee and Edinburgh and four local trips, covered by the Dundee stock, across to Tayport and back. Despite the rapid growth of Newport as a dormitory suburb and the building there of fine churches, local Sunday services were, as they had been in 1879, 'tailored' to enable attendance at worship in Dundee.

To avoid inconvenient delays at Leuchars, passengers travelling between Newport line stations and destinations in the south were permitted use of Dundee Tay Bridge at no extra charge.

The Newport line was single track throughout except between the North and South signal boxes at Tayport and from the station end of the 148 yard long Wormit tunnel to the junction with the main line. In the Down direction, the line from Tayport to East Newport rose steeply at gradients of 1 in 83 to 1 in 72 for about 2½ miles to within a short distance of the latter station. It continued more or less level through and for a quarter mile beyond this station before starting to fall at gradients of 1 in 103 in 1 in 193 for about one mile past West Newport. After levelling to 1 in 313 for a quarter mile, the descent steepened to 1 in 66 for 507 yards almost to the mouth of Wormit tunnel, through which the line continued to fall at 1 in 178. The line was curved for the greater part of its length, especially between East and West Newport where speeds were restricted to 25 m.p.h.

With the coming of the Newport Railway, Tayport became a through station. It was by far the largest station, both in respect of area and accommodation, north of Cupar. East Newport as built had no loop, but it would seem that the necessity for one had become apparent even before the fall of the Tay Bridge. A

Down platform and loop were constructed during August 1878. West Newport was never more than a halt, to which an agent's house was added around the turn of the century. Plans to build a station at Wormit were not made until as late as June 1887, some two months after the second bridge was opened.

Wormit station, only yards from the Tay Bridge, was to provide the setting for a serious railway accident on the evening on Saturday, 28 May, 1955. A picnic special returning from Tayport, headed by an ex-L.M.S. Class 5 engine running tender first and pulling eight bogie coaches, derailed at the west end of Wormit tunnel. The engine over-turned and four coaches were derailed and severely damaged. The cause of the accident, which killed the fireman and two unauthorised footplate passengers, besides injuring 42 others, some seriously, was attributed to the train's speed, possibly 55 m.p.h., over the sharp curve in the tunnel. Both the driver and guard were considered to have been under the influence of drink.

By April 1910, the weekday service had been increased to 21 trains outwards from Dundee and 23 inwards. Of the outward workings, five terminated at Leuchars and the remainder at Tayport. Nineteen of the trains arriving in Dundee originated at Tayport. All trains stopped at every station with minimum journey times of 21 minutes to and 23 minutes from Tayport. On Sundays there were three return workings to Tayport and two to Leuchars Old.

A deterioration in the standard of service during and after the 1914-18 War was reflected in a report which appeared in the 'Dundee Advertiser' of 20 January, 1920:—

At a special meeting of Newport Town Council last night, the Provost and all the members spoke out strongly against the overcrowding in dark and dirty railway carriages on the Dundee and Tayport railway. The Provost said that during the War they were prepared to be patient and considerate, but their patience had been abused. For a long time the overcrowding on the trains had been notorious, and now the lighting had become inefficient. Whole carriages were run dark. He had had an interview with the District Manager, who had received him courteously, but the interview was unsatisfactory. The travelling public was not going to tolerate an inefficient service. He moved that the Council protest against the inefficient service, pointing out the unsatisfactory state of affairs.

Baillie Buick, who seconded, complained about the filthy state of the carriages, in which empty bottles, papers, etc., are to be seen in the forenoon trains.

Councillor Barry Robb made a special appeal for the restoration of Sunday trains and of family tickets. He said that people had bought or rented houses at Wormit because of the pre-War train service and fares.

The motion was approved and the Town Clerk instructed to communicate with the North British Railway Company.

In the timetable for Summer 1948, there were slightly fewer weekday trains—17 to and from Dundee and the frequency interval had become more irregular. For example, two hour gaps in the morning and afternoon departure times from Tayport were separated by services leaving at 12.15 p.m., 1.14 p.m., 1.32 p.m., 1.44 p.m., and 2.49 p.m. Similarly, no trains left Dundee between 8.47 and 11.40 a.m. nor between 2.15 and 4.16 p.m. The Sunday service had however been resumed with four trains in both directions.

No major timetable revisions occurred until after the line was truncated between East Newport and Tayport in May 1966, except that some d.m.u. sets, which by 1960 had begun to compliment steam hauled trains, worked through from Tayport to Arbroath. After the Tay Road Bridge opened in August 1966, possible closure of the 'Newport Railway' was increasingly mooted. It was suggested that with only 14 weekday trains in each direction—the last of which left Dundee at 7.46 p.m. and Newport at 8.11 p.m.—British Railways were deliberately seeking to discourage passengers. Whether or not this was the case, services were withdrawn in 1969.

The target date for closure was originally 6 January, 1969 but the Traffic Commissioners stipulated that firstly a turning circle for buses must be provided at Wormit. This was done on the site of the former Wormit goods yard.

At 7.46 p.m. on Saturday, 3 May, 1969, a diesel train pulled out of Tay Bridge station with fewer than 20 passengers, but when it reached its destination at Newport, hundreds of people

153

lined the platforms and dozens boarded her for the return journey. Two pipers marched up the platform to the guard's van heading a 'funeral procession'. Behind them were six other members of Newport Round Table complete with top hats and tails bearing a black coffin and a wreath.

The train on its return journey was greeted by exploding fog-warning detonators at every station. All along the line in Newport, between the East and West stations, people unprepared to brave the fog and drizzle stood at the windows of their homes as the train passed. When the train entered No. 2 platform at Tay Bridge station a large congregation was waiting to welcome it. The funeral party formed up and headed with due solemnity for the Tay Road Bridge from which it was expected that a burial at sea would take place.

Newport Round Table composed a few lines "in memoriam" with apologies to William McGonagall:—

> Damnation to the undertakers of the Newport railway
> Hoping the Lord will their labour not repay
> It proved a blessing to people
> For ninety years all but a few day,
> Who lived in nearby Newport
> On the bonny braes o' the silvery Tay

10

Fife and the North British—1862 to 1879

DESPITE being separated by the waters of the Forth, the E. P. & D. very soon lost all vestiges of its former independent parochial existence. In particular, new locomotives appeared on all the North British lines throughout Fife.

A high proportion of the engines acquired from the E. P. & D. in 1862 and listed below had already given sterling service for many years and were due for scrapping or heavy rebuilding:—

TABLE 10

N.B.R Engines Acquired from the E. P. & D. in 1862[1]

Note	Wheel Arrangement	Coupled Wheels	Builder	No. Deliv'd	Deliv'd	Withdrawn
1	0-4-2	5ft.	R & W Hawthorn	10	1847-48	1870-71
2	0-6-0	4ft. 6in.	R & W Hawthorn	10	1847-48	7 by 1869
3	0-6-0	5ft.	Burntisland	8	1856-63	After 1880
4	2-2-2	6ft.	R & W Hawthorn	4	1848	3 in 1871
5	0-4-OST	3ft. 6in.	Neilson & Co.	4	1858-59	After 1880
6	0-6-0	5ft.	Neilson & Co.	3	1850-51	After 1880
7	0-4-0	4ft. 6in.	Hawthorn of Leith	3	1855-61	1878/89/99
8	0-4-2	5ft.	Neilson & Co.	2	1849	1868 & 73
9	0-4-0	4ft.	Hawthorn of Leith	2	1847	Both 1870
10	0-4-0	4ft. 6in.	Hawthorn of Leith	2	1857	1878 & 1909
11	2-4-OT	5ft. 6in.	R & W Hawthorn	2	1850	1874 & 82
12	2-2-0	4ft.	R & W Hawthorn	2	1847	1870 & 77
13	0-4-0	4ft.	R & W Hawthorn	1	1847	1871
14	0-4-0	3ft. 10in.	R & W Hawthorn	1	1847	1874
15	0-4-0	4ft.	Hawthorn of Leith	1	1847	1875
16	0-4-2	4ft. 6in.	Hawthorn of Leith	1	1857	1891
17	2-2-2	6 ft.	Burntisland	1	1861	After 1880

[1]For notes, see appendix 4, p. 243

By 1871, twenty-six of the fifty-seven locomotives inherited by the North British had been withdrawn and substituted either by new engines or older ones transferred from other parts of the system and relegated to less exacting duties.

During the middle 1860's 24 handsome new 2-4-0 passenger engines with 6 ft. coupled wheels were built to replace the Hawthorn 2-2-2s of 1847. Their brass domes, which were placed over the firebox had a flared top, whilst the short plain smokebox carried a copper-capped chimney. There were no brakes on the engines themselves, speed being controlled by the tender handbrake. Of the 24 engines which formed this class, four of twelve built by Neilson & Co. during 1866-67 saw regular service in Fife. They were allocated to Ladybank, from where they worked to Perth and Glasgow via Kinross.

Goods traffic on all sections of the N.B.R. network was rapidly increasing and the original engines becoming hard pressed to cope with it. Between 1860 and 1867, 62 powerful 0-6-0 locomotives, varying in several minor structural respects, were built for Hurst by Hawthorn of Leith, R. Stephenson and Dubs & Co. Many were distributed throughout the Fife Peninsula where they would be seen until the early 1900s.

Lighter 0-4-2 class engines, built by Beyer Peacock between 1859 and 1862, became a familiar sight heading local passenger trains on Alloa, Kinross and Ladybank services. They had lavish brasswork, open splashers and footplate arrangements, and the boilers were interchangeable. All of the class were rebuilt by 1895 and continued in service until the Great War.

In 1869 work commenced at Cowlairs on the first of eight 2-4-0 express passenger engines under the supervision of Thomas Wheatley. Their front 6 ft. 6 in. coupled wheels had paddle box splashers pierced with eight slots, while the rear driving wheels had box splashers linked to the front splashers by continuous coupling rod splashers. A scanty weatherboard with two circular spectacles was connected to the box splasher by small side sheets. These engines were, in particular, employed on Glasgow-Dundee trains.

The engine which gained immortality by going down with the first Tay Bridge—No. 224—was one of two designed by Wheatley and built at Cowlairs in 1871. Although perhaps austere to look at, these inside frame 4-4-0 engines with their large 6 ft. 6 in. coupled wheels gave an impression of fleetness.

Possibly this was because their driving wheels were closely set, whilst by contrast, the unusually small 2 ft. 9 in. solid bogie wheels were spaced six feet apart.

North British amalgamations in 1865 gave the company access to coalfields both in Fife and Lanarkshire for which a new class of mineral engine was designed to cope with the additional traffic. There were 38 0-6-0 engines in the class built at Cowlairs between 1867 and 1873. Many of the engines varied in small details from each other due to the fact that parts of old engines were incorporated. Among the first 18, a number had domeless boilers and wheels with only ten spokes. Double sandboxes were provided for forward and reverse running but there was only one handbrake and that was on the tender. The latter 20 in the series were given cabs with curved sidesheets and short roofs. All sheds serving the Fife coalfield received an allocation of this new class.

The first goods locomotives to be built by Thomas Wheatley at Cowlairs were two 0-4-0 engines assembled in 1868 from pieces of scrapped locomotives. They had inside cylinders and frames and were capped by a plain stovepipe chimney. The engine and wooden framed tender had separate hand brakes and both were fitted with deep buffer beams which were provided with an additional pair of buffers to cope with narrow gauge colliery wagons. These much-loved little engines were rebuilt by Reid in 1911 and survived until 1925, when they could still be seen employed between Alloa and Alloa harbour and as shunters at Methil docks.

Six light 0-6-0 ST shunters were built at Cowlairs in 1874 for duties at the Forth and Tay ferry stations. Broughty Ferry and Newport got one each, and Burntisland and Granton two each. The Granton engines not only shunted ferry traffic but also worked passenger trains to and from Edinburgh.

In 1877 absorption of the Leven & East of Fife Railway brought into the North British stock 5 small four-wheel outside cylinder tank engines, three of which were built by Hawthorn of Leith in 1857 and two by Black Hawthorn & Co. of Gateshead in 1874.

Such was the variety of locomotives which a traveller in Fife during the early 1870s might expect to encounter. It was a time of change, with new and relatively old engines passing each other head on as they worked increasing loads.

As the number of train movements increased quite dramatically so did the onus on permanent way staff. During the early hours of one October morning, fire destroyed the wood and cast iron bridge carrying the railway across the Cupar-Auchtermuchy road at Collessie. So completely was the woodwork destroyed that part of the rails was found lying on the road below. That a sound substitute bridge was opened to traffic within 33 hours reflects the high efficiency of the lineside gangers, who were often provided with cheap inferior materials. No time allowances would be made for faults or delays and within five hours of the bridge reopening no fewer than 16 heavy goods and mineral trains passed over the new structure, in addition to ordinary traffic.

Fire contributed to many mishaps including one which, by reason of its unusual circumstances, is of particular interest. Late on a Friday afternoon in October 1866 fire broke out in the luggage van of an Edinburgh-Dundee train when it was passing between Cupar and Dairsie. After attempting unsuccessfully to extinguish the flames, the guard was forced to leave his van and cling to the hand rails and steps outside. As the fire worsened it became increasingly difficult to remain with the train even though it would reach Dairsie in a matter of moments. His waxed moustache and eyebrows scorched by the intense heat, he was poised to jump when an explosion from inside caused splinters of burning wood to be projected onto the roofs of adjacent carriages where several small fires started. Upon arrival at Dairsie, willing helpers unclasped hands too weak to let go and dragged the semi-conscious guard away from his charge only a few seconds before the fire erupted with great fury. The baggage van—which was not the last vehicle—was rapidly isolated and, for want of water, burnt to the axles. Although the carriages were only superficially damaged, large quantities of valuable passenger luggage were lost. It was subsequently ascertained that the fire was initially started by chemicals from a bottle in a parcel leaking onto the van's floor.

Permanent way faults, mostly due to broken rails, caused considerable anxiety throughout the early and mid-1870s. It was North British policy to renew only 40 miles of rails each year and never to use new rails when old rails would suffice. Old rails were regularly shipped from Scottish east coast ports to be re-rolled at mills in north east England. Upon their return they were invariably set in re-cast chairs—a practice which was not ended until late in 1877. At the same time it was decided for safety reasons to discontinue the use of iron rails on main lines. During the considerable time required to remedy these weaknesses, it was necessary to run trains at reduced speeds for considerable distances and had the first Tay Bridge weathered the storm, its full potential as a link between Fife and the north could not initially have been realised.

For many years staff morale was bad. Staff turnover in the signals and telegraphs department rose to 113 per cent in 1873 and young lads with barely a few weeks training were often found in charge of complex signal boxes. This may well have been a contributing factor in a serious accident at Cowdenbeath in which over 60 passengers sustained injuries. The following graphic account appeared in the *Fife Herald* of 9 February, 1865:—

> On Monday morning there was a collision between the Dunfermline and Kinross trains. A siding is set apart on the south side of Cowdenbeath station for the Kinross trains. The first train from Kinross, comprising a composite carriage, 3rd. class carriage and brake van arrived at the junction at 7.10 a.m. and was shunted into the siding. While waiting in the siding upon the return of the Dunfermline train from Thornton, at 8.30 a.m., the engine was sent to Lochgelly to clear out a mineral lye and returned with 6 wagons shortly after 8.00 a.m. The engine and wagons were backed into a siding already well filled. It was then the duty of the pointsman to shift the points to allow the Dunfermline train to run into the station on the main line. This he neglected to do. The distance between the points and the terminus of the siding is about 120 yards, but about half this space was already occupied. The tender of the stationary train stood outermost and took the brunt of the ensuing collision.

Fortunately, there were no passengers on this train, two carriages of which were pushed up the embankment into a large wooden erection just vacated by waiting passengers in anticipation of the imminent safe arrival of their Dunfermline train. There were about 60 passengers on the Dunfermline train, all of whom were more or less injured. But for good fortune, far more disastrous consequences would almost certainly have resulted.

Although very important alterations and additions to the main line timetable were introduced in May 1871, consisting chiefly of a separation for the first time of Dunfermline and Leven passenger traffic into local trains running independently of through services to Perth and Dundee, journey times were not significantly different from those ten years earlier.

TABLE 11

Average Journey Times from Waverley

	To Perth	To Dundee
1861	2 hrs. 45 mins.	3 hrs. 30 mins.
1871	2 hrs. 44 mins.	3 hrs. 18 mins.

By contrast with modern practice, Sunday journeys were markedly quicker:—

TABLE 12

Average Sunday Journey Times from Waverley

	To Perth	To Dundee
1861	2 hrs. 38 mins.	3 hrs. 10 mins.
1871	2 hrs. 38 mins.	3 hrs. 05 mins.

Sunday trains called at all stations except Edinburgh Trinity and Thornton, whilst on weekdays most omitted at least several of the lesser stations.

Problems of defective rails and incompetent signalling staff could not be completely remedied before the opening of the Tay Bridge, which enabled the North British to compete with the Caledonian. Drastic cuts in journey times were achieved by running trains non-stop over comparatively long distances, use of the far shorter route via St Fort and the elimination of transfer times at Tayport and Broughty Ferry.

Fast speeds were not desirable until the middle 1880s when the old signalling arrangements were disposed of and the block system, with all its expensive structures and trained staff, substituted throughout Fife. A report in the *Fife News* of 15 September, 1888, describes improvements at Ladybank station, where the platforms were doubled in width by removal of two of the four lines of rails which originally intervened. The article comments that with installation of the block system here, this busy junction need no longer be considered the most dangerous part of the main line.

Only a short time later, almost twenty years of planning and setback were successfully crowned at Queensferry and the main line through Fife became an integral part of that which ran the length of Britain's eastern coast.

Although the river Forth at the Queensferry was not more than a mile wide, had an island in the centre and good rock foundations upon which to build a bridge, the site was rejected by the N.B.R. as early as 1863. When the Company began to think seriously on how the ferry might be replaced by a bridge, Thomas Bouch chose in preference a site some four miles upstream near Charlestown, where the expanse of water was twice as wide but far less deep. Depth of water was not, however, to be the main problem—far more serious was the uncertainty of the river bed. Towards the close of the last Ice Age, melt-water from retreating glaciers filled in the Forth Valley with silt to a great depth and, as a result, when Thomas Wyllie made test borings during the 1860s he found the river bottom extremely uncertain. In May 1862, two bores were sunk 166 feet at low tide without clearing the silt, and in 1865 another was sunk to 231 feet but did not reach solid rock.

However, Bouch still considered that a bridge at this site would be a practical proposition and he estimated the cost of its erection at £500,000. Given that the bridge would save annually somewhat over £150,000 on the operation of the ferries, repairs to piers and maintenance of steamers, the North British directors readily agreed to giving the plan their approval.

During the autumn of 1864 notices were published of an

application to Parliament for statutory powers to construct a lattice girder bridge 2 miles and 367 yards long which would carry a single line of railway on 61 piers more than 100 feet above the river. In midstream there would be four great spans of 500 feet each, rising to a maximum height of 195 feet above river level. The ironwork would rest on stone piers sunk down to 25 feet below the silt bottom, thus making the total height of the structure 285 feet from its foundation to the topmost tip.

Strong opposition and many searching questions, mainly from the Alloa Harbour Trust did not succeed in undermining Bouch's display of great public confidence in the project—a display which got the Company its Act.

The North British, some of whose members still had lingering doubts, felt that before committing itself to so large a sum of money it should erect one of the pillars to confirm the accuracy of the estimates and the suitability of the riverbed for the foundations. Work on this pillar was put in hand in June 1866, when a great crowd assembled at Burntisland to watch an enormous timber raft, measuring 60 ft. by 80 ft. and 7 ft. thick, launched and towed out into the Forth. On this raft was to be built a brickwork shell for the pier, so that when the masonry was high enough, the hollow centre could be filled with 10,000 tons of iron to make it settle securely on the river bed. The raft was moored in position off Charlestown and bricklayers began to build the pier, working from two mooring tugs especially fitted out as living quarters for them.

On 3 August, 1866, as the workmen were preparing to sink the raft, they were visited by Richard Hodgson, the Company Chairman, together with other directors who ordered that work was to stop immediately and the raft towed back to Burntisland and dumped. All the workmen were dismissed. The experiment had cost the North British £34,390 and had proved nothing, but the company knew that if it had allowed the pier to be put in place and then called off the project, it would have been even more costly to demolish the unwanted pillar.

The abandonment of the Forth Bridge was a result of financial troubles, troubles found to have arisen from "a careful and most ingenious fabrication of imaginary accounts begun and carried on from time to time for the purpose of supporting the falsified half-yearly statements of revenue and general misrepresentation of affairs".

Towards the end of October 1864 a public meeting was held in Dundee attended by all parties desirous of promoting the construction of a railway bridge across the Tay, and thereby giving Dundee an alternative connection with the national railway network. In its editorial of Friday, 30 September, 1864, the *Dundee Courier,* bitterly attacking the many instances of gross impertinence and incivility by the Scottish Central's servants, noted that two of the town's largest firms had taken to sending all their goods by the North British and concluded that if the North British ever attempted to establish an independent connection with the town, they would be met with the warm support of every Incorporation in it, not excepting the Town Council itself.

The North British was desperately anxious to obtain at least a firm commitment for the project before a contemplated amalgamation between the Scottish Central and Caledonian Railways could have time to make very decided changes for the better on the main line to Perth and the South.

Addressing the many leading Dundee merchants and manufacturers present at the October 1864 meeting, Provost Parker began by recalling how some twelve months previous a project for 'throwing' a bridge downstream across the Tay had been defeated, not on account of its own merits, but for fear of the possible effects on the Docks and Harbour. The new plan, he emphasised, was for a bridge higher up the river—a bridge which would confer great and general advantages on the town of Dundee and its neighbouring district.

Mr Bouch, who had arrived using crutches, was then introduced and invited to detail the nature of the scheme. On the south side of the river, the railway would be extended to run west from Ferry-Port-on-Craig along the coast beside the road, climbing as it approached Newport so as to get the elevation to 'spring' the bridge. The bridge would commence at Newport and cross the river to a point near the Craig Pier, attaining an elevation of 100 feet above the water. On the Dundee side, in order to form a junction with the Dundee and Perth line, the railway would be carried on an elevated curve running for a considerable distance towards the Magdalen Yard, where the necessary connection could be formed. An angular piece of ground at the Craig Pier, covered at high water, would, having been embanked and recovered from the tide, be used for the purpose of building a central station for all the railways serving Dundee. Out of this central station a junction line was to pass close to the entrance of the then Dundee and Perth station, and crossing the corner of Dock Street, travel along raised arches through the Greenmarket towards Trades' Lane, descending gradually until it attained a junction on the level with the Scottish North Eastern Railway.

In an ironical opinion, Mr Bouch considered crossing the Tay to be a very ordinary undertaking and not to be compared with the great and difficult task of bridging the Forth. The eminent engineer estimated the cost of the bridge, which would be very similar in character to that once proposed by Mr Blyth for crossing the Tay at Mugdrum, at £180,000. He continued:—

"Assuming then the estimate is correct—and of course it is upon that that the commercial question turns—I have had made out for me from the books of the Companies a statement of the whole of the existing traffic from Fife by railway into Dundee. We will consider the question—first, with regard to the existing traffic only, and without adding a single penny for that traffic which may be expected to be created when the new line is opened, and we find that, at the rates which we would get under the Bill by charging a four-mile rate for the ferry, and deducting the expense according to the offer we have of working the line at 25 per cent., there would be left something like £17,000 and that sum would pay a dividend of upwards of 5 per cent. on the capital of £350,000. That, however, does not include the traffic from the Scottish North Eastern, or any of the traffic that will arise by the completion of the Forth Bridge—giving, as it will do, another access between Dundee and Glasgow, some

164

portion of which traffic is sure to be secured. Taking then, the present traffic, and adding to it a moderate sum for the other traffic we will secure, we may reckon upon a sum of £25,000 which will yield a dividend of 8% to the shareholders."

During the following month the Tay Bridge and Dundee Union Railway gave formal publication of its intention to apply for an Act of Parliament in the 1865 Session.

Unlike arrangements being made to incorporate the Scottish North-Eastern into the Caledonian Railway system, about which the general public could hardly object, opposition by certain public bodies to the scheme set out above was considered well-founded both on behalf of particular and general interests. The plan by which the proposed line would pass through the town had certain very objectionable features, such as high embankments, which the Town Council thought it necessary to resist.

New plans for bridging the Tay were published by the North British itself almost a year later in November, 1865. The site of the crossing was to be a mile or so further up river, the line from the south entering upon the bridge at the east side of Wormit Bay. Reaching the northern landfall, trains would be carried twice across the Dundee and Perth line whilst running east to the centre of the town, where they would cross Union Street and terminate at a large central station to be erected partly on the site of the Town House. The route from thence to the east was to be almost identical to that proposed in the previous year—the railway being carried south of Castle Street, across Trades' Lane and out to the north of the existing Arbroath line. Dock Street was to be shifted to the south of the new line, so completely opening up the new docks by taking away their confined north quays. The fact that both the North British and Caledonian companies both now contemplated their own central station gave rise to hopes that one or other of the schemes would be carried out, although a site for the Caledonian United Station was yet to be finalised. The Bridge Scheme and Union Junction Line, together with a direct line to Leuchars and another via Newport to Tayport was estimated at almost £1 million—almost equivalent to a year's income on the East Coast lines. Like the Caledonian, the North British was lavish in the properties which it scheduled for demolition. Many of those between Nethergate and Fish Street and in the Vault were old properties unhealthily crowded together, which, if removed, would have conferred a benefit on the town. The gradiosity of the scheme and the enormity of its cost proved to be the greatest objections successfully urged against it.

It was not until 1870 that a scheme for bridging the Tay received Parliamentary approval. The total cost of this, a more modest scheme, was to be £339,742, of which £229,680 was required for erecting the bridge. At a special general meeting of the North British shareholders, held in Edinburgh on 12 November, 1869, assurances were given to objectors, most of whom also held Caledonian stock, that the Tay Bridge scheme was not an 'aggression' on the Caledonian Railway. By an agreement of 1865, the Caledonian company had obtained the Mid-Calder line without North British opposition, in return for which the latter company would at a future time be entitled to carry out the Tay Bridge scheme unopposed. On 12 December, 1869, the shareholders voted overwhelmingly for the bridge and, without waiting for an Act of Parliament, the company accepted a tender already submitted by Messrs. Butler and Pitt of Yorkshire. A time limit of three years was set, but the job was to take nearly three times as long. The contractors had hardly begun work when Pitt died and the firm asked to be relieved of the contract. No other contractor could be found until in May, 1871, Charles de Bergue & Co. of London agreed a price of £217,099. Upon the death of de Bergue in 1873, Hopkins, Gilkes & Co. Ltd. of Middlesborough agreed to complete the undertaking.

The foundation stone having been laid at Wormit on 22 July, 1871, there followed six years of problems, redesigns, accidents and deaths. No sooner had Hopkins, Gilkes & Co., resumed the work, following the death of de Bergue, than sand was found in the river bed where Bouch's plans indicated solid rock. This discovery meant that Bouch had to redesign the bridge and

166

incorporate new building techniques. Girders from Middlesborough and iron columns cast in a special foundry at Wormit were ferried out into the river as very slowly the structure took shape.

Winter weather conditions caused frequent stoppages and there were many accidents resulting in loss of life or serious injury. One particular accident on the night of Friday 2 February, 1877, bore ominous forebodings of the subsequent disaster also the result of a freak storm and was vividly described in the *Perthshire Advertiser*:—

> While the gale on Friday night was at its height a most unfortunate accident occurred to the Tay Bridge. At the time when the storm burst forth in the afternoon, the usual gangs of men were employed on the piers and girders in the middle of the river in the concreting and other operations. Some idea of the suddenness and force of the storm may be gathered from the fact that it was impossible to get a steamer near the piers to release the workmen from their precarious position, and 54 men were left upon the girders, and, as it turned out, had to spend a fearful night there. Captain Whyte, of the steamer Excelsior, did everything that was possible to relieve them, and about eight o' clock his vessel was beating up the river in the face of a terrific gale, which at times was so violent that although the engines were working at their fullest capacity the ship drifted astern. As the steamer approached the bridge she encountered large quantities of planking and loose timber carried off the tops of the girders by the strength of the wind, and which threatened to get in about the paddles. About this time—a quarter past eight o' clock—there was a momentary lull in the force of the wind, followed by a quick and furious blast of wind, which sent the spray and waves flying on the deck of the steamer. A terrific crash was heard in the direction of the bridge, and the whole air was lighted up for a few seconds by great bursts of fire. It was found that two of the large girders, each weighing 200 tons had been blown down, that the pier on which they mutually rested had been snapped asunder like a thread, and the strong ironwork crumpled up like burnt paper.

The first official crossing of the bridge by a train, apart from ballast trains used by the contractors took place on 26 September, 1877. On that day the locomotive *Lochee* ventured across hauling four carriages containing N.B.R.

directors, officials of the Tay Bridge undertaking and local dignitaries. The special train, preceded by a pilot engine with Thomas Bouch on its footplate, took quarter of an hour to complete the crossing to the Esplanade, where it was greeted by many thousands of people.

Eight months later, on 31 May, 1878, what was then by far the largest bridge in the world was officially opened for passenger traffic. Two separate parties had the privilege of making the inaugural journey northwards, one from Dundee and the other from Edinburgh. The party from Dundee crossed by the steamer *Auld Reekie* to Tayport where they boarded a special train for Leuchars. Here they met with the Edinburgh contingent. From Leuchars, the *Lochee* steamed uphill towards the new bridge with a train-load of 1,500 people seated in 23 First Class carriages. Seven minutes after passing Wormit the train was welcomed at the north end of the bridge by a crowd estimated to number 15,000. Within the station itself, several hundreds had congregated to welcome the occupants of the train on their arrival. As the train drew to a halt the band of the 1st Forfarshire Volunteers struck up 'See the Conquering Hero Comes'. John Stirling, Chairman of the N.B.R., was the first passenger to leave the train and be welcomed by the City's Provost. After various speeches, the band led a procession of those invited to a celebration luncheon in the Great Hall of the Albert Institute. Included on the menu was the new 'Tay Bridge Sauce', specially invented for the occasion by one of the city's pharmaceutical chemists! Both Stirling and Bouch were given the Freedom of the Burgh at the lunch, after which the guests were driven away in horse-drawn carriages. The Edinburgh party left Tay Bridge about half past four.

On the same day the N.B.R. issued its new timetables and handbills. These detailed seven trains a day in each direction— basically the same service as before, but with a full hour cut off the journey time. Regular passenger services started on 1 June, 1878, and during the summer months many city dwellers delighted in picnicing near St Fort or Leuchars and travelling by the Tay Bridge.

11

The Main Line 1879-1939

AT ABOUT three minutes to 2 o' clock on the afternoon of 20 June, 1879, a Royal Train conveying Queen Victoria departed from Ballater for Windsor. The *Dundee Argus* gives the following graphic account of the train's progress through Dundee and Fife:—

In Dundee at five o' clock the Old Steeple bells rang out a merry peal, which was continued until the Queen had left the town. Crowds of people began to throng the vicinity of the Tay Bridge Station an hour before the advertised time of arrival, and those who were not fortunate enough to have admission tickets gratified their curiosity by watching the preparations which were being made at the platform. The Royal train was signalled at Camperdown Junction six minutes before six o' clock, and three minutes later it drew up there, and entered the line leading through Dock Street Tunnel to the Tay Bridge Station. On either side of the railway near Camperdown Crossing there was a large assemblage of spectators, and the Queen repeatedly bowed in response to their hearty cheers. Two minutes later the train emerged from the tunnel at West Dock Street, and the hundreds of spectators who had collected on both sides of the cutting cheered most vociferously. The train drew up within the station at exactly six o' clock. The platform was covered with crimson cloth and a judicious arrangement of stove plants gave the station a pleasing aspect. The Queen was greeted by the Provost who presented Her Majesty with an Address of Welcome, on vellum with the seal of the Corporation attached.

Seven minutes sufficed for the transfer of the train from the Caledonian to the North British officials, and at seven minutes past six o' clock the train steamed away from the platform, two minutes behind time. The engine, named *Netherby*,[1] is one of the Company's newest locomotives and fitted with the Westinghouse brake. The journey along the Bridge occupied eleven minutes and between the large girders and the south end of the Bridge the train moved very slowly—the speed being reduced to something like three miles an hour. As soon as the foremost carriages of the train entered upon the

---

[1]The *Netherby* was a 4-4-0 engine designed by Drummond and built at Cowlairs in 1878.

169

land line, a band of boys from the Mars training ship struck up the National Anthem while some 100 of their companions presented arms. Her Majesty, who was standing close to the carriage window, at once recognised the young sailors, and appeared to be much gratified by their loyal reception. At the same time, a Royal Salute was being fired from the Mars, which lying off Woodhaven Pier, attracted special attention on account of her fine dressing. On reaching the Fife side, the speed of the engine was increased, so that Leuchars was passed at 6.35 p.m. and the train halted half a mile south of Ladybank at 6.53 for five minutes to change engines.

Ladybank South signal box set the road for Kinross and the Devon Valley Line, by which the train was to proceed to Stirling. Here engines were again changed and after a stay of six minutes the train moved away towards Carlisle.

The gala atmosphere inspired by this royal crossing of the Tay together with the knighthood of Thomas Bouch so enhanced a Company, too modest to be great, that nobody could doubt that it would only be a matter of time before the Forth was bridged. Indeed, such a bridge had been authorised by Parliament as early as August 1873, but the North British had delayed construction in order to hasten completion of its mammoth project up on Tayside.

Within a month of successfully completing the Tay Bridge an agreement had been concluded between the North British, the North Eastern, the Great Northern and the Midland companies whereby each would guarantee sufficient traffic to equal a 6% dividend on the construction costs.

Designed by Thomas Bouch, the structure was to resemble two great suspension bridges set end to end, with the division between the two parts at Inchgarvie Island—a small barren outcrop practically mid-way between North and South Queensferry. The pillars to support the bridge were to be all of 600 feet tall and each of the two spans 1,600 feet long. Along each span a single railway track would carry fast expresses or lumbering goods trains 150 feet above high water level.

To comply with the Act work had to begin by 1 October, 1878, but the companies involved tried to persuade the Board of Trade to allow them to lower the height of their bridge, so

170

cutting both length and cost. Because the Board's refusal did not become known until towards the end of September, the ceremonial laying of the foundation stone on Inchgarvie Island by Mrs Thomas Bouch had to be hurriedly arranged and took place with a minimum of formality. Once the pier had reached high water mark and the terms of the Act were thus complied with, work was abandoned until 4 April, 1879.

Throughout the summer and autumn of 1879, William Arrol, whose modest company had successfully tendered for the ironwork of the bridge, busily prepared to begin construction. Undeterred by the Tay Bridge collapse, Arrol acquired sufficient ground near South Queensferry upon which to build extensive workshops and ancillary plant, whilst across the river a brick-works was set up at Inverkeithing to utilise local deposits of clay. However, in July 1880, a month after the Commissioners of Inquiry into the Tay Bridge Disaster presented their report, contracts for the Forth Bridge were cancelled and the project abandoned.

Whilst the Abandonment Bill was still before Parliament, the three English companies involved reappraised the potential for an east coast route to northern Scotland and representatives met at York to consider engineering feasibility reports. Over a working dinner, heads of agreement were drawn up, and after a hastily convened meeting of North British shareholders in Edinburgh, the Abandonment Bill, which had already completed its Commons stages, was withdrawn.

On 30 September, 1881, the Chairmen and General Managers of all four companies met in Edinburgh to discuss a plan for a cantilever bridge laid before them by Messrs. Fowler and Baker. Within two hours they had instructed that a Parliamentary Bill for the Bridge should be drafted in time for the forthcoming Session, during which it met with little real opposition, as the Government's inspecting officers had already been having regular discussions with the designers.

The present Forth Bridge received the Royal Assent on 12 July, 1882 and in December of that year several hundred workmen arrived at Queensferry to begin work on one of

Scotland's most famous landmarks. South Queensferry was the principal construction base, for it was near the main Edinburgh-Glasgow railway and had a branch line running right to it. Eventually more than 60 acres were covered by huge workshops, stores, houses for workmen, yards and railway sidings.

A long wooden pier was built in the shallow waters off the southern shore and this was gradually extended for nearly half a mile out into the Firth. A railway was built on it and joined to the Queensferry branch by a 65 foot bridge. On one section of this line, where the gradient was particularly steep, a stationary engine was used to haul laden trucks up from the jetty. This pier, besides being used for unloading construction materials, was also used by the contractors' little fleet of vessels. On the east of the site of the Bridge, slipways were erected to launch the giant caissons for the piers. When the last of the main piers was completed in March, 1886, work on the great cantilevers began. As these grew upward and outward the girders to carry the permanent way were put in, so that they furnished an extra platform from which more of the work could be done. These girders were so strong that they could project 100 feet over the Firth and still bear the weight of a three ton crane and its load at their tip.

Whilst work at Queensferry was speeded on by the use of recent scientific advances including electric light and a telephone line laid across the river bed, reconstruction of the Tay Bridge was well in hand. Construction of the existing bridge commenced in June 1882 and was completed five years later. The bridge, which is sited 60 feet upstream of its predecessor's visible stumps, consists of 85 iron spans and is 2 miles 364 yards long. Where the 72 approach spans are separated by 13 through spans, more commonly known as the central girders, there is a clear headway of 79 feet for the passage of ships.

Girders from the original bridge were incorporated into the new bridge as outside girders in the approach spans. To do this, pontoons were constructed with a platform on telescopic supports, so that the height could be varied to suit the levels of the bearings of the girders. The pontoon was moored under an old span at low water and floating on the rising tide it lifted the span, which was then towed between the new piers and lowered by hydraulic jacks into its new position. None of the original girderwork was used in the 13 central spans, and the huge lattice spans, each weighing 514 tons were built complete on pontoons in docks on the south shore of the Firth. A temporary lifting column constructed in the interior of each pier took 21 days to lift each span 77 feet to its final resting position on top of the piers. Lifting was accomplished by means of hydraulic jacks, one at each corner of the span, which raised it a few inches at a time.

The bridge was opened for goods traffic on Monday, 13 June, 1887—the first train being a heavy goods at 1.00 a.m. from Dundee to Bothwell Junction—and for passenger trains a week later.

Preliminary testing of the Forth Bridge took place on 22 January, 1890. Two trains of wagons were taken out over the 2,765 yard bridge simultaneously. The trains, each with three engines, stood abreast on the 660 yard South Approach Viaduct and at a given signal proceeded gingerly as far as Inchgarvie. To any workman looking down from on top of the 361 feet high main cantilever towers the sight must have been enthralling. The exact weight produced by the six engines and 104 wagons was 1,800 tons. This experiment was repeated on several days prior to the opening ceremony performed by H.R.H. The Prince of Wales on 4 March.

The Royal party, which had remained overnight at Dalmeny, residence of the Earl of Roseberry, drove to Forth Bridge Station (later to be renamed Dalmeny) where the Royal train was waiting. Shortly after 11.00 a.m. the party boarded the carriages, the Prince being ushered to a seat at the very end of his Special Saloon attached at the rear of the train. Sheltered from the inclement weather, His Royal Highness smoked a cigarette as the train sedately made its crossing some 158 feet above High Water Mark. Having inspected the structure from the Firth, the Prince returned to the bridge deck where he drove home the last rivet. Applying a silver key to the riveting apparatus, a silver rivet was immediately sent home by hydraulic pressure. After the distinguished party, which numbered about 500, were re-seated, the train proceeded slowly back across to the southern granite approach or 'entrance' where a second halt was made. It was here, with the wind increasing and heavy drizzle falling, that the Prince unveiled a plaque declaring the bridge open. As quickly as dignity would permit, the party made landfall and were thereafter entertained to a 'sumptuous' lunch.

Standing majestically was a bridge which had cost £3¼ million, taken seven years to build and occupied generally 3,000 men. No fewer than 57 workmen lost their lives whilst assembling over 54,000 tons of steel, 21,000 tons of cement and 140,000 cu. yards of masonry.

In order to take full advantage of the new bridge in rivalling the Caledonian Railway, the North British had for some time been engaged on the following permanent way schemes:—

1. A six mile direct line from Corstorphine to Dalmeny, where it met a most useful four mile spur coming in from the main Edinburgh-Glasgow line at Winchburgh Junction.
2. Construction of a line from the Forth Bridge down to Inverkeithing.
3. Provision of a seven mile connection between Inverkeithing and Burntisland.
4. Doubling of the North Queensferry-Dunfermline line from Inverkeithing to Townhill and the section between Kelty and Mawcarse—distances of five and nine miles respectively.
5. Installation of a two mile loop line between Cowdenbeath and Kelty.
6. The building of a ten mile double track route from Mawcarse to Bridge of Earn through Glenfarg and an intermediate station with sidings to serve the village of that name.

Undoubtedly the most difficult of these sections to engineer was that between the Forth Bridge and Inverkeithing. Immediately after crossing the Bridge, the line descends through a deep whinstone ridge, the initial part of which had to be tunnelled. Upon emerging into the first of two deep cuttings a most exceptional difficulty was encountered—the crater of an extinct volcano! When the 70 ft. deep orifice had been filled in with rubbish, the pressure of the material deposited raised the ground on the north side of the railway by 17 feet. Having passed the site of the volcano and through the second 70 ft. cutting, trains cross the 65 ft. high Jamestown Viaduct before tunnelling under part of Inverkeithing to reach the station. Although only two miles in length, this section cost no less than £110,000.

On the North Queensferry-Dunfermline line, the station at Comely Park in Dunfermline was removed to a position nearer the town centre and redesigned to provide a wide main platform with an island platform opposite.

Immediately after the opening ceremony, the Bridge was used by both goods traffic and the local passenger service between Edinburgh and Dunfermline, although until completion of the direct line to Corstorphine trains continued to travel via Kirkliston. At the same time services from Dunfermline to Edinburgh using the North Queensferry-Port Edgar ferry were withdrawn. The ferry-boats, which continued to ply across the Firth, were used by North Queensferry passengers who were left without a station for six months. The line from Burntisland to Inverkeithing passed the Board of Trade's examination on 16 April, 1890 and was opened for goods traffic thereafter. Because construction problems were expected to delay opening of the Glenfarg route until mid-May, it was announced that goods traffic from Aberdeen and the North, travelling via Dundee and Thornton, would on and after 1 May, 1890 be conducted across the Forth Bridge instead of the Burntisland ferry. It was not until the beginning of June, however, that main line passenger trains commenced to use the Bridge. The following paragraph has been extracted from the *Fife News* of 4 June, 1890:—

Early trains were got promptly away and on Monday morning Cupar station was visited by a few early risers who saw the express which left Edinburgh for Dundee at 5.30 a.m. fly past them at 6.29 or 11 minutes early.

The table below details northbound passenger trains to be seen leaving Burntisland during August 1889:—

TABLE 13

Passenger Train Departures from Burntisland
August 1889—Weekdays

Depart	For	Calling At
7.25 a.m.	Thornton Jct.	All stations. Arrive 8.02 a.m.
7.47	Dundee	Kirkcaldy, Thornton (u), Markinch, Ladybank, Springfield, Cupar, Dairsie and Leuchars. Dundee arr 9.15 a.m.
7.52	Dundee	All stations via Tayport except Wormit. Dundee arr. 10.26 a.m.
10.00	Thornton Jct.	All stations. Arrive 10.37 a.m.
10.25	Dundee & Aberdeen	Kirkcaldy, Thornton, Ladybank, Cupar and Leuchars. Dundee arr. 11.44 a.m.
10.46	Dundee	All stations. Dundee arr. 12.40 p.m.
1.52 p.m.	Thornton Jct.	All stations. Arrive 2.29 p.m.
2.27	Dundee	Kirkcaldy, Thornton, Ladybank, Cupar, Leuchars, St Fort and Dundee Esplanade. Tay Bridge arr. 3.53 p.m.
4.30	Thornton Jct.	All stations. Arrive 5.07 p.m.
4.55	Dundee	Kirkcaldy, Thornton and then all stations via Tayport. Dundee arr. 6.57 p.m.
5.00	Thornton Jct.	All stations. Arrive 5.37 p.m.
5.35	Dundee	Kirkcaldy, Thornton, Cupar and Leuchars. Dundee arr. 7.10 p.m.
7.54	Dundee	All stations. Arrive 9.50 p.m.

Notes to these trains

Express trains for Dundee left Glasgow at 7.00 a.m., 9.05 a.m., 1.10 p.m., 4.35 p.m., and 7.25 p.m. Calling only at Larbert, Alloa, and Dunfermline, they reached Thornton in 1 hour 40 minutes at an overall average of 37 m.p.h. North of Thornton, the 7.00 a.m. and 9.05 a.m. trains both preceded trains from Burntisland by 5 minutes and, stopping only at Cupar and Leuchars, covered the 28½ miles to Dundee in 53 minutes.

Connections for Perth left Ladybank not more than 2 minutes after the departure of all Burntisland-Dundee trains except the 10.25 a.m. and 2.27 p.m.

As from 2 June, 1890, there were twelve rather than eight passenger departures from Edinburgh to Dundee. Seven of the eight trains which travelled via St Fort completed their journeys in less than two hours; the four fastest taking 1 hr. 25 mins., 1 hr. 30 mins. and 1 hr. 40 mins. to cover the new 59¼ mile route. The first of these four trains, which left Waverley at 5.30 a.m., made no stops, whilst the second called only at Kirkcaldy. However, both the 9.35 a.m. and 9.00 p.m. expresses, although taking only ten minutes longer, were required to pick up and set down at no fewer than four and five intermediate stations. Before the Forth Bridge was opened, the journey could not be completed in less than 2 hrs. 10 mins., but that included delays of seven minutes at both Granton and Burntisland and a thirty minute ferry passage!

Six trains from London crossed the Bridge daily. During a stoppage at Waverley, varying in length from 10 to 25 minutes, the trains were divided—one section going by way of Glenfarg to Perth whilst the other continued to Dundee and Aberdeen. A similar number of trains between Glasgow and Dundee were re-routed across the new bridge and conveyed a Dunfermline portion which was detached, or attached, at Dalmeny. Alloa was served by a new service from Glasgow to Perth via the Devon Valley line and Glenfarg.

The Forth Bridge enabled the N.B.R. to design a timetable which for the first time could properly cope with steady growth amongst manufacturing industries in the major urban centres, where population had been expanding rapidly since the mid-19th century. As the turn of the century approached, the railway's passenger potential was becoming far less evenly spread throughout Fife.

Civil Parish Populations

1861, 1881 and 1901

Parish	1861	1881	1901
North East Fife District			
Abdie (Newburgh)	1,381	983	664
Auchtermuchty	3,285	2,333	1,884
Collessie (Ladybank)	1,530	1,989	2,161
Cupar	6,750	7,404	6,768
Dairsie	638	693	464
Ferryport-on-Craig	2,013	2,818	3,445
Kettle (Kingskettle)	2,474	2,054	1,759
Leuchars	1.903	2,185	2,499
St Andrews & St Leonards	7,605	8,604	9,410
Strathmiglo	2,261	2,061	1,618
TOTAL	29,840	31,124	30,672

Parish	1861	1881	1901
Central and West Fife Districts			
Auchterderran	3,457	4,332	8.626
Ballingry	736	1,065	4,156
Beath (Cowdenbeath)	2,390	5,442	15,812
Burntisland	3,670	4,821	5,599
Cameron	1,362	1,003	738
Dunfermline	21,187	26,568	31,697
Kirkcaldy and Abbotshall	11,293	14,963	21,908
Markinch	5,375	5,863	6,803
Scoonie (Leven)	3,257	3,730	6,342
Wemyss	6,003	7,307	15,031
TOTAL	58,730	75,094	116,712

In the same year as the Edinburgh & Northern Railway opened, Michael Nairn, a Kirkcaldy entrepreneur, started to manufacture floor coverings. His factory, which was known by local cynics as "Nairn's Folly", became so successful that others followed his example and before the end of the century Kirkcaldy was recognised as the linoleum centre of the world.

178

Within the same period four extensive foundries were erected and hundreds of steam engines manufactured, mainly for overseas buyers. The proprietor of one such foundry, noted for its marine engines, established a thriving shipbuilding business at Abden near Kinghorn. Here, many railway passengers must have had their curiosity excited by a gigantic 50 ton travelling crane, possibly the only one of its kind in Scotland. The crane, 52 feet high, was supported partly on the railway embankment and partly on cast iron pillars. Amongst the many vessels built at Abden was the twin-funnelled *William Muir* which saw service on the Burntisland and Queensferry crossings for almost sixty years.

Only a short distance north of Abden were the Binnend Shale Oil Works. At the third Annual Meeting of its proprietors, held in May 1885, it was stated that during the year 125,000 tons of shale had been raised and 116,000 tons of this was used to make 3,578,000 gallons of oil. However, two great difficulties beset the company:—

1. the want of coal on the spot
2. the expense of conveying this and other traffic between the somewhat remote works and Burntisland.

To avoid carting fuel and oil for a mile overland to Burntisland, work began in September, 1886 on a short railway to join the main line at Kinghorn. Construction of the 1½ mile track, although involving a 36 ft. deep cutting at Midroad and a bridge across the road which skirts Kinghorn Loch, was finished by the end of the following May. Unfortunately, deposits of suitable shale were over-estimated and the branch was destined to have only a brief working life.

By 1904 the main lines provided the means of access to sidings and short branches serving no fewer than 82 collieries and over 90 assorted factories throughout the Peninsula. During summer weekends and trades holidays train control on these same access routes was further complicated by many special workings.

179

During the 1914-18 War, especially heavy demands were placed upon the Peninsula's railways; in particular on the east coast main line and its branch from Inverkeithing to the great naval base at Rosyth. Military training centres were established at Inverkeithing, Kinghorn, Tillicoultry, Kirkcaldy, Dunfermline, Kinross, Perth, Leven, Ladybank, Cupar, St Andrews and Wormit. From these centres thousands of officers and men for overseas were transported south by both special and ordinary trains, whilst specials conveyed horses from Cupar and other Scottish depots to Swaythling, the collecting depot for the Continent. Large garrisons were stationed on both banks of the Tay and Forth, as well as on several islands in the Forth, to protect the railway bridges—a measure which meant even more traffic for the railway.

Upon demobilisation in 1919, special trains running every day between Edinburgh and Kinross dispersal camp brought, and took away again, over 72,000 soldiers during one single four month period.

Throughout the War special leave trains were run weekly from Rosyth, while the daily Euston-Thurso naval train followed the 'Waverley' route between Carlisle and Perth from May 1917 until April 1919. This train usually consisted of 14 vehicles, although on occasions it was run in two or even three parts. In December, 1918, when the whole of the Grand Fleet personnel were granted leave, as many as 32 special trains had to be run out of or into Rosyth Dockyard and Port Edgar every day.

Construction of Rosyth Dockyard was far from complete on the outbreak of war and 24 workmen's trains arrived daily at the Dockyard station from Edinburgh, Dunfermline and Kirkcaldy. Between their schedules, the branch was required to handle exceptionally heavy coal traffic from South Wales.

Throughout the first year of the ensuing peace long overdue locomotive repairs, coal shortages and permanent way maintenance resulted in many short-comings. In December, 1919, 22% of engines in the N.B.R.'s stock were on the non-effective list, and between 12 October and 14 December of that year,

180

685 Sunday specials ran over the company's system because engines were not available on weekdays.

By the autumn of 1920 most of the post-war problems had been overcome and gradually prestige trains re-appeared on the Edinburgh-Aberdeen route. Of those engines rostered for this service during the inter-war years, the 4-4-2 Reid Atlantics and Gresley 2-8-2 P2s gave many fine performances the like of which had never been seen before. Details of runs by such Atlantics as *St Johnstoun, The Lord Provost,* and *Hazeldean* and Gresley's powerful *Cock O' the North* and *Earl Marischal* are to be found in a number of books as well as contemporary railway journals.

The two tables below show how Fife passengers were able to benefit increasingly from a shortening of journey times provided by a greater frequency of long distance and local trains:—

TABLE 14

October 1920

Northbound Journey Times
(in minutes from Waverley)

		Edinburgh-Aberdeen Expresses			Other main line trains		
		Train No.				*Av.*	*Fastest*
Distance		*1*	*2*	*3*	*No.*	*Time*	*Time*
25.71	To Kirkcaldy	42+	—	42	13	57	43
39.09	To Ladybank	—	—	66	9	95	76
44.46	To Cupar	74	67	79	7	104	87
50.68	To Leuchars	86	—	91	7	117	99
59.18	To Dundee	105	88	109	7	141	118

+On Sundays, when no stop was made at Haymarket, the journey to Kirkcaldy took 38 minutes.

Two additional trains, departing Waverley at 4.25 a.m. and 2.20 p.m., ran non-stop to Dundee in 85 and 84 minutes respectively.

TABLE 15

July 1938

Northbound Journey Times
(in minutes from Waverley)

			Train No.					Av.	Fastest
Distance		*1*	*2*	*3*	*4*	*5*	*6*	*No.* Time	Time

Distance		Train No. 1	2	3	4	5	6	No.	Av. Time	Fastest Time
25.71	To Kirkcaldy	40	37	37	35	37	41	18	50	41
39.09	To Ladybank	—	—	—	—	—	—	8	88	70
44.46	To Cupar	72	71	—	—	65	67	6	98	80
50.68	To Leuchars	84	81	74	67	75	78	6	111	91
59.18	To Dundee	100	97	89	82	91	93	6	130	106

Edinburgh-Aberdeen Expresses+   *Other main line trains*

Train No. 1 *The Night Scotsman* ex King's Cross
Train No. 2 Includes a 9 minute wait at Kirkcaldy for through carriage from Glasgow.
Train No. 4 *The Flying Scotsman* ex King's Cross
Train No. 5 Through train from King's Cross.

One train, departing Waverley at 4.05 a.m. ran non-stop to Dundee in 80 minutes.

+Even before 1935, when the full stud of 2-8-2s were introduced, it had been possible to adopt a fixed standard of timing over the route, irrespective of the load, so that for a great part of the year comparatively light trains ran to times designed for maximum loadings, with a great deal of time in hand.

Reduced journey times from Edinburgh to Perth and from Glasgow to Dundee gave shorter distance passengers less time to enjoy travel in Pullman coaches—an additional luxury introduced during inter-war years. Throughout the Edwardian era, Pullman car services had been almost entirely restricted to the south of England, but in 1914, Lord Dalziel, owner of the Pullman Car Company, signed a contract with the Caledonian Railway to provide and operate all restaurant cars on its network. In the summer of 1914 ten new Craven—built Pullman Cars were supplied for work on the principal services from Glasgow to Aberdeen and Edinburgh (Princes Street) to Perth. Pullman operations in Scotland later became competitive, as the L.N.E.R. began to introduce Pullman cars singly on services within Scotland between cities also served by L.M.S. Pullman restaurant cars. In 1933, however, the Pullman contract with the L.M.S., was not renewed and all the cars, having been purchased by the L.M.S., were repainted in its standard livery and renumbered in normal stock.

At varying times from 1929 Pullmans were incorporated in L.N.E.R. Edinburgh-Perth section workings. Such a car was attached to the Perth portion of *The Night Scotsman* from King's Cross due to proceed out of Waverley at 7.30 a.m. and reach Perth five minutes before nine o' clock. Whilst a fitting breakfast was being served, intermediate calls were made at Dunfermline (Lower) and Kinross. The car returned to Edinburgh at 12.25 p.m. appended to the 8.30 a.m. working from Inverness. A second return journey from Edinburgh commenced at 4.10 and terminated at 9.34 p.m.

A Pullman restaurant car service was provided as far as Dundee on the 1.07 p.m. Glasgow (Queen Street)-Aberdeen via Fife express. As Kirkcaldy was not reached until 2.29 and Leuchars 3.02 p.m., Fife passengers had liberal time to relax over lunch. The return working left Dundee at 5.50 p.m. on a 2 hr. 34 mins. scheduled train.

Strangely, Pullman cars never provided a regular service on the east coast line between Edinburgh, Dundee or Aberdeen!

12

The Decline of Steam Engine Workings

IN THE decade immediately following railway and coal nationalisation the Fife Peninsula was a veritable paradise for any steam enthusiast. By reason of its location within Scotland, even the casual visitor would almost certainly encounter some locomotives working far from their home depots. Whether he visited the large sheds at Thornton and Dunfermline, or any of the seven to which they were parent, it would be difficult to escape noticing a multitude of pugs working like busy bees for the N.C.B. and private industries. The many engines operated at Rosyth Dockyard and several other defence establishments were rather less accessible to view.

Only by the combined efforts of all these engines and their crews could any part of the rail network have been made to function effectively.

BRITISH RAILWAYS

Express passenger and freight trains travelling between Edinburgh and Aberdeen by the East Coast Main Line continued, as in pre-war years, to be hauled by engines from Ferryhill, Dundee and Haymarket depots. In 1950 these depots had the following allocation of 4-6-2, 2-6-2 and 4-6-0 locomotives, from which to roster their most important trains:—

Class	Wheel Arrangement	Ferryhill (61B)	Dundee (62B)	Haymarket (64B)
A2	4-6-2	3	2	32+
V2	2-6-2	11	10	7
B1	4-6-0	2	9	5

+Includes Classes from A1 to A4

By the summer of 1955, there had been no significant changes in this distribution, except for the allotment of 3 WD

2-8-0s to Ferryhill and 6 to Dundee. Class A2 Pacific *Blue Peter* was one of its class resident in Aberdeen, whilst sister engines *Sun Chariot* and *Tudor Minstrel* continued as representatives in Dundee. The number of Haymarket based Pacifics had risen from 32 to 37.

From 1959, type 2 diesels, working in tandem, were phased in on some of the Aberdeen express workings and, by comparison with records taken during 1958/59, far surpassed the uphill speed performances of A2 Pacifics. Although no steam engines ever proved ideally suited for the particularly difficult route across Fife, regular through steam workings continued, alongside progressive dieselisation, until the mid-1960s. A report in the *Railway Magazine*, as late as February 1967, notes that No. 60532 *Blue Peter* and Class V2 No. 60836 had been recently seen on freight and occasional passenger trains between Aberdeen and Edinburgh, mainly replacing failed diesels. It was also observed that Class A2 *Sayajirao* had done similar work until put into storage at Dundee in August 1966.[1]

In March 1953 Thornton Shed ranked the fifth largest in Scotland in overall numbers of engines, having only four fewer than Perth South. It retained this position in 1959, but lacking only two members to equal Perth. During the same period, Dunfermline slipped from twelfth to thirteenth placing. Of the 37 locomotives at Thornton in 1966, only 10, however, were actually fired.

Despite this run-down, steam working continued throughout the Peninsula until late in 1967. Freight working, especially around Thornton, and the regular coal trains from Fife to Perth and beyond remained in the hands of Thornton's 'Bls' and WDs'. Two passenger services with steam rosters, which survived into 1967, were the 11.35 and 18.42 Glasgow (Buchanan Street) to Fife trains. They were usually hauled by Class 'Bl' Nos. 61029, 61072, 61140, 61180 and 61345, but three B.R. Standard Class '5' locomotives also participated.

---

[1]For a table listing comparitive steam locomotive allocations between 1950 and 1960 see appendix 1 on p.240

Thornton's remaining two 'J36s' survived withdrawal until June 1967, when they had the honour of being the last B.R. steam engines in service in Scotland and were also reputed to be the oldest on the British network. Although there still remained six steam locomotives at Dunfermline, two 2-8-0s, 4-6-0s and 0-6-0s, none of these had been worked for some time. Alloa shed stood empty, with its roof removed; steam working having ceased at the beginning of 1967. The last steam locomotive noted in the area was a 'WD' 2-8-0 which worked a coal train down to Kincardine Power Station on 4 February, 1967.

THE N.C.B.
The National Coal Board, which came into being on 1 January, 1947, acquired no fewer than 55 standard gauge steam locomotives dispersed over 29 collieries throughout the Peninsula. In addition, there were a further three engines of 4 feet 4 inch gauge which had worked on the recently closed Fordell Railway. These were re-gauged at Cowdenbeath Workshops between 1952 and 1954.

Closely associated, but nevertheless autonomous, was the Ministry of Fuel and Power's Directorate of Opencast Coal Production. They operated four RSHN 0-6-0 saddle tanks at their Balgonie, Earl's Seat and Kelty Disposal Points. The foremost was closed in 1948 and its two engines re-allocated to Earl's Seat and Kelty. On 1 April, 1952, the sites and engines were handed over to the N.C.B.

An analysis of the N.C.B.'s engines shows a preponderance of 0-4-0 STs built by Andrew Barclay, Sons & Company Ltd. at their Caledonia Works in Kilmarnock. No fewer than 41 of this type had been built there, three as early as 1890 and a further six during the decade which followed. Seven 0-4-0 ST engines, supplied by Kilmarnock rivals Grant, Ritchie & Company to private coal companies between 1890 and 1905, were still doing a good day's work in 1947. By far the oldest engine, however, was an 0-6-0 ST which had found its way from the G.N.R. works at Doncaster in 1875 to Wellesley colliery, Methil.

Throughout the years after nationalisation, Barclay's continued as the principal suppliers of both 0-4-0 and 0-6-0 saddle tanks, whilst a smaller number of acquisitions originated from RSH Newcastle, Hudswell, Clarke & Co. Ltd., and the North British, Hyde Park Works.

Eight years later, in 1955, there were 57 steam locomotives, working with the aid of two Ruston & Hornsby diesel mechanical engines, at a total of 28 pits. This figure does not include nine 0-4-0 STs, either in store or under repair at Cowdenbeath and Dysart Central Workshops.

Although by 1965 there had been nine pit closures and, there were in total ten fewer locomotives at work, steam still dominated the coal-mining scene. Of the 40 steam locomotives deployed, 29 had been built by Barclay's—17 during the years prior to 1914 and 8 since nationalisation. With only three exceptions, the mines in the Fife Peninsula remained entirely dependent on steam haulage for marshalling coal trains. At all but four there were two engines to rely upon, whilst the two most productive pits—the Michael at East Wemyss and Wellesley at Methil—had an assortment of five and six 0-6-0 tanks and saddle tanks respectively.

There followed a policy of rationalisation throughout the industry with a massive programme of pit closures and consequent steam redundancies. By July 1973 there remained only four collieries—Comrie, near Oakley, Frances, near Dysart, Seafield, near Kirkcaldy and Valleyfield—together with Bowhill Coal Preparation Plant and Cowdenbeath Central Workshops. All but 6 of the 40 steam locomotives had either been scrapped or, after an overhaul at Cowdenbeath, transferred to locations outwith the area. In the three years 1967-1969 alone, no fewer than 22 were disposed of. Two went to Kinneil and one to Bedlay, but the remainder were either scrapped on site or acquired by a firm of Thornton scrap merchants.

Early in 1976 steam was still to the fore at Comrie pit; its three engines apparently used on a rota basis. They were all 0-6-0 STs—one built by Bagnall in 1945 and two by Hunslet during 1954/55. With production at Comrie increasing and a nearby smokeless fuel plant winning shipping orders to Scandinavian countries, the pugs could be observed in full cry as they laboured uphill, past a private signal box, with heavy trains, comprising perhaps forty wagons of Seafield coal and a blue ex-Caledonian brake van, en route from Oakley Exchange Sidings to the fuel plant.

In the same year steam repairs were still being undertaken at Cowdenbeath Workshops. Going further east to the Frances pit, two Barlcay 0-4-0 STs could be seen. The younger, built in 1949 was still working, while its elder companion, dating from 1908, was spare, perhaps resting after being sent to Bowhill in 1974 to handle traffic, when both the North British diesel hydraulics there were having their transmission systems repaired.

DEFENCE ESTABLISHMENTS

In the same year that coal-mining was nationalised, steam was in regular use at the Royal Naval Stores Depots at Donibristle, near Inverkeithing, and Lathalmond, by Dunfermline.

At the former a Barclay 0-6-0 ST built in 1920 survived until 1951, when it was replaced with an 0-4-0 ST built in 1915 by the same firm. The railway was completely dieselised in 1956, but closed together with its depot in 1959.

Lathalmond had a Barclay 0-6-0 T, acquired new in 1917, and a Bagnall 0-4-0 ST received direct from its makers in 1941. The Barclay engine was transferred to Rosyth Dockyard in 1948 and replaced by a similar Bagnall. Two four-wheeled diesel-mechanical engines, delivered in 1961 and 1964, worked the traffic alone, after the steam engines were scrapped in 1965 and 1969. The line closed in 1971.

Two years after the end of the 1939-45 war, Rosyth Dockyard was home for 8 steam locomotives. Four were Barclay 0-4-0 STs, delivered new between 1915 and 1919, whilst three were 0-6-0 pannier tanks, built for immediate delivery by Bagnall in 1940. A 1928 Hunslet 0-6-0 ST was the odd one out. Before the Dockyard took delivery of F.C. Hibbard diesels in 1955, it acquired two additional steam engines in 1948 and 1949. These were both Hunslet 0-4-0 STs built in 1941. There was no steam working after 1961, by which year all ten steam engines had either been scrapped or transferred to other establishments.

Only a few miles west of Rosyth is situated the Royal Naval Armament Depot at Combie, where there are tracks of both standard and 2 feet 6 inch gauge. The standard gauge was, by 1947, already dieselised, while the last three narrow gauge fireless steam engines—two 0-2-2s and an 0-4-0 built by Barclays in 1915—were scrapped about the same year.

Since the sale of its Kerr, Stuart 0-4-2 ST to a firm of Clydeside shipbreakers in 1948, the railway from Leuchars Junction into the R.A.F. aerodrome has been operated by a variety of 0-4-0 diesels. Presently, there is a solitary Ruston and Hornsby 0-6-0 diesel hydraulic built in 1961 and ironically property of the Army Department!

THE PRIVATE SECTOR

During the immediate post-war years steam engines could be seen working on twelve industrial sites throughout the Peninsula. Many did not survive for long.

The lengthy branch which climbed steeply up a long curve from the main line at Springfield to Cults Limeworks had been dismantled by 1950 and its 1935 Barclay 0-6-0 ST sold.

Until scrapped about 1950, traffic at Kirkcaldy Harbour was worked by the Corporation's own 0-4-0 ST, rebuilt by Andrew Barclay in 1912 from a Fletcher Jennings 1874 model. Amongst imports at Kirkcaldy taken inland by rail, was esparto grass destined for the Tullis Russell Ltd. paper mills at Markinch. Here, a 2 feet gauge 0-4-0 fireless locomotive, built by Andrew Barclay in 1917, was operated until about 1953 when rail traffic within the works ceased.

Away to the west in Clackmannanshire, the Glenochil Yeast Factory at Menstrie dispensed with steam working in 1947. That year they took delivery of a Ruston and Hornsby diesel and retired their 1894 Barclay 0-4-0 ST after over 50 years service with them. Rail traffic to this factory stopped in 1969.

The Forth Paper Mills at Kilbagie, near Kincardine, replaced their only steam engine—a Barclay 0-4-0 ST of 1916 vintage—with a new Ruston and Hornsby diesel in 1951. It served for 16 years before railway links were severed in 1967.

For many years an 1879 0-4-0 ST Barclay worked at the Alloa Glass Company's Killiebank Works until replaced by a similar engine from the same makers in 1950. This new replacement engine was scrapped on site in 1967, over a year after the plant closed.

Two steam engines disposed of in 1952 were an 1892 0-4-0 ST Barclay, which for sixty years had worked at Cameron Bridge distillery, and an 1889 Fletcher, Jennings & Co. 0-4-0 T, owned by Caldwell's Paper Mill in Inverkeithing. Whilst rail traffic at Cameron Bridge was given over to the sole charge of a new Ruston and Hornsby diesel, Caldwell's retained a 1918 Avonside Engine Company 0-4-0 ST, until selling it to a Lanarkshire firm for scrap in 1961. Two 0-4-0 diesel mechanicals—one acquired in 1950 and the other in 1962—continued to work at the mill until railway services were discontinued in 1972.

Amongst the most photographed industrial steam engines in Fife must have been those worked by the British Aluminium Co. Ltd. at Burntisland. As many as three were in use until the early 1970's. Then, in April 1973, engine No. 1—an 0-4-0 ST Peckett built in 1915—left after 58 years service for the Lochty Private Railway near Anstruther. Its departure had been preceded by that of a similar engine, six years its younger, which was transported to H.P. Bulmer Ltd. at Hereford early in 1972. There remains a Barclay 0-4-0 ST delivered new in 1937 and now used if either of two John Fowler 0-4-0 diesels, acquired in 1971, should fail.

For many years a conspicuous landmark seen by travellers on the East Coast Main Line has been the sugar beet factory at Cupar. In 1926, the year of its opening, a new Barclay 0-4-0 ST was purchased. A second similar engine followed the next year. When the factory closed at the end of the 1972 season, the first engine remained on site, permanently out of use, while the second had been sold for scrap early in 1964, immediately after the arrival of its substitute—a John Fowler 0-4-0 diesel hydraulic. This engine subsequently went to the Corporation's Kings Lynn factory.

Readers who have travelled on the branch line from Leuchars to St Andrews may be curious to know whether steam was ever used at the Guardbridge paper mills, amongst the largest and best known in Fife.

Although the writer can find no record of this being so, the unusual use of an English Electric battery powered locomotive for standard gauge working until 1973 is worthy of note.

THE WEMYSS PRIVATE RAILWAY

A pre-war history, outlining the growth of this significant and extensive industrial railway, far greater than any other in the Peninsula, has already been set out in an earlier chapter.

As a result of certain legal peculiarities, the line was unique amongst those worked by other colliery companies and could not, as contemplated, be taken over by the N.C.B. in 1947. Instead, its operation was administered jointly by representatives of the Wemyss Estates and N.C.B. It was determined that all the smaller old engines, used for shunting at the collieries, be transferred from the Wemyss Coal Co. stock to the Coal Board, but that a class of five 0-6-0 Ts, supplied by Andrew Barclay during the 1930's especially for longer journeys, would be retained.

The Barclay side tanks were joined in 1954 by an ex-Caledonian Railway 0-6-0 T and in the early 1960's three ex-WD austerity 0-6-0 STs augmented the number. The ex-Caledonian tank, outshopped from St Rollox in 1899, together with one of the Barclay side tanks acquired in 1934, were scrapped in 1959 and 1964 respectively.

Although only the Michael and Lochhead collieries remained in production by 1967, it was considered prudent to purchase a final austerity from the Army Department, so as to ensure the railway's ability to cope with the very high level of production at the Michael colliery.

191

Following a tragic underground fire in September of the same year, the Michael was abandoned, thus causing traffic carried on the private railway to fall to trifling proportions. After closure of the Michael, several engines were put into storage. One continued to work the four miles from Lochhead colliery to Denbeath (Methil) washing plant during the morning shift only, while at least one engine was provided throughout the week to work coal, now sent from Seafield for export, between Methil West Yard and the washery.

When mining at Lochhead ceased in March 1970, the railway lost whatever future it may possibly have had. None of the engines remained at Methil after 1970. One of the three ex-WD austerities acquired in the early 1960's had been scrapped in October 1969 and three of the Barclay tanks were scrapped on site in May 1970. A sister engine, W.P.R. No. 20 has survived and travelled under its own steam to the S.R.P.S. depot at Falkirk in October of that year. One month later, the remaining three engines—two ex-WD austerities and a Barclay side tank—were taken to Thos. Muir's scrapyard at Thornton.

THE LOCHTY PRIVATE RAILWAY

This railway runs east from Knightsward over the last one and a quarter mile stretch of the former 15 mile East Fife Central Railway. Officially opened on 14 June, 1967, visitors were able to watch A4 Pacific No. 60009 *Union of South Africa* steam majestically up and down a shorter three-quarter mile track. Passenger services began operating on summer Sunday afternoons from 1968.

Today, 'No. 9', as she is commonly known, is no longer at Lochty, but still under the same ownership. When, in 1973, British Rail gave their approval for private steam engines to use certain sections of their lines, the engine and its tender were taken separately by road through the streets of St Andrews and Cupar to be re-railed at Ladybank. Between working excursion trips, principally from Edinburgh via Stirling to Perth, No. 9 is stabled in the former Markinch Goods Shed. Her route

17   The fallen girders wallowing in the Tay after their collapse in 1879. *Briitsh Rail*

18   NB 0-6-2T No. 65 photographed at Burntisland. In the background part of the engine shed known affectionately as the 'Citadel' is seen.
British Rail

19 Introduced by Gresley in 1936 Class V2s became widely used throughout Fife. Here No. 60953 is seen at Kirkcaldy in 1953. *British Rail*

20   Both NB No. 65 and LNER No. 9210 shown here in Burntisland belonged to a class introduced by Reid at Cowlairs in 1910. *British Rail*

21 0-6-0ST No. 146A seen at Ladybank in 1907 not long before its withdrawal. Built in 1874 at Cowlairs and allocated originally to Granton.
British Rail

22 No. 1256 at Perth was built at Cowlairs by Wheatley in 1873, and rebuilt twice—by Holmes in 1890 and Reid in 1914. Withdrawn in 1925 after 52 years service. *British Rail*

23   No. 9608 *Foch* seen at Perth. Built by Holmes in 1888 for goods and mineral haulage. *British Rail*

24   Battery driven shunting locomotive at Guardbridge Paper Mill. *Keith Jones*

25　Former NCB No. 47 and WPR No. 15 engines await their fate in a Kirkcaldy scrapyard. *Author's collection*

26 Former Wemyss private railway saddle tank engine at Lochty coupled to a Gresley designed observation coach. *Ian Johnstone*

27 Kirkcaldy station rebuilt in 1960 reflects a modern trend in railway architecture. *Author's collection*

28   A *merry-go-round* train at Cardenden. *Author's collection*

availability is now very much restricted by the absence of turntables or suitable triangles—the Inverkeithing triangle necessitates 20 miles of running tender first, at a maximum of 40 m.p.h. on every trip from home. Indeed on a recent trip which terminated at Kirkcaldy, it was necessary to run light engine with tender leading back to Inverkeithing, so as to be able to reverse to Markinch.

Today, passenger services at Lochty are hauled by a Bagnall 0-6-0 ST built in 1944 and acquired by the Wemyss Private Railway from the War Department in 1965. She was latterly extricated from Thornton scrapyard. Beside her can be seen standing a former British Aluminium Works engine from Burntisland—an 0-4-0 ST Peckett built in 1915 and delivered to Lochty in April 1973. A Ruston Hornsby 88 h.p. diesel, donated by The North British Distillery Co. in the same year completes the engine stock.

It is gratifying that the thrill of steam and its distinctive odour may yet be enjoyed by both residents and visitors to the Fife Peninsula.

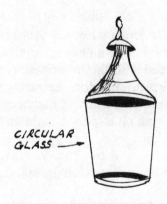

CIRCULAR
GLASS →

13

Post-War Freight Changes

THIS chapter examines how the changing economy of the Fife Peninsula, a national rationalisation of the railway network and a movement away from the wagonload concept have together resulted in significant post-war changes in the fields of mineral, general goods and through train workings.

During the years since 1945 there have been two major re-orientations of coal movements in the Fife Peninsula. The first of these came about as a result of a dramatic drop in shipments through Methil and Burntisland and the consequent change of flow from eastwards to mainly westwards as the traffic was worked throughout by rail. A second change began in the 1960s following concentration of coal output on a handful of economically productive pits and the construction of large coal-fired electricity generating stations at Kincardine and Longannet—the latter supplied by 'merry-go-round' trains from as far as Ayrshire.

To meet the National Coal Board's plan to increase the output of the Fife and Clackmannan pits to over 11 million tons during a 10-15 year period, the Railway Executive decided, as early as 1948, to proceed with the first phase of marshalling yard development in the district. Before the war, when over half the coal mined was exported by sea, it had been possible to work trainloads direct from pit to port without any need to re-assemble the wagons 'en route'. Traffic was not normally despatched from the pits until the ship was available and, consequently, the provision of intermediate standage facilities had been unnecessary.

The decision to develop marshalling yards involved the expansion of former small mineral marshalling yards at Oakley and Kelty. Oakley Yard, located between Alloa and Dunfermline had been provided to handle output from the nearby Comrie Colliery, then considered to be the most modernised in Scotland.

Because of the increasing westerly flow of coal traffic and an expected rise in output from the immediate area, the following additional facilities were provided: four through reception and departure lines on the north side of the main line; head shunt, ashpit, coaling and water facilities, a new signal box together with new office and messroom accommodation. The earthwork required the excavation and tipping of over 40,000 cubic yards of material to form an embankment. A 55-lever mechanical interlocking frame in the new signal box, together with existing apparatus in the old box, controlled six colour-light signals on the main running lines and another colour—light signal for train movements from the new reception sidings to the Up line, whilst ten new semaphore signals controlled movements to and from the additional sidings. At a later stage a 70 ft. turntable was to be provided to obviate engines proceeding light to Dunfermline to turn, after arrival with empty wagons from western locations.

Developments at Kelty, on the main line between Dunfermline and Perth, included the extension of twelve existing dead-end sidings and their conversion into through sidings as well as provision of a new signal box. The latter was constructed of steel and capable of being raised in the event of subsidence. Besides operating all the points and signals controlled from the old box, the new 120-lever mechanical interlocking frame operated an additional 15 pairs of points, six colour-light and 20 semaphore signals.

According to the summer, 1955, Working Timetable, a total of 17 trains were booked to arrive and depart on weekdays from both Oakley and Kelty. Of the departures from Oakley twelve were westbound via Alloa Bridge to Cadder Yard or the large steelworks and power stations in the Clyde valley. There were three short-haul journeys from nearby Blairhall Colliery to Thornton and one each to Perth North Yard and Portobello. Trains ran between Kelty and Perth, Craiginches, Thornton Junction, Dundee and Niddrie. Although only one shunt and assist engine was stationed at Oakley to work the yard and assist trains when required east to Whitemyre Junction, no fewer than four similar engines were allocated to Kelty, where their working week was from Mondays 6.00 a.m. until Saturdays at 2.00 p.m. Included in their duties was the piloting of heavy trains up the long Glenfarg bank.

Whilst the above yards were being developed near the western and northern fringes of the mining district, coal and goods traffic originating in, or destined for, east and central Fife, continued to be handled in six small yards or groups of sidings near Thornton Station, also, four at Burntisland, Townhill (near Dunfermline) and Methil. Work was retarded by the need for double handling and inter-yard working and by scattered and inadequate facilities. These problems were remedied in 1957 when a new mechanised marshalling yard was brought into use near Thornton Junction.

Construction of the yard on a 78 acre site, 2½ miles west of Thornton Junction and immediately north of the main line to Dunfermline, began in 1953. The main earthworks, involving movement of 430,000 cubic yards of material, having been completed, a start could be made on laying 26 miles of track and the construction of a control tower, three signal boxes and various administrative and staff buildings.

The yard comprised three Down and three Up reception lines, a hump engine line, and 35 sorting sidings. Up and Down through lines, quite independent of passenger lines, encircled this extensive yard, where equipment provided also included a 70 ft. electricity operated turntable, brake-van sidings and wagon repair facilities. Total standage of the reception lines and sorting sidings was 375 and 2,311 wagons respectively. Important innovations included the incorporation of secondary retarders and experiments in the field of automatic retarder control.

The site at Thornton was selected for the following reasons:—

1.   Its commanding position in relation to the principal and secondary railway routes traversing Fife.
2.   The location of the homes of staff.
3.   Regard to the possibility of mining subsidence

196

4.   Location of an existing motive power depot nearby.
5.   Close proximity to new collieries and opencast sites then under construction.

Rothes Colliery, where production was expected to reach 5,000 tons per day by 1960, was directly connected to the east end of the Yard, whilst the Westfield Opencast Site—one of the largest in Britain—could be reached by just a four mile long mineral line. At the former, no fewer than 10 standard gauge tracks passed through the preparation plant. Together with running roads there was a capacity of 1½ days full standage and 1½ days empties.

Principal traffic flows from Thornton Yard were north-easterly via the Tay Bridge to Dundee and Aberdeen, northwards to Perth and Inverness, and west to the areas surrounding Glasgow. In volume, the flows were approximately equal.

In 1954 the Scottish Region announced that a new marshalling yard would be built at Alloa to deal with coal traffic from new pits being sunk in Clackmannanshire and west Fife. When construction was completed at an estimated cost of £500,000, Alloa Yard, located on the west side of the town, would have available 15 sorting sidings and 5 reception sidings, together capable of handling 1,500 wagons a day.

Before 1960 these first two phases in an overall plan to modernise the handling of mineral and goods traffic had been completed, in blissful ignorance of the contraction and consolidation programme which the N.C.B. were about to put into effect.

The ten years between 1957 and 1967 were characterised by a rapid decline of the coalmining industry, a decline which brought about crucial changes in production, manpower and in the pattern of productive units. Within a mere ten years of the opening of Thornton Yard, the industry in Fife had been reduced from twenty-four collieries to only seven and a potential growth industry of the fifties had been pruned to almost the level of insignificance. Only four collieries, Michael and Seafield in east Fife and Comrie and Valleyfield in the west of the county, were expected to continue operating into the

1970s. The foremost, however, was 'sealed off' after a disastrous explosion in 1967. Railway travellers could hardly but be aware of the increasing decay and dereliction associated with an exhausted coalfield, especially as they passed through central Fife where blighted areas exceeded 2,000 acres. By 1968 Thornton Yard was shut each weekend from 6.00 a.m. on Saturdays until 2.00 p.m. on Mondays.

Continued production at Seafield, Comrie and Valleyfield pits, with the possibility of future expansion, resulted from their own economic viability and a potential capable of going a long way to satisfying an insatiable demand from the two new generating stations at Kincardine and Longannet. Westfield opencast mine was also to provide an important source of suitable coal.

Conspicuous by its twin 400 feet chimneys, Kincardine was formerly opened by H.M. The Queen on 12 October, 1960. Reception sidings adjacent to the main line and extensive marshalling sidings within the site boundary easily handle some 300 hopper wagons, with bottom-door discharge, supplying most of the 8,000 tons of coal consumed every day,

Only two miles further east along the same coastal line lies Longannet—altogether a far greater complex. Although four new drift mines supply 12,000 tons of coal each day along a 5½ mile underground conveyor belt, a further 8,000 tons is required daily to maintain the plant's high level of output. Merry-go-round trains therefore operate from Seafield, which provides over 5,000 tons, Westfield, Dora and pits as far distant as Ayrshire. Although Seafield has been equipped with appropriate overhead bunkers, the layout enforces terminal loading so that true merry-go-round operating is ruled out.

The writer has had the privilege of touring Longannet and being able to watch the arrival and discharge of coal wagons. Approaching along the single track from the west, the train which our party watched slowed to a walking pace for two reasons; first for the guard to phone the ultra-modern signal box that his train had cleared the main line, and secondly, to pass between a series of metal posts equipped to count the

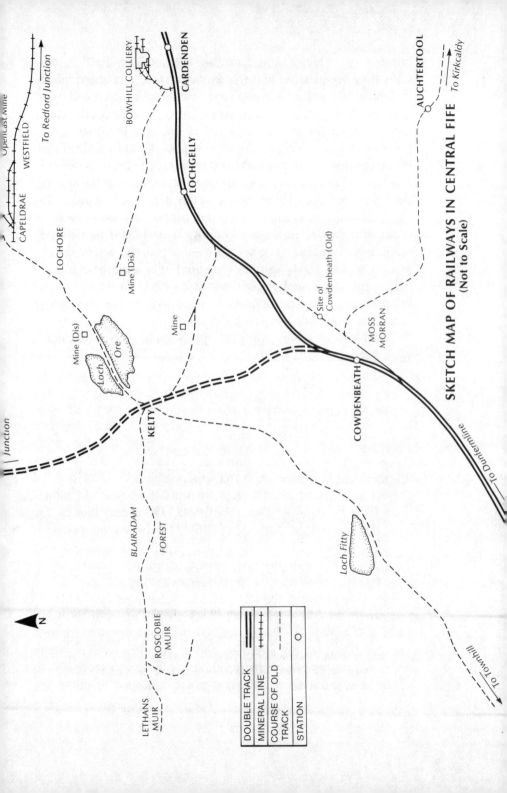

SKETCH MAP OF RAILWAYS IN CENTRAL FIFE
(Not to Scale)

N

To Kirkcaldy
AUCHTERTOOL
To Dunfermline
To Townhill

CARDENDEN
LOCHGELLY
COWDENBEATH
KELTY

BOWHILL COLLIERY
Opencast Mine
WESTFIELD
CAPELDRAE
LOCHORE
To Redford Junction

Mine (Dis)
Mine
Mine (Dis)
Loch Ore

Site of Cowdenbeath (Old)
MOSS MORRAN

Loch Fitty

BLAIRADAM FOREST
ROSCOBIE MUIR
LETHANS MUIR

Junction

DOUBLE TRACK
MINERAL LINE
COURSE OF OLD TRACK
STATION

number of vehicles and transmit the total to staff in the unloading hopper shed quite a distance ahead. The hopper shed is almost 100 yards long and spans two tracks, separated by a platform along which are positioned various electronic devices. On reaching a colour-light signal at the entrance to the shed, the train must stop whilst its driver activates the automatic slow-speed control, which enables his train to proceed at no more nor less than a ½ m.p.h. As the train progresses, rams at the side of the track unfasten three safety catches on each wagon, so permitting the opening lever to be tripped manually with a brake stick when the wagon is above a particular part of the underground recess. Its contents discharged, the wagon doors are closed and safety catches reapplied by a series of clams at the far end of the shed. All of the train's 41 hopper wagons were handled in a little less than 45 minutes without the train once having stopped after entering the shed.

The following tables listing merry-go-round train movements were prepared in 1977:—

FROM LONGANNET P. S.

Train No.	Departs	Arrives	
6U74	07.00	08.10	Seafield Colliery
6U77	08.15	09.37	Westfield O.C.
6B36 SX	10.48	13.34	Millerhill Yard
6U75	11.37	12.35	Seafield Colliery
6B96 MX	12.23	—	Barony Colliery, Ayrshire
6U78	14.00	15.22	Westfield O.C.
6U76	16.35	17.35	Seafield Colliery
6F23 SX	19.22	—	Falkland Junction, Ayrshire
6V59	20.30	22.15	Thornton Yard
6U81	21.15	23.00	Seafield Colliery

Train No. 6B36 uses 2 Class 26 locos to haul 29 wagons and proceeds via Townhill.

Train No. 6B96 uses 2 Class 20 locos to haul 26 wagons and proceeds via Townhill Yard, thence to Stirling.

Train No. 6F23 uses 2 Class 20 locos and proceeds via Townhill Junction to Stirling.

200

TO LONGANNET P. S.

Train No.	Departs	Arrives
6U71	04.54 Seafield	06.02
6U83	05.19 Westfield O.C.	06.54
6U60 SX	06.19 Bilston Glen	10.00
6U72	09.12 Seafield	10.56
6U65 MX	21.10 Barony Clly.	11.34
6U84	11.42 Westfield O.C.	13.14
6U73	14.02 Seafield	15.09
6U61 SX	11.53 Killoch Clly.	
	or 12.06 Barony Clly.	17.39
6U85	17.29 Westfield O.C.	19.01
6U82	19.26 Seafield	20.36

Train No. 6U60 reaches Longannet from Millerhill by Townhill Junction.

Train No. 6U65 runs from Stirling through to Townhill Yard, where it arrives at 02.21.

Train No. 6U61 runs from Stirling direct through Kincardine.

NOTE: Except where otherwise stated, all trains convey 41 wagons and are hauled by three 1,000 h.p. Class 20 locomotives, two in multiple at one end one at the other. WT communication is provided between the leading and trailing locomotives. Each hopper wagon is of 26-32 tons capacity, the high capacity being obtained by fitting 26 ton wagons with capes.

More recently, local newspapers have given prominence to plans to extract over 700,000 tons of coal from a 287-acre site at West Moss, immediately south of Cowdenbeath. Work on the site began in the autumn of 1978 just as the rundown of the smaller adjoining Dora site commenced to take effect. Merry-go-round trains, capable of carrying 850 tons in 28 wagons now make three daily trips to Longannet.

Not all the coal produced at Seafield and Westfield is despatched to Longannet. Some 14,000 tons is consigned daily to Cockenzie power station, a short distance east of Edinburgh, and to Leith Docks, where new handling facilities were installed prior to switching coastal shipments away from Methil.

Agriculture has always formed the principal source of Fife's general merchandise traffic. During the 1950s, long before closure was decided upon, upwards of 100,000 tons of sugar beet was conveyed in over 11,000 wagonloads every year to the refinery at Cupar—and this within the three month harvest period. Closure of Cupar in 1971 has been compensated for by a particularly satisfying recapture of most of the extensive seed potato traffic to England and the Continent. In recent years, between October and April, rakes of white Interfrigo and Transfesa vans have appeared with increased frequency alongside loading banks at Cupar, Ladybank and Markinch, awaiting arrival of consignments by road from the east of Fife. A photograph published in the January, 1977 issue of *Rail News* portrays a giant 58-ton Polybulk wagon, owned by Traffic Services, being loaded on to the train ferry *St. Germain* at Dover. The wagon, on a regularly worked route, is one of several containing grain collected from Alloa and bound for La Spezia on the coast of north-west Italy. Sometimes the wagons travel via Dunkerque and may be berthed on the ferry alongside through loads of whisky from Markinch.

Two other important sources of revenue involve the carriage of aircraft fuel and liquified gas. In 1977, a typical year, almost 38,500 tonnes of aviation fuel was forwarded in 1,434 tanker loads from B.P.'s Grangemouth refinery to R.A.F. Leuchars. And then there were some 1,200 tonnes of 'materials' despatched from the fighter station in 185 wagons!

Liquified Gas is used to boost the quality of gas derived as a by-product of coal at Westfield. The line from Thornton Yard signal box is worked in accordance with Electric Token Block Regulations and trains must not exceed 20 m.p.h. Prior to any movement within the plant, three barrier wagons, kept in an adjacent siding, must be attached between the locomotive and those vehicles which require to be deposited or removed.

Doubtless in what must be a succinct coverage the writer may have made many unjustifiable omissions. One working which must, however, be mentioned is the movement of alumina in bulk from Burntisland to Fort William and Ballachulish. After a hard fight, the Scottish Region successfully fended off road competition and in 1965 concluded a five year

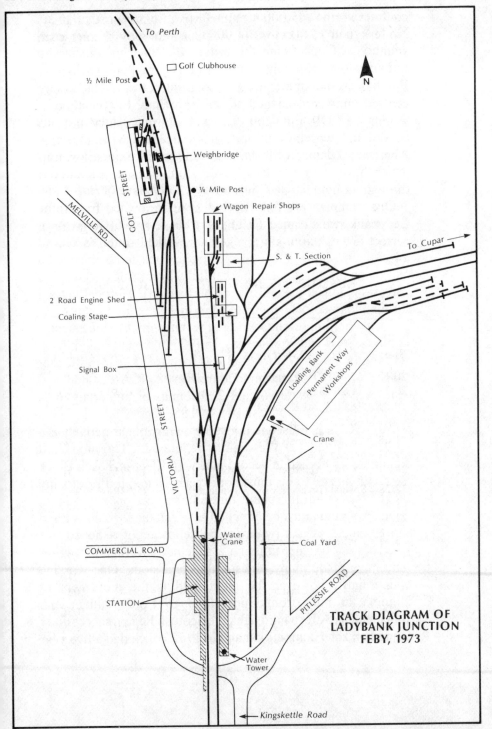

To Perth

Golf Clubhouse

½ Mile Post

N

Weighbridge

MELVILLE RD.

GOLF STREET

¼ Mile Post

Wagon Repair Shops

To Cupar

S. & T. Section

2 Road Engine Shed

Coaling Stage

Loading Bank

Permanent Way Workshops

Signal Box

VICTORIA STREET

Crane

Water Crane

COMMERCIAL ROAD

Coal Yard

PITLESSIE ROAD

STATION

TRACK DIAGRAM OF LADYBANK JUNCTION FEBY, 1973

Water Tower

Kingskettle Road

contract worth £165,000 with the British Aluminium Company. No less than 75,000 tons of alumina were moved north each year.

The volume of freight traffic carried by the main line across Fife has risen dramatically as a consequence of the oil 'boom' centred on Aberdeen and the Moray Firth. At the time of writing, in 1979, timetables show eleven mandatory and two conditional workings through from Edinburgh to Dundee/Aberdeen together with three services to Inverness. Several, which have timing loads of over 1,000 tonnes, are worked throughout by a single Class 40 or 47 locomotive.

One summer evening, during a sojourn with friends at Ladybank, we sat up all night and, from a window giving a perfect few of the re-aligned junction, compiled the following log:—

THURSDAY 13th JULY/FRIDAY 14th JULY, 1978

Time	Train From		To	Loco- motive(s)	Timing Load incl Loco. (Tonnes)
20.10	15.45	Oxwellmains	Dundee East	26.016	715
20.21	19.23	Perth Yard	Millerhill	25.077	510
20.30	18.00	Oxwellmains	Craiginches	26.003	793
21.05	19.37	Millerhill	Inverness	40.166	867
21.08	20.10	Dundee West	Millerhill	26.028	690
21.23	Special	Leith	Montrose	25.241/215	1210
21.54	18.20	Aberdeen	Millerhill	47.271	910
22.28	Special	Invergordon	Edinburgh	25.049	—
22.50	22.13	Thornton Yd.	Craiginches	26.088	610
22.52	15.35	Burghead	Doncaster	40.062	660
23.04	19.03	Oxwellmains	Craiginches	25.094	793
23.09	22.12	Dundee West	Millerhill	25.230	676
00.11	17.48	Inverness	Millerhill	40.166	710
00.50	14.10	Doncaster	Muir of Ord	40.149	1033
01.08	23.33	Millerhill	Craiginches	37.235	1050
01.22	20.00	Muir of Ord	Doncaster	40.160	660
01.34	19.45	Oxwellmains	Inverness	26.001	683

02.02	22.48	Aberdeen	Millerhill	47.053	910
02.40	15.15	Doncaster	Burghead	40.158	1069
03.05	02.20	Dundee East	Oxwellmains	26.016	510
03.30	21.30	Inverness	Millerhill	26.001	715
03.33	02.02	Millerhill	Dundee West	25.230	510
04.04	23.30	Aberdeen	Thornton Yard	26.022	783
04.16	18.50	King's Cross	Aberdeen	47.183	Freightliner
05.25	03.52	Millerhill	Perth Yard	25.077	660
05.44	04.08	Millerhill	Craiginches	47.053	1143
06.36	03.50	Craiginches	Oxwellmains	26.003	510
06.51	06.22	Thornton Yd.	Craiginches	· 26.022	710

Oxwellmains, which handles bulk cement traffic, is near Dunbar and 31 miles east of Edinburgh, on whose south-eastern outskirts lies Millerhill Yard. Trains for Burghead would pass Craiginches, a mile south of Aberdeen, on their way to Alves Junction beyond Elgin, from where they take to a 4½ mile branch line.

The first of the special trains to pass during our night's vigil comprised 22 wagons, carrying 66 pipes, each 40 feet long and 48 inches in diameter. It represented a small part of a mammoth transport contract worth more than £1 million from the British Gas Corporation. The contract involved moving 50,000 similar pipes from coating plants in Leith and Immingham to depots along the route of underground pipelines being laid in eastern Scotland.

For details of the second special we are indebted to our friend Guard A. Mitchell of Perth. The train-belled 2.6.2. throughout-conveyed an 80-ton transformer of width 9 ft. 3 ins. over side girders of wagon and extreme height of 12 ft. 4 ins. above rail level. The Transformer Wagon—MC 901801—was accompanied by an Equipment Van, Brake-van for Loads Inspector and Brake-van for Guard on its four hour journey through to Millerhill. Although its maximum permissible speed was 35 m.p.h., the train was not to exceed 5 m.p.h. through Inverkeithing and North Queensferry Tunnels and when crossing Jamestown Viaduct and the Forth Bridge.

The London-bound Freightliner, which currently passes Ladybank at 16.08 with a noticeably higher load factor than its Down counterpart, carries a considerable number of insulated meat and fish containers. Indeed, its schedule was framed primarily to meet the Smithfield and Billingsgate market requirements.

Looking towards the future, the introduction of Dundee—Dover Speedlink services in 1977, with the possibility of further such services to come, suggests that more and more freight traffic originating in Dundee and areas further north will travel south via Perth and the West Coast Main Line, rather than through Fife.

LAMP INSIDE

14

Post-War Passenger Changes

WHEN British Railways' Scottish Region inherited railways in the Fife Peninsula, it took over the task of operating 234 passenger route miles together with the management of 75 stations. At the time of writing, thirty years on, corresponding figures are 81 and 18.

North of the main industrial zone which spreads across the Peninsula, traffic potential on the rural routes was poor. Even before the end of 1955, year of the revolutionary Modernisation Plan, the following 48 miles of single-track route had been closed to passengers:—

Line	Closure Date
Ladybank—Mawcarse Junction	5 June, 1950
Glenburnie Junction—St. Fort	12 February, 1951
Alva—Cambus	1 November, 1954
Methil—Thornton	10 January, 1955
Bridge of Earn—Ladybank	19 September, 1955

Besides the 15 intermediate stations on the above lines, Crossgates, Dairsie and Causewayhead stations were also eliminated from the timetable and closure of Kingskettle first proposed.

Dundee (Esplanade) station, at whose abandoned platforms trains from Fife are still often required to await passage of Perth—Dundee services, before being permitted down from the Tay Bridge, closed late in 1939, but was later given a temporary lease of life—albeit a short lease. The station was re-opened to help handle large crowds attending the Royal Highland Show held at Dundee over four days in June, 1957.

Services on the Glenburnie Junction—St. Fort and Bridge of Earn—Ladybank routes were, at their cessation, sparse, only two trains each way on weekdays. Whilst an ex N.B.R. Reid 4-4-2 tank engine has been noted leaving the Tay Bridge, tender first, with a train for Newburgh comprising two Gresley non-corridor coaches, the last train between Perth and Dundee by that route was made up of four ex-N.B.R. coaches hauled by ex-Caledonian McIntosh 4-4-0 No. 14447. On the latter line, the 'last' train to leave Ladybank was composed of two former L.N.E.R. non-corridor coaches hauled by a Reid N.B.R. D34 *Glen* class No. 62472 *Glen Nevis*. Following closure of the N.B.R. shed at Perth, soon after nationalisation, services to Ladybank had, however, been operated by a wide variety of coaching stock and motive power. One train seen arriving at Ladybank in May, 1955 consisted of three crimson and cream L.M.S. corridor coaches in resplendent formation behind ex-Caledonian McIntosh 0-4-4T No. 55226.

Examination of an 1948 passenger timetable shows that Thornton Junction was at that time the busiest station in the Fife Peninsula. On weekdays (excluding Saturdays) no fewer than 27 journeys commenced from this station, at which 24 trains terminated and a further 34 called 'en route'—a total of 85 train movements. Once every year Thornton station was virtually overwhelmed with visitors. This was on the Friday of the Fair Week, when Thornton Games would attract a crowd of 50,000 or more. There was no possibility of coping with the multiplicity of 'specials' from centres throughout Central Scotland in addition to regular traffic so temporary platforms were added to the station for use on that day.

Twenty or so miles to the north-east of Thornton is Leuchars Junction, which in 1948 handled up to 73 passenger trains daily. All trains between Dundee and Edinburgh or Glasgow called here, including five restaurant car expresses to and from Aberdeen. A shuttle service from St Andrews connected with these trains and with an infrequent service to Dundee via Tayport.

Withdrawal of passenger services between Leuchars and Tayport on 9 January, 1956 was the first small step towards depriving Leuchars of its function as a junction.

A considerable part of the traffic on the St Andrews branch consisted of passengers travelling between Dundee and St

Andrews. Until 1966, the effective barrier of the river Tay could only be crossed by road vehicles at Perth, involving a detour of 53 miles, or by means of ferries subjected to the vagaries of weather and tide. The ferry services were very considerably curtailed during construction stages of the Tay Road Bridge and were finally suspended when the new bridge opened on 18 August, 1966. Between 1963 and 1966 this curtailment caused many additional passengers to travel by rail, but after opening of the new bridge ease of private and public road travel resulted in an appreciable reduction in rail travel.

The average number of passengers using the services at St Andrews station daily during two census periods was as follows:—

	Mondays-Fridays		Saturdays	
	March 1967	Sept. 1966	March 1967	Sept. 1966
Joining	361	608	390	519
Alighting	351	560	405	576

The branch was served by the following twin-unit diesel multiple trains:—

	Mondays-Fridays			Saturdays		
To or From	Leuchars	Dundee	Arbroath	Leuchars	Dundee	Arbroath
From						
St Andrews	13	6	1	13	5	1
To						
St Andrews	16	6	—	17	5	—

No trains ran on Sundays

By mid-1967 the line was included in the British Railways Network for Development Map as a 'grey' line, and as such, passenger services were subject to regular review.

Guardbridge station closed on 6 September, 1965 and freight services were withdrawn on 20 June, 1966, with the single exception of one trip train serving the private siding at Guardbridge Paper Mill, about one mile from Leuchars.

Withdrawal of passenger train services came into effect on 6 January, 1969, when the entire branch line was closed along

209

13 Sketch plan of Abernethy station, 1973

SKETCH PLAN OF ABERNETHY STATION—1973

(Not to Scale)

Newburgh

Profile of Ramp and Loading Bay

Road Down

Gate

Ramp

Loading Bay

Ramp

Wooden Hut

¼m

Grass Track

Metal Division

Ramp

ROAD

Bridge No. 25

PUBLIC

Town Centre

No Evidence of Station Buildings

Bridge of Earn

Ramp

Platform

Steps

Platform

Ramp

Wooden Fence at Back of Platforms

N

UPLIFTED TRACK	-----
LAMP POST	●
MILE POST	⌷

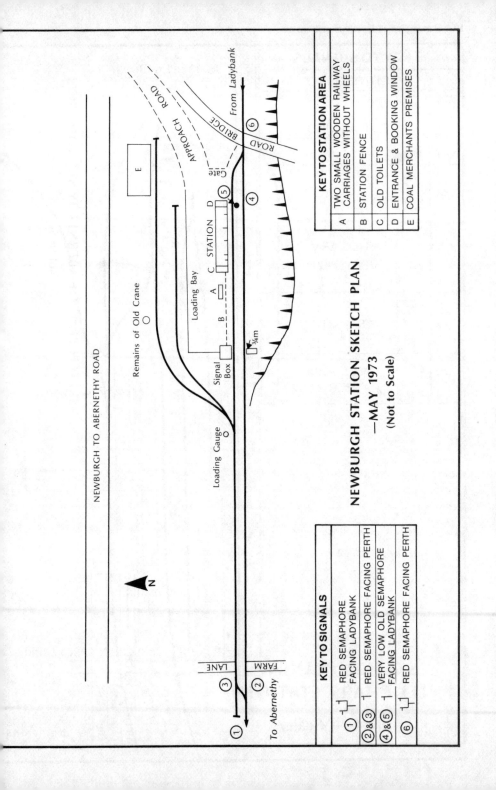

NEWBURGH TO ABERNETHY ROAD

Remains of Old Crane

Loading Gauge

Loading Bay

Signal Box

¾m

To Abernethy

FARM LANE

From Ladybank

ROAD BRIDGE

APPROACH ROAD

Gate

STATION

A B C D

N

NEWBURGH STATION SKETCH PLAN

—MAY 1973

(Not to Scale)

KEY TO SIGNALS

①	RED SEMAPHORE FACING LADYBANK
②&③	RED SEMAPHORE FACING PERTH
④&⑤	VERY LOW OLD SEMAPHORE FACING LADYBANK
⑥	RED SEMAPHORE FACING PERTH

KEY TO STATION AREA

A	TWO SMALL WOODEN RAILWAY CARRIAGES WITHOUT WHEELS
B	STATION FENCE
C	OLD TOILETS
D	ENTRANCE & BOOKING WINDOW
E	COAL MERCHANTS PREMISES

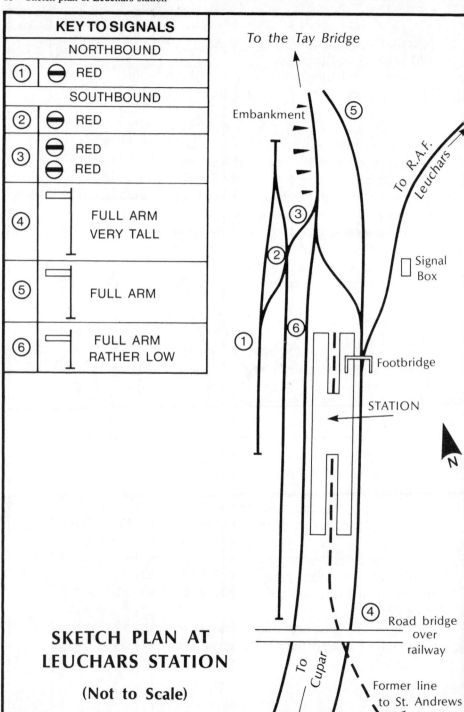

KEY TO SIGNALS

	NORTHBOUND	
①	⊖	RED
	SOUTHBOUND	
②	⊖	RED
③	⊖ ⊖	RED RED
④		FULL ARM VERY TALL
⑤		FULL ARM
⑥		FULL ARM RATHER LOW

To the Tay Bridge

Embankment

To R.A.F. Leuchars

⑤

③

②

①

⑥

Signal Box

Footbridge

STATION

N

④   Road bridge over railway

To Cupar

Former line to St. Andrews

SKETCH PLAN AT LEUCHARS STATION

(Not to Scale)

with Leuchars South signal box. So, the first branch line to be operated by the E.P.&D. Rly. disappeared from the map after 120 years of constant use.

There are still times when Leuchars station handles capacity crowds. Every year it plays host to an increasing number of visitors attending the Open Day at R.A.F. Leuchars. Bargain fares usually apply to any special excursions whilst a frequent service also runs between Dundee and Leuchars. In 1978 two excursion trains, one from Falkirk and the other Edinburgh, terminated at Leuchars, whilst three specials, from Middlesborough, Darlington and Newcastle passed through Leuchars to Dundee. From here, passengers returned to Leuchars on the shuttle service, together with those from Dundee to whom over 3,300 tickets were sold. Eight additional staff were on duty at Leuchars to assist with crowd control and to direct passengers to a temporary level crossing at the north end of the island platform.

Although its passenger train movements were modest, by comparison with those of Thornton or Leuchars, Kinross Junction was easily the busiest hub of activity in a wide area north of the Fife coalfields, where passenger services were far less intensive.

Seven trains from Edinburgh and a similar number from Perth pulled into the junction on weekdays; three ran to and from Ladybank and three in each direction from Kinross by the Devon Valley line to Alloa and on to Glasgow. Two of the services between Edinburgh and Perth included through carriages to Inverness via Carrbridge.

The station's island platform was attractively laid out with flower beds and an ornamental pool shaped to represent Loch Leven and its islands. The original station had been located at the junction between the lines from Cowdenbeath and Alloa, but was moved to the north side of the present A977 road in 1890 when the line from Mawcarse to Cowdenbeath was doubled.

During the post-war years innovation and variety were a prominent feature of the Kinross scene. Between May 1959 and

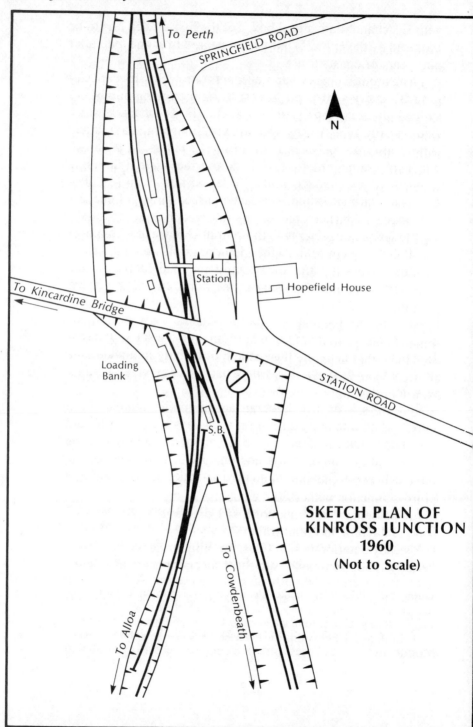

To Perth

SPRINGFIELD ROAD

N

Station

Hopefield House

To Kincardine Bridge

Loading
Bank

STATION ROAD

S.B.

**SKETCH PLAN OF
KINROSS JUNCTION
1960
(Not to Scale)**

To Cowdenbeath

To Alloa

its closure on 15 June, 1964 most passengers on the Devon Valley line travelled by railbus. Two Wickham vehicles worked this line with one through journey in each direction so the buses could be stabled on alternate nights at Perth and Stirling. Frame trouble caused the Wickhams to be replaced at an early date by slightly larger Park Royal 50-seater buses. There were in the winter of 1959 four trains between Alloa and Kinross together with a through steam-hauled Glasgow-Perth working via Alloa Bridge. The railbuses were poorly patronised, a factor which may have assisted them to breach the summit of a four mile unbroken climb at 1 in 70 east of Dollar.

Access to Kinross from the north, through Glenfarg, also called for a high standard of driving ability. Until dieselisation, the principal passenger trains, often comprising upwards of eight vehicles, required careful coaxing up the continuous 6½ miles at 1 in 74 and 75 between Bridge of Earn and Glenfarg summit. Trains were most frequently hauled by Thompson and Peppercorn A1 Pacifics or Gresley A4s and V2s, but they sometimes appeared behind B.R. Standard Class 5 4-6-0s or even the rather ungainly Ivatt 4MT 2-6-0s. Such engines were allowed 35 minutes to cover the 17¼ miles separating Perth from Kinross, but in the reverse direction journeys were 10 minutes shorter. With the gradual introduction of diesel multiple units from 1960 some southbound journey times were reduced to as little as 24 minutes.

Before its complete closure on 5 January, 1970 and almost immediate removal from the path of an advancing motorway, Kinross Junction witnessed the passage of the only scheduled *Deltic* passenger[1] working north of Edinburgh:—the Perth to London daytime motorail train.

A steady deterioration in Glasgow-Fife services throughout the early 1950s became the subject of special concern especially

[1]During early 1978 a Haymarket *Deltic* was rostered to run Light Engine from its depot to Perth, by way of Ladybank, and return to Waverley with empty coaching stock to form the morning Edinburgh-Plymouth departure. The 12 carriages had been worked to Perth the previous evening for over-night cleaning.

to local authorities and Chambers of Commerce. Representations were made to the B.R., drawing attention to a number of faults, in particular inadequacy of service and bad time-keeping.

It was noted that except for a brief summer period, when an augmented service operated, Glasgow could not be reached earlier than 9.50 a.m. Once in Glasgow, passengers from the Dunfermline area could not return by any of the Fife Coast express trains because none of them stopped to provide a connection at Inverkeithing. Further, the last through service back to Fife left the now obliterated Buchanan Street as early as 7.35 p.m. Aggravation was also caused by the uneven spacing of trains throughout the day. For example, departures from Kirkcaldy were at 8.03 a.m., 10.22 a.m., 10.56 a.m., 2.59 p.m., 3.51 p.m., 6.52 p.m. and 8.26 p.m.

Use of corridor coaches was also requested.

Persistent pressure by interested parties resulted in British Railways agreeing to increase the daily number of weekday trains in each direction from seven to twelve commencing on 6 May, 1957. A summary of the much improved timetable, to extend for a trial period of a year, is set out below:—

TABLE 15

Glasgow-Fife Services Commencing on Monday, 6 May, 1957

Glasgow (Buch. St.) Dep.	(Queen St.) Dep.	Falkirk (G'ston) Dep.	Dunf'line (Lower) Arr.	Kirkcaldy Arr.	Terminus of train
—	7.37 a.m.	8.12	8.57	10.02+	Ladybank
8.42 a.m.	—	9.20	10.19+	10.21	Dundee
(New) 9.43 a.m.	—	10.20	11.21+	11.16	Kirkcaldy
(New)11.35 a.m.	—	12.13	1.08+	1.14	Leven
12.40 p.m.	—	1.19	2.28+	2.26	Kirkcaldy
(New) 2.20 p.m.	—	2.58	3.57+	4.03	Thornton
3.50 p.m.	—	4.27	—	5.29	Leven
—	4.14 p.m.	—	5.46	6.16+	Dunf'line
5.06 p.m.	—	5.43	6.57+	6.49	Ladybank
(New) 6.40 p.m.	—	7.19	8.00	8.31+	Thornton
—	7.40 p.m.	—	9.19+	9.23	Thornton
(New) 9.00 p.m.	—	9.37	10.19+	10.34	Ladybank

+Change at Inverkeithing

216

Fife-Glasgow Services

Commencing on Monday, 6 May, 1957

Train starts From	At	Kirkcaldy Dep.	Dunf'line Dep.	Queen St. Arr.	Buch St. Arr.
(New) Markinch	6.50 a.m.	7.16	7.18+	—	8.58
Thornton	7.30 a.m.	8.02+	8.26	—	9.57
(New) Leven	8.45 a.m.	9.20	9.27+	—	10.53
Dundee	7.34 a.m.	10.22	10.23+	—	12.10
Thornton	10.30 a.m.	10.57+	11.22	—	12.46
(New) Kirkcaldy	12.05 p.m.	12.05	12.09+	—	1.44
(New) Markinch	1.25 p.m.	1.48	1.56	—	3.35
Dundee	1.46 p.m.	2.59	2.46+	4.53	
Crail	2.30 p.m.	3.50	3.56+	—	5.22
(New) Thornton	3.59 p.m.	4.04+	4.52		6.20
Thornton	6.56 p.m.	7.09	7.04+		8.47
Thornton	7.47 p.m.	8.26++	8.48		10.21

+Change at Inverkeithing ++Change at Dalmeny

As a result of the alterations, residents around Fife's East Neuk lost the 'Fife Coast Express', its five coaches from the pre-war *Silver Jubilee* streamliner considered to be a gloomy reminder of its former greatness. Its departure from Queen Street was at 4.07 p.m., and with stops only at Burntisland, Kirkcaldy, Leven, Elie and Anstruther, St Andrews was reached at 6.53 p.m. Refreshment facilities for these long distance commuters were withdrawn in 1952. In the city-bound direction, the *Fife Coast Express* was away from St Andrews at 7.15 a.m. in time to reach Glasgow by 9.50. During the currency of the winter timetable, a nameless Down express ran from Glasgow at 4.07 p.m. in the same times, but only as far as Leven. There was no corresponding return service.

Some of the trains introduced in the above timetables did not attract the anticipated custom and were withdrawn. Indeed, the timetable commencing on 6 May, 1957 represents the Glasgow service at its best. By 1959/60 only ten trains ran direct to Fife, nine calling at Kirkcaldy and a mere one at Dunfermline. Three of the Kirkcaldy trains provided possible Dunfermline passengers with no connection at Inverkeithing whilst a further two

217

required a wait of over twenty five minutes. An equal number of trains ran to Glasgow—six by way of Kirkcaldy and four via Dunfermline. This frequency of weekday trains was maintained until the middle 1960s. During this period a change was made to Queen Street rather than Buchanan Street as the principal Glasgow terminus.

Farther to the west, shuttle railbus services connected Alloa with Larbert, where connections could be made with Stirling-Glasgow trains. These services were withdrawn on January 29, 1968—the same day as the last through Glasgow to Alloa train ran.

By 1968 most travellers between Fife and Glasgow had to journey into Edinburgh (Haymarket) and there change to the Swindon-built Edinburgh-Glasgow buffet car expresses. To their credit British Rail did not alter the fare structure, despite a longer journey.

Only a solitary direct service now survived. This departed from Thornton at 7.07 a.m. and calling at all stations reached Glasgow at 8.59—probably too late for office and shop workers! The return journey commenced at 5.09 p.m. Good connections both to and from Dunfermline were available at Inverkeithing. Protestations enabled this remaining vestige of a once major service to continue its weekday pilgrimage until 1 January, 1973.

Commencing on Monday, 4 April, 1960, a regular diesel multiple unit service, involving some 40 additional trains, was provided between Edinburgh and Kirkcaldy/Dunfermline. In essence, the new service provided an hourly fast and slow train crossing the Forth to and from both of the Fife towns.

Fast trains, leaving the Waverley at 3 minutes past each hour, and calling only at Haymarket and Inverkeithing, reached Dunfermline (Lower) in 28 minutes. Successive arrivals either continued to Dunfermline (Upper) or to Perth. With two exceptions the Perth trains then called at all stations. The exceptions were both locomotive hauled Edinburgh-Inverness expresses. Trains which departed from Edinburgh at 33 minutes past each hour also stopped at Dalmeny and North

Queensferry giving an alternating two-hourly service calling at all stations to Thornton or Stirling.

The Kirkcaldy route was served by fast trains from Edinburgh at 10 minutes past each hour. From Kirkcaldy they continued to Dundee making frequent stops on their way. Trains which departed from Waverley 30 minutes later, called in addition at Dalmeny, North Queensferry, Aberdour and Kinghorn. These terminated either at Kirkcaldy or Thornton Junction.

Also, on the 4 April, 1960, four new diesel hauled express trains—two in each direction—were inaugurated to run between Edinburgh and Aberdeen. In order to curtail their journey times to exactly three hours, all stops in Fife were eliminated. However, the former 7.30 a.m. Waverley to Aberdeen train continued to run as far as Dundee, where passengers who had joined at Kirkcaldy, Thornton, Cupar or Leuchars could make a same platform connection with the new express. In the evening, the 5.00 p.m. from Edinburgh, due in Aberdeen three hours later, ran in place of the more leisurely 4.15 p.m. and offered a saving of 70 minutes. Again, Fife passengers were obliged to change at Dundee. New connecting facilities were likewise made available at Dundee for those who took advantage of the 7.30 a.m. and 4.00 p.m. Aberdeen departures.

Diesel units were now also introduced on direct services linking Edinburgh and Glasgow with resorts in East Fife but the few local services which originated at Thornton continued, as yet, to be steam rostered.

The Forth Road Bridge, opened to traffic in September, 1964, had a prompt and lasting effect upon railway passenger traffic between the Lothians and Fife. Actual and percentage decreases recorded for the Edinburgh to Dunfermline and Kirkcaldy services are summarised below:—

TABLE 17
Effect of the Forth Road Bridge on Rail Services
Edinburgh-Dunfermline Service

Date	Tickets Sold	Decrease	% Decrease
January, 1964	15,780	—	—
January, 1965	11,730	4,050	25
January, 1966	10,390	1,340	11
June, 1964	19,270	—	—
June, 1965	12,490	6,780	35

Edinburgh-Kirkcaldy Service

Date	Tickets Sold	Decrease	% Decrease
January, 1964	20,690	—	—
January, 1965	18,920	1,770	8.5
January, 1966	18,900	20	1
June, 1964	22,870	—	—
June, 1965	18,320	4,550	14

These figures are based upon sales of single, cheap day return and weekly season tickets

Whilst these decreases were taking place, it is an impressive fact that in 1965 alone, W. Alexander (Fife) Ltd. and Scottish Omnibuses Ltd., joint operators of new bus services linking these Fife towns with Edinburgh, carried a total of 1,480,850 passengers across the bridge. In the first three months of 1966 there was a comparitive increase of no less than 24%!

That Edinburgh-Dunfermline passenger traffic was affected much more than on the Kirkcaldy route reflected differences in journey times. Seventy minutes from Kirkcaldy to Edinburgh by bus did not compare favourably with forty-three minutes by rail, whereas fifty-five minutes as against thirty-three in the case of Dunfermline presented less of a discouragement to potential bus travellers.

In 1964, between 8.00 a.m. and 6.00 p.m., there was a daily weekday service of 19 trains in both directions on the Dunfermline and Kirkcaldy routes. However, as from Monday, 6 September of that year, off-peak Edinburgh-Fife services were re-organised to run at hourly in place of half-hourly intervals. The d.m.u's, which had been introduced in 1960, continued to be well patronised during peak periods but as little as 10% of seating capacity might be occupied at other times. It was considered economical to withdraw six return services from the Kirkcaldy route and eight from amongst those serving Dunfermline. Additionally, two Edinburgh-Dundee services were now to reverse at Thornton and Kirkcaldy.

The timetable for the year commencing May 1968 contains details of the final services on three lines which closed that

220

year:— Dunfermline-Stirling, Leuchars-St Andrews and Dundee-Newport East. It also describes workings for the last full year of services between Cowdenbeath and Perth and Leven and Thornton. These were all routes which were losing popularity and had been 'run down' over the preceding ten years. The timetable did introduce a promising improvement by innovating direct connections between the west and north-east of Fife. Hitherto, passengers from Dunfermline and intermediate stations had been required to change at Thornton into Edinburgh-Dundee trains. Now four of the fourteen local services starting from Dundee or Arbroath diverged after Thornton onto the secondary route via Dunfermline and regained the main line at Inverkeithing. Northbound, five of the sixteen locals made the same deviation, whilst maintaining the standard ninety minutes journey time. Many of the trains which ran by way of Dunfermline called only at a limited number of stations and, although opting for a more circuitous route, might nevertheless be considered to rank as expresses. One instance is the 8.40 a.m. from Edinburgh, which having stopped at Haymarket, called only at Inverkeithing, Dunfermline, Cowdenbeath, Markinch and Cupar. Edinburgh bound, the 1.20 p.m. from Dundee ran non-stop between Leuchars and Thornton—20 miles in 23 minutes—and then called only at Cowdenbeath before reaching Dunfermline in exactly one hour.

In 1968 Dunfermline (Lower) was, as yet, a close rival to Kirkcaldy in terms of arrivals and departures. This can be seen in the table below showing the numbers and destinations of Down arrivals at both stations:—

TABLE 18
Comparitive Numbers and Destinations of Trains Arriving
at Kirkcaldy and Dunfermline (Lower)—Down Lines

Kirkcaldy		Dunfermline	
Destination	Numbers	Destination	Numbers
Kirkcaldy	11	Dunf'line (Lower)	1
Thornton	2	Dunf'line (Upper)	2
Leven	8	Stirling	6
Dundee/Arbroath	10	Thornton	4
Aberdeen	3	Perth	11
		Dundee	5
	34		29

The distance between Dunfermline's Lower and Upper stations, is a mere half mile 'as the crow flies', yet it took six minutes for a train to wind its way for 2½ miles through the town's eastern suburbs.

Services from Kirkcaldy to Leven were augmented by two additional workings which commenced at Thornton and provided connections from Dundee trains.

Once the following closures had been effected, Dunfermline lost the hustle of activity associated with a busy junction station:—

Line	Closed as from
Dunfermline-Stirling	7 October, 1968
Cowdenbeath-Perth	5 January, 1970

Despite an ultimate frequency of 10 trains per day, the branch from Thornton Junction to Leven carried no passengers on or after 6 October, 1969 and the booking offices at Sinclairtown, Dysart and Thornton ceased issuing tickets. British Railways, in defending closure of the Leven branch and intermediate stations from Kirkcaldy, stated to the Transport Users Consultative Committee that between 1964 and 1967 season ticket sales had fallen thus:—

Leven	24%	Cameron Bridge	15%
Thornton	28%	Dysart	23%
Sinclairtown	20%		

Despite three major economy exercises introduced in 1963, in which there had been a saving in both equipment and mileage, the line, it was contended, no longer continued to pay. The saving had been achieved without any significant reductions in train numbers.

In October, 1968 the number of season ticket holders at the following stations were:—

Leven	32	Cameron Bridge	5
Thornton	9	Dysart	24
Sinclairtown	64		

It was pointed out by the Railway's representative that in the same month 136 season tickets were issued at Kirkcaldy to persons living in the areas of the doomed stations. Their closure came just four years after closure in September, 1965 of the long connection from Leven around the coast to St Andrews.

With closure of Thornton Junction, the railways of the Fife Peninsula lost their personal 'Crewe'; only a widening of the space between tracks has been left to commemorate a station which at one time was so busy that it needed two inspectors, one foreman, thirteen porters and eight ticket collectors to man it.

Early in the same year the fate of a truncated remnant of the original main line, which now terminated at Newport (East) was sealed. Tayport station had remained open for the sale of tickets and handling of parcels, even though buses were substituted for the rail link in May, 1966 so as to facilitate construction of access roads leading to the new Tay Bridge.

Thus the 1970/71 timetable contained many fewer tables and times. Because Thornton and all intermediate stations were now redundant, all local services to Edinburgh commenced from Kirkcaldy. There started a phased withdrawal of certain weekday services on Saturday mornings, those at peak-hours being particularly affected. As a little compensation, a new Saturdays only facility was the incorporation of through First and Second Class accommodation to Blackpool North in the 7.45 a.m. from Dundee to Edinburgh. This direct service was available from Kirkcaldy and Inverkeithing on seven Saturdays between June 27 and August 5, but its life was short and it did not operate again after the summer of 1972.

As from Monday, 6 October, 1975, the two daytime services between Edinburgh and Inverness, diverted by way of Falkirk and Stirling since the closure of Glenfarg, were re-routed via Kirkcaldy and Newburgh with calls at Inverkeithing and Kirkcaldy in both directions. British Rail in a publicity state-ment emphasised that the re-routing had been decided upon because of a bigger population market for rail travel in the industrial areas of Fife. The change would provide east and west Fife with direct links to Perth and the North. Journey times between Edinburgh and Perth were identical to those operating when the trains ran via Stirling, despite a saving of almost fifteen miles—a reflection of the many severe speed restrictions in Fife. Maximum permissible speed between Ladybank and Hilton Junction is 45 m.p.h., but drivers must slow to 15 m.p.h. when passing Clatchard Craig Rock at Newburgh and not exceed 20 m.p.h. whilst negotiating Ladybank Junction. The then 08.15 from Inverness averaged 45.5 m.p.h. on its run down to Perth, but with the same engines, usually two Class 26s working in multiple, the average dropped to 37.5 m.p.h. for the remainder of the journey! A third working between Perth and Edinburgh was introduced in May, 1977.

Yet a further improvement took effect from 9 January, 1978, when, in response to local lobbying, the 09.40 Edinburgh-Perth and 20.10 return services commenced calling additionally at Ladybank.

Close scrutiny of post-war timetables has revealed that through trains between Fife and English destinations have never been more numerous than in the years since 1973—a year which heralded the major development of North Sea oil. Table 18 details the running of these trains in 1974 and, in particular, highlights the large number of calls they made between Edinburgh and Dundee. Indeed, the 23.15 from King's Cross and the Up *Aberdonian* were even given the paths of former d.m.u. local workings!

Experiments in combining long-distance express passenger needs with those of local commuters were abandoned by the Scottish Region at the conclusion of the 1974/75 timetable. Thereafter, train No. 1S77 was named *The Night Capitals* and provided with buffet car facilities. Departing Waverley at the later time of 07.40, it called only at Inverkeithing, Kirkcaldy, Cupar and Leuchars.

In the Up direction, the 08.55 from Aberdeen had its title transferred to the mid-morning departure, even though it now only called at Kirkcaldy and Inverkeithing.

The 08.45 from Leeds City to Edinburgh was extended to Dundee where, after calls at Inverkeithing and Kirkcaldy, it arrived at 14.26. On its return journey, which commenced at 16.15, similar stops were made.

TABLE 19

Through Train Services between Fife and England
6 May, 1974 to 4 May, 1975

Mondays to Fridays

Train No.		1	2	3	4	5	6
Aberdeen	Dep.	08.55	10.45	16.23	19.20	19.45	21.20
Dundee	"	10.25	12.15	17.48	21.05	21.35	22.52
Leuchars	Dep.	10.40	12.30	18.03	21.21	21.51	23.07
Cupar	"	10.48	12.38	—	—	22.02	—
Ladybank	"	10.56	—	—	—	—	—
Markinch	"	11.05	—	—	—	—	—
Kirkcaldy	"	11.16	13.03	18.31	21.57	22.32	—
Inverkeithing	"	11.35	13.22	18.49	—	22.55	—
Waverley	Arr.	11.57	13.44	19.09	22.38	—	—
King's Cross	"	17.55	20.00	23.01 York	06.28	06.50	07.06

Train No. 1 *The Aberdonian.*
No. 5 Sleeping car passengers only.
No. 6 *The Night Aberdonian* Conveys Sleeping car passengers only.

Train No.		1	2	3	4	5
King's Cross	Dep.	22.15	23.15		12.00	14.00
York	"			07.15		
Waverley	Dep.	05.20	07.15	11.40	18.05	20.24
Inverkeithing	"	05.41	07.34	12.00	—	20.41
Kirkcaldy	"	06.04	07.55	12.19	18.40	21.01
Cupar	"	06.30	08.25	—	19.07	—
Leuchars	"	06.41	08.34	12.48	19.16	—
Dundee	Arr.	07.01	08.52	13.08	19.35	21.46
Aberdeen	"	08.44	10.16	14.37	21.01	23.16

Train No. 1 *The Night Aberdonian.* Conveys second class seating accommodation from Edinburgh.
No. 2 Conveys sleeping cars and stops additionally at Burntisland, Markinch, Ladybank and Springfield.
No. 4 *The Aberdonian.*

The 20.00 overnight sleeper from King's Cross ran non-stop between Edinburgh and Dundee at a very early hour and so provided six through workings in both directions.

225

Apart from minor adjustments of a few minutes in the times of some trains, the only other alteration involved passengers on the Down *Aberdonian*, who could no longer alight at Cupar or Leuchars. These latter two deletions were re-instated in the following timetable, from which the Leeds-Dundee working disappeared.

Despite important permanent way improvements during years since the last war, serious speed restrictions continue to operate on account of curves and mining subsidence. On the principal line north the following maximum permissible speeds apply:—

Between	Down Line m.p.h.	Up Line m.p.h.
Haymarket West Jn. and Dalmeny	75	75
Dalmeny and Falkland Road	60	60
Falkland Road and Dundee Tay Bridge	70	70

Certain speed restrictions between Dalmeny Junction and Kirkcaldy may be exceeded by up to 10 m.p.h. by multiple-unit trains, provided they do not have attached additional vehicles having a wheelbase of less than 15 feet.

Between Haymarket West Junction and Kirkcaldy locomotive hauled trains are restricted to 50 m.p.h. or less for a total distance of 8 miles 18 chains. Speed across the Forth Bridge must not exceed 40 m.p.h. and 25 m.p.h. over Burntisland viaduct, while Kinghorn tunnel, with its notorious reverse bend, is not to be entered at more than 30 m.p.h. North of Kirkcaldy, some 10 miles 60 chains are restricted to speeds not in excess of 60 m.p.h.—the maximum permitted in both directions over the 4¼ mile section between Leuchars and Tay Bridge South signal box. Restrictions crossing the Tay are lower than those over the Forth. From the south end curve to the north end of the high girders train speeds must be kept below 35 m.p.h. and then reduced to 25 m.p.h. over the remaining mile and a quarter.

Timetable planners have had constantly to allow for these restrictions when trying to prune journey times.

Until comparitively recently, when pits in the area closed, fears of subsidence required constant attention at Thornton. Mr

O.S. Nock, in a contribution to the February 1962 *Railway Magazine* describes how, on a journey from Edinburgh to Dundee, the train had to pass through the station at walking pace. Indeed, at one time there was a squad of men whose constant duty was to ballast the rails to the correct level since they sank appreciably overnight, whilst miners worked so near the surface that they could assess the time by the rumbling of trains overhead!

Probably the most elaborate permanent way improvement was effected in September, 1965, when a completely redesigned junction was installed at Inverkeithing, then one of the busiest but most notorious junctions in Scotland. The existing junction was greatly restricted by a narrow road overbridge but this was replaced with construction of the Forth Bridge approach roads. Complete realignment of the tracks became possible and the speed restriction was raised from 25 to 40 m.p.h.

Unfortunately only southbound trains which did not stop at Inverkeithing could thereby benefit from a faster approach to the two mile arduous 1 in 70 climb up onto the Forth Bridge. Ironically, all the heaviest trains did stop there and drivers had to use years of expertise in coaxing their charges away up through and beyond North Queensferry tunnel.

A study of the locomotive performances recorded by Cecil J. Allen and O.S. Nock, which appeared in the January 1936 and February 1937 issues of *Railway Magazine*, gives some indication of handling requirements. All the trains recorded were hauled by P2 2-8-2 *Cock O' the North* and with one exception had gross loads exceeding 500 tons. Even though none of the trains stopped at Inverkeithing, only two of the six tabulated succeeded in maintaining a speed of above 20 m.p.h.

Getting up to the bridge was rather more of a problem than exceeding permissible speeds. And not all drivers made it. At about 10.50 p.m. on the evening of 7 March, 1954, the 6.55 p.m. Aberdeen-King's Cross express, consisting of 13 bogie coaches hauled by Class A4 No. 60024, began slipping inside North Queensferry tunnel. The engine stopped momentarily before running back over catch points which derailed the last three

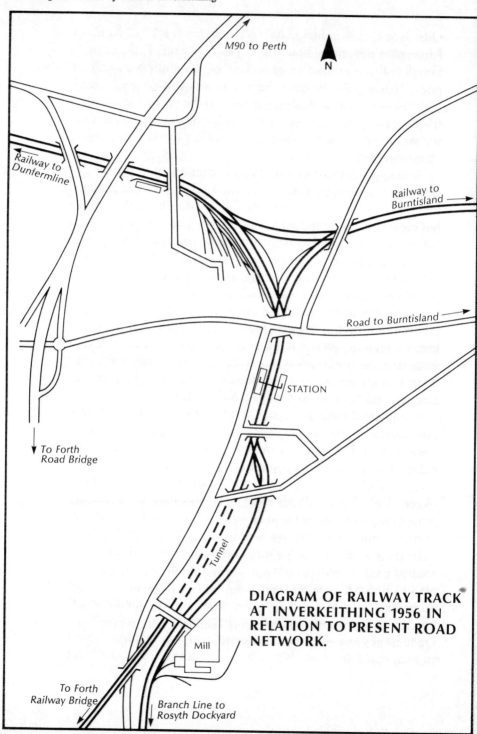

M90 to Perth

N

Railway to
Dunfermline

Railway to
Burntisland

Road to Burntisland

STATION

To Forth
Road Bridge

Tunnel

DIAGRAM OF RAILWAY TRACK
AT INVERKEITHING 1956 IN
RELATION TO PRESENT ROAD
NETWORK.

Mill

To Forth
Railway Bridge

Branch Line to
Rosyth Dockyard

vehicles. Both lines were blocked and that the buck-eye couplings remained connected undoubtably saved the last two coaches from being precipitated down an embankment. At the ensuing enquiry it was noted that, during the period from 1 January, 1952, no less than 3 passenger, 1 fish and 26 freight trains had failed to negotiate the incline at various places, 12 of the failures occurring in this particular tunnel.

Since the introduction of more powerful diesel locomotives, this obstacle to faster running has been eliminated. Improved signalling is also intended to provide for time-saving. Complimentary to the introduction of Inter-City 125s will be completion of the Edinburgh and East Scotland resignalling scheme. This will take the Waverley control area north to fringe boxes at Cupar and Newburgh. Also included in the Edinburgh SC[1] area will be the loop from Inverkeithing to Thornton.

The timetable which became effective on 2 May, 1977, introduced a new pattern of services devised over several years. It skilfully incorporated a network of regular interval trains with closely integrated connections which provided faster and more frequent accessibility between Glasgow or Edinburgh and major population centres in eastern Scotland. Growth in passenger traffic potential, which has been closely allied to development of the North Sea oil industry, was sufficient to justify an additional daytime train in each direction on both the Glasgow and Edinburgh services. Major stations between Dundee and Aberdeen are now served by no fewer than 15 through trains, excluding overnight sleepers.

Recasting of the Edinburgh-Dundee medium-haul d.m.u. services made it possible for passengers from almost all stations in Fife to connect at Dundee with every northbound express. Trains on the local service continued to leave Waverley at 15 minutes past every hour, but, in addition to calling at Inverkeithing, Kirkcaldy and then at all stations except Springfield, now stopped at every station. Springfield was served by only three peak-hour trains. Generally, journey times were increased by eight minutes with arrival in Dundee at 52

[1]Signalling Centre

minutes past the hour following departure. This arrival time gave a very good connection with Aberdeen expresses, departing at 8 or 10 minutes past every hour. Hitherto irregular departure times from Dundee had prevented such timely connections.

Exactly 30 minutes after their arrival at Dundee the d.m.u.'s returned to Edinburgh, carrying passengers who may have transferred from either Glasgow or Edinburgh expresses due to arrive from the north at approximately 8 minutes past every hour. Express trains for Edinburgh arrived shortly after every even hour and, with four exceptions made an additional call at Leuchars and two also stopped at Cupar.

With all but two through services from King's Cross, express trains to Aberdeen departed Waverley at 45 minutes past every even hour. Stopping only at Inverkeithing and Kirkcaldy, they provided a faster journey time to the two most patronised stations in Fife than the Dundee d.m.u.'s. Sufficient was the demand to justify complementing this fast service with two-hourly interval multiple units terminating at Kirkcaldy. They departed from Edinburgh at 45 mintues past every odd hour and together with all other local services crossing the Forth officially provided only Second Class accommodation.

By 1977 early Mark II coaching stock had been introduced on all Aberdeen services with locomotive power normally being provided by Class 40 or 47 engines. Restaurant cars and buffets serving hot dishes to order, which were still available on some services following a 'cut back' in January, 1976, disappeared completely. Their substitution by a buffet service of drinks and snacks on all trains could be considered a more equitable arrangement.

On the secondary route to Dunfermline, Cowdenbeath and Cardenden the pattern of services has remained unchanged. Although there are regular hourly-interval trains to and from Cowdenbeath, only four peak-period trains work in each direction between there and Cardenden. Three of the departures from Cardenden, the latest being at 08.01, originate as empty coaching stock worked from Thornton Yard, whilst the fourth travels as far north as Lochmuir box, where it traverses onto the

Up line and commences uplifting passengers at Markinch. The four arrivals from Edinburgh appear within the space of an hour—the first at 17.49. From Cardenden the first two work back empty to Cowdenbeath where they again enter revenue service. Those that follow are taken out of service and stabled at Thornton Yard. There are only two workings to Lochgelly and Cardenden on Saturdays.

Soon after a promotion visit to Edinburgh, Dundee, Aberdeen, Inverness and Perth, the first scheduled HST services began to run north from Edinburgh. From 2 October, 1978, the 09.00 (12.30 Sundays) Aberdeen to London and 11.55 (13.00 Sundays) London-Aberdeen services were operated by these sets.

With the introduction of the 1979/80 timetable on 14 May, 1979, and corresponding acceleration of services south of Edinburgh, it was intended that the first of two through Kings Cross-Aberdeen HSTs, the 12.00 *Aberdonian*, should leave Waverley as early as 16.55. Calling only at Dundee (18.06), Aberdeen would be reached at 19.27—a mere 7 hours 27 minutes out from Kings Cross. The second HST would depart from Kings Cross three hours later and leaving Edinburgh at 20.05 arrive in Aberdeen at 22.38. This train would make an additional stop at Kirkcaldy at 20.37.

North of Fife passengers, travelling home by the 12.00 departure, were given ample time to change at Waverley into the 16.50 Aberdeen express (Saturdays excepted). Routed via Cowdenbeath, this 'slower' train was timed to rejoin the main line at Thornton Station Signal Box five minutes after the 16.55 had passed. Cupar and Leuchars were its only stops in Fife. Passengers for intermediate stations to Kirkcaldy, except Dalmeny, could travel by a d.m.u. service leaving Edinburgh at 16.58.

Southbound, HST departures from Aberdeen were to be at 08.35 and 10.25, the latter calling at Kirkcaldy.

Although the nature of the route through Fife is such that really high speeds are not possible, some of the HST timings are worthy of note. The 16.55 from Edinburgh is booked to run the

37 miles 56 chains between Inverkeithing and Leuchars in 40 minutes, pass to pass, whilst the 08.35 from Aberdeen averages just over 55 m.p.h. on the 34 mile 26 chain stretch from Tay Bridge South to Burntisland. Some further journey time reductions, even if modest, may still be possible when certain line speed improvements—during the course of routine renewals—are made.

However, the rock collapse at Penmanshiel tunnel on 17 March, 1979, of necessity meant a lengthy postponement in implementing the full East Coast HST programme.

CIRCULAR GLASS ⟶

A Chronology of Railway Developments

17 September 1847	The Edinburgh and Northern Railway officially opened from Burntisland to Lindores and Cupar.
30 December 1847	Completion of the Moncrieffe tunnel.
22 May 1848	The Scottish Central Railway opened from Stirling to Perth.
18 July 1848	Extension of services from Lindores to Hilton Junction.
13 December 1849	Dunfermline reached by a branch from Thornton Junction.
17 May 1850	Commencement of passenger services between Cupar and Ferry-Port-on-Craig.
28 August 1850	Start of Dunfermline-Alloa passenger services.
3 June 1851	The Devon Valley line opened from Alloa to a temporary terminus at Glenfoot near Tillicoultry.
1 July 1852	Opening of the St Andrews Railway between Leuchars and St Andrews and of the Stirling and Dunfermline Railway from Alloa to Stirling.
17 June 1853	Leven Railway authorised between Thornton and Leven.
1 July 1853	The Stirling and Dunfermline Railway's bridge across the Forth and independent station at Stirling opened.
	Commencement of passenger workings on the Alloa Junction to South Alloa branch.
3 July 1854	Opening of the line to Leven and its harbour.
23 July 1855	Authorisation of the East of Fife Railway from Leven to Kilconquhar.
14 July 1856	Act passed incorporating the West of Fife Mineral Railway.
6 June 1857	The Fife and Kinross Railway opened between Ladybank and Strathmiglo.
8 July 1857	Opening of the East of Fife Railway to Kilconquhar.
9 March 1858	Extension of the Fife and Kinross Railway to Milnathort.
20 August 1858	Passenger and goods services began to operate from the Fife and Kinross terminus at Hopefield, Kinross.
16 September 1858	The Edinburgh Perth & Dundee Library Committee reported an annual surplus of £28 and an increased borrowing of the 1,300 volumes at the Burntisland library.

20 June 1860	Using its own engine, operated by the Edinburgh Perth and Dundee, the Kinross-shire Railway opened a link from Cowdenbeath to a temporary terminus at Kinross.
20 August 1860	A new joint station occupied by the Fife & Kinross and Kinross-shire railways was established at Kinross.
22 July 1861	Amalgamation of the Leven and the East of Fife railways to form the Leven & East of Fife Railway.
1 August 1861	West of Fife Mineral Railway amalgamated with the Charlestown Railway & Harbour Company to form the West of Fife Railway & Harbour Company.
29 July 1862	The Edinburgh Perth & Dundee Railway, with which the Fife & Kinross and Kinross-shire Railways had amalgamated in 1861, was absorbed, along with the West of Fife Railway, by the North British Railway.
1 May 1863	Worked by the North British, the Devon Valley Railway was opened from Kinross to Rumbling Bridge.
3 June 1863	Opening of the branch from Cambus to Alva.
1 September 1863	Extension of services from Kilconquhar to Anstruther.
3 May 1869	Extension of the Devon Valley line east to Dollar.
1 May 1871	Completion of the link between Dollar and Rumbling Bridge.
1 August 1877	Both the Leven & East of Fife Railway and the St Andrews Railway were absorbed by the North British Railway.
1 November 1877	Dunfermline connected by rail to North Queensferry pier.
1 June 1878	Public opening of the Tay Bridge.
12 May 1879	The Leuchars-Tayport line was extended to Newport and on the following day to join with the main line at Wormit.
11 August 1879	The Alloa Railway Company was authorised to bridge the Forth at Alloa and construct a three mile extension from the Caledonian's South Alloa branch.
28 December 1879	The Tay Bridge Disaster.
26 August 1880	Powers obtained to link Anstruther with St Andrews.
1 August 1881	The Wemyss and Buckhaven Railway opened from Thornton.
27 April 1883	Agreement reached between the Caledonian and North British Railways whereby the latter was

	granted running powers over the new line from Alloa to Alloa Junction and as far as Greenhill on payment of £3,000 p.a.
1 September 1883	Opening of the Anstruther & St Andrews Railway from Anstruther to Boarhills.
December 1883	A new station opened at Anstruther enabled the original terminus to become part of a busy goods station.
14 July 1884	The Caledonian Railway acquired the Alloa Railway.
20 December 1884	Introduction of a Postal Sorting Tender carrying mail through Fife. Converted from a second class carriage, two of the three compartments were changed into one and fitted out as a sorting room. It was withdrawn on 3 August 1888 after disagreement with the G.P.O.
1 October 1885	Opening of the line across the Forth at Alloa.
12 December 1885	New passenger station opened at Leven.
5 May 1887	Extension of the Wemyss and Buckhaven Railway to Methil, where, on the same day, the first wet dock was opened.
1 June 1887	The first passenger trains ran between Boarhills and a new through station at St Andrews.
13 July 1887	The present Tay Bridge was opened to traffic.
1 May 1889	Opening of Dundee (Esplanade) and Wormit stations.
26 July 1889	Acquisition of the Wemyss & Buckhaven Railway by the North British Railway.
4 March 1890	H.R.H. The Prince of Wales opened the Forth Bridge.
2 June 1890	Both the direct line from Dalmeny to Saughton Junction (Edinburgh) and the Winchburgh spur opened.
17 August 1890	The N.B.R. scrapped six of its Forth ferry steamers.
2 February 1892	Bridge of Earn station, situated on the Ladybank side of the Glenfarg line, was rebuilt west of the junction.
18 December 1893	The line from Kincardine Junction to Kincardine opened.
1 September 1894	Opening of the rebuilt Charlestown branch.
17 September 1894	Kilbagie station opened for passengers and goods.
3 March 1896	Opening of a railway between Invertiel Junction, south of Kirkcaldy, and Foulford near Cowdenbeath.

235

18 August 1898	The East of Fife Central Railway, from East Fife Central Junction to Lochty, opened for goods traffic.
January 1900	Methil's second dock, partially brought into use in July 1897, was fully completed.
12 October 1904	Closure of Alloa Bridge by storm damage until 1 June 1905.
1 July 1906	An extension of the railway east from Kincardine to Dunfermline was opened.
13 August 1906	A new passenger station came into use at Newburgh.
14 January 1909	Work to double the Thornton-Leven line commenced.
25 January 1909	Newburgh & North of Fife Railway opened for all traffic.
20 March 1911	Extension and heightening of Cupar station platforms, previously 26 inches below the step of modern carriages, was completed, Hitherto, most trains stopped twice and passengers used steps.
22 January 1913	Formal opening of the third and largest dock at Methil.
30 June 1913	Seven suffragettes and two males, occupants of a car seen near Leuchars, were held responsible for a fire which totally destroyed Leuchars Junction station at 1.30 a.m.
14 April 1914	Collision at Burntisland between the night London-Aberdeen express and a fast goods from Carlisle to Dundee. The *Atlantic* class express engine 'bounced off' the goods engine and in overturning crushed its crew who had safely jumped clear.
1 July 1915	Rosyth Dockyard station opened.
18 August 1915	After only two years, Methil's third dock closed for extensive repairs which were to last for four years.
28 March 1917	Rosyth Halt opened to passengers.
29 March 1919	All passenger trains began using the deviation line via Cowdenbeath (New) station.
15 August 1920	Alloa Bridge closed by storm damage until 1 March 1921.
31 August 1920	Restaurant cars were withdrawn from Fife Coast Expresses.
1 September 1921	Closure of Loch Leven station.
3 October 1921	Passenger services withdrawn from Leuchars (Old) station.
1 December 1921	Clackmannan Road station closed

236

1 November 1926	Dunfermline to Charlestown branch closed to passengers.
7 July 1930	Alloa-Dunfermline via Culross line closed to passengers.
22 September 1930	Sauchie, Halbeath, Kelty, Blairadam, Boarhills, Kingsbarns, Stravithie and Mount Melville stations closed.
2 January 1932	Last day of passenger services between Leslie and Markinch.
July 1933	Despite extensive use by heavy northbound coal trains avoiding Glenfarg bank, the Up line was removed between Bridge of Earn and Ladybank, excepting that section from Newburgh to Glenburnie
2 October 1939	Closure of Dundee (Esplanade) station.
10 August 1946	Last shipment of coal loaded at St Davids Harbour.
December 1946	Closure of the Fordell Railway between Fordell village and the L.N.E.R. main line near Crossgates.
24 September 1949	Crossgates (Fife) station closed to passenger traffic.
7 November 1949	Passenger and goods services withdrawn from West Wemyss.
3 June 1950	Termination of Kinross-Ladybank passenger services.
10 February 1951	Last passenger trains ran between Newburgh and St Fort.
11 September 1954	Proposals for a new marshalling yard at Alloa announced.
20 September 1954	Closure of Dairsie station.
1 November 1954	The Alloa-Cambus branch closed to passengers.
10 January 1955	Last passenger trains ran from Thornton to Methil.
28 May 1955	Derailment of excursion train at Wormit station.
4 July 1955	Causewayhead station near Stirling closed.
17 September 1955	Passenger services ceased between Ladybank and Bridge of Earn when Pickersgill 4-4-0 No. 54494 departed Ladybank with the 6.02 p.m. working.
9 January 1956	Passenger trains withdrawn between Tayport and Leuchars.
13 September 1958	Bogside, East Grange and Falkland Road stations closed.
13 May 1960	St Fort to Glenburnie Junction ceased to be a through route as the section from Glenburnie Junction to Lindores was 'axed'. Glenburnie signal box closed and the line to Newburgh was thence singled.

237

17 November 1963	Closure of the freight line from Invertiel to Cowdenbeath.
13 June 1964	Last passenger services on the Devon Valley line and from Bridge of Earn, Glenfarg, Mawcarse and Milnathort stations.
1 August 1964	Closure of the East of Fife Central Railway.
8 October 1964	Withdrawal of the thrice-weekly freight trip working between St Fort and Lindores.
6 September 1964	St Andrews-Leven passenger services were withdrawn whilst Guard Bridge and St Fort stations closed.
11 January 1966	The Perth-Ladybank line was blocked by a massive rockfall at Clatchard Craig quarry, where a large outcrop towered menacingly over the rails near Newburgh. The mammoth task of clearing and renewing the trackbed, begun in the autumn of 1966, was completed on 16 January 1967.
19 January 1967	Closure of Alloa sub-shed.
2 September 1967	Kingskettle station deleted from the timetable.
18 September 1967	The Newport-on-Tay (East) to Tayport section, have closed on 22 May 1966 to permit access to the new road bridge, special buses operated from the railhead to Tayport station closed in September 1967.
29 January 1968	Railbus services ceased between Alloa and Larbert.
7 October 1968	Dunfermline (Lower)-Stirling trains were 'axed' and all intermediate stations closed.
4 January 1969	Withdrawal of all Leuchars-St Andrews services.
5 May 1969	Local Dundee-Newport-on-Tay (East) trains withdrawn.
6 October 1969	Sinclairtown, Dysart, Thornton, Cameron Bridge and Leven stations closed.
5 January 1970	Last passenger trains between Cowdenbeath and Perth.
April 1970	Closure of Thornton (62A) and Dunfermline (62C) engine sheds. The stabling point at Townhill wagon repair shops received the latter shed code and an allocation of locomotives.
4 May 1970	Permanent closure of the main line from Cowdenbeath to Milnathort which had been kept open as a single line to handle seed potatoes.
8 February 1971	Demolition of Alloa bridge began.

238

16 February 1972	Tokenless block working was commissioned between Ladybank and Hilton Junction, whilst Bridge of Earn signal box (no longer at a junction) was phased out.
May 1972	The crossing loop at Newburgh was lengthened and both lines signalled for two way working.
December 1972	The line from Thornton to Kirkland Yard was singled.
8 January 1973	Withdrawal of the only Kirkcaldy to Glasgow direct daily working.
21 April 1973	Work commenced on demolition of Ladybank engine shed and adjoining track rationalisation.
6 October 1975	Re-routing of some Perth-Edinburgh trains via Ladybank.
1 October 1977	All Fife d.m.u. services became second class only.
2 October 1978	Inauguration of London to Aberdeen HST services.
29 June 1979	Signing of a £5 million contract to rationalise track and extend full colour light signalling from Dalmeny as far as Cupar, Dunfermline and Cowdenbeath. By 1981, control of 170 main signals and 80 ground frames will have been transferred from local boxes to Edinburgh Signalling Centre through remote interlocking relay rooms at North Queensferry, Inverkeithing, Burntisland, Kirkcaldy, Thornton, Markinch, Ladybank, Charlestown, Cowdenbeath, Townhill and Redford.
6 October 1979	Withdrawal of freight facilities from Newburgh prior to removal of the passing loop.
	Closure to all traffic of the Alloa-Dunfermline direct line between Kincardine Junction and Bogside. The Up loop at Oakley was secured out of use, all signals removed and Oakley signal box closed. One train regulations were introduced between Townhill Junction and Bogside, the staff custodian being the signalman at Townhill Junction. Access to the Exchange Sidings at Oakley are now controlled by a 2-lever ground frame released by the section train staff.
February 1980	No's 1 to 5 sidings and the east end headshunt at Alloa New Yard were secured out of use pending removal.

Appendix 1

Table of Steam Locomotive Allocations for Selected Years

Depot No. 62A, Thornton
(Sub-sheds:— Anstruther, Burntisland, Ladybank and Methil)

Dates and Allocations

Class	Wheel Arrangement	31/8/50	21/3/53	14/5/55	14/2/59	-/1/66
B1	4-6-0	5	7	8	15	7
K2	2-6-0	—	3	2	2	—
D30	4-4-0	6	6	6	1	—
D29	4-4-0	2	—	—	—	—
D34	4-4-0	5	5	5	5	—
D49	4-4-0	5	5	5	6	—
J35	0-6-0	11	8	7	6	—
J36	0-6-0	3	3	3	3	2
J37	0-6-0	14	13	13	11	7
J38	0-6-0	13	13	—	15	13
J67	0-6-OT	4	3	—	—	—
J69	0-6-OT	—	—	1	—	—
J72	0-6-OT	—	—	2	1	—
J83	0-6-OT	6	6	6	4	—
J88	0-6-OT	8	8	8	5	—
C15	4-4-2T	2	3	1	—	—
N15	0-6-2T	6	9	8	—	—
WD	2-8-0	22	19	15	20	8
Total		112	11	90	94	37

Depot No. 62C, Dunfermline
(Sub-Sheds:— Alloa and Kelty)

Class	Wheel Arrangement	31/8/50	21/3/53	14/5/55	14/2/59	-/1/66
B1	4-6-0	—	—	1	3	3
K2	2-6-0	—	3	3	3	—
D30	4-4-0	1	2	3	2	—
D33	4-4-0	2	1	—	—	—
J35	0-6-0	10	10	9	10	—
J36	0-6-0	8	6	6	7	1
J37	0-6-0	12	11	11	8	3
J38	0-6-0	11	11	—	4	9
J88	0-6-OT	5	3	3	2	—
C15	4-4-2T	3	2	1	—	—
N15	0-6-2T	9	9	9	2	—
Y9	0-4-OST	1	1	1	1	—
V1/3	2-6-2T	2	2	2	2	—
WD	2-8-0	12	8	11	9	9
Total		76	69	60	53	25

Appendix 2

Grant-Aid for Passenger Services

For more than a decade all passenger services operated in and through the Fife Peninsula, with the exception of Aberdeen-London services, have been unremunerative. However, because of their social importance to the community, losses incurred by them have since 1969 been met by government grant aid. Until December 1973, the amount of aid was specific to each service but in 1974 all services were grouped together and became no longer individually identifiable.

Details of the 1972 deficit and train/passenger miles included in the Grant Aid Application were as follows:—

	Annual Deficit £000	Deficit per Pass. Mile p	ci' Deficit per Train Mile p	Annual Loaded Train Miles '000	Annual Pass. Miles '000
Edinburgh-Dundee via Kirkcaldy	414	0.9	55	747	44,257
Edinburgh-Dundee via Dunfermline	351	1.6	85	414	22,314

Appendix 3

Passenger Stations in the Fife Peninsula

Shown below are the total number of passengers using each of the stations during representative weeks in summer 1978 and winter 1977.

	1978 August	1977 November
	(Weekly totals)	
Aberdour	2,811	2,716
Burntisland	7.283	3,393
Cardenden	444	400
Cowdenbeath	6,313	5,519
Cupar	4,675	5,047
Dunfermline	13,363	15,029
Inverkeithing	17,929	20,519
Kinghorn	3,933	2,053
Kirkcaldy	33,123	29,155
Ladybank	2,044	1,603
Leuchars	5,768	5,123
Lochgelly	419	438
Markinch	2,446	2,265
North Queensferry	2,411	1,901

Figures are not available for Springfield or Rosyth Halt, the former being totally unstaffed and the latter staffed only during peak hours.

Appendix 4 *(See Table 10, p. 155)*

1 Designed for passenger duties, these engines formed part of the bulk order with which to open the line. Five of them underwent major repairs at Perth in 1856-57 by arrangement between the E.P. & D. and Scottish Central Railways.

2 These formed the first batch of goods engines to be supplied to the Edinburgh & Northern Railway.

3 The last two of these engines were completed by the North British.

4 The survivor of these express passenger engines was withdrawn in 1884 having been rebuilt at Burntisland in 1866.

5 These engines had particularly small wheel-bases (5 ft. 4 ins.) and worked exclusively on the West of Fife Mineral Railway.

6 These were ordered as 'heavy luggage engines' at a cost of £2,360. They had outside frames and a wheelbase of 7 ft. 3 ins. plus 6 ft. 7 ins.

7 One was built for the E. P. & D.'s Granton section in 1855 and another, bearing both E. P. & D. and N.B.R. numbers for administrative purposes, became the property of the independent Leslie Railway until that company's stock was handed over to the N.B.R. in 1869. The third engine was built for the Kinross-shire Railway and worked by the E. P. & D.

8 Descriptions of these engines are lacking.

9 These two engines were built especially for the Edinburgh-Granton section.

10 Built for the Fife and Kinross Railway, these two engines were not numbered by their original owners but carried on their four-wheeled tenders the names *Loch Leven Castle* and *Falkland Castle.* They were subsequently used by the N.B.R. as station pilots at Perth, Burntisland and Tayport.

11 One was entirely rebuilt at Burntisland in 1867 as a Hurst 0-4-2 well-tank whilst its companion later emerged as a 2-2-2 engine with 5 ft. 6 in. wheels.

12 One was rebuilt at Burntisland in 1860 as an 0-4-0 engine with 3 ft. 10 in. wheels.

13 Nothing further is known about this engine.

14 This engine was rebuilt in 1870 as a saddle tank.

15 Built initially for the Granton section, this engine was rebuilt at Burntisland in 1860 as an 0-4-2 with 4 ft. 6 in. wheels. On withdrawal it was sold to the Glentore Colliery near Cowdenbeath.

16 This engine built for the Charlestown Railway, absorbed by the West of Fife Mineral Railway in 1861, was rebuilt as an 0-6-0 at St Margarets Works in 1866.

17 Delivered in 1861 as a Single and named *Oakley,* this engine was rebuilt in 1868.

Sources and Bibliography

E&NR. Minute Books

EP&DR. Minute Books

EP&DR. Agreement Book

EP&DR. Batches of miscellaneous documents held in West Register House, Edinburgh.

NBR. Service and Public Timetables.

BR (Scotland). Sectional Appendices

BR (Scotland). Selected Working Timetables.

'A Regional History of the Railways of Great Britain Vol. 6 The Lowlands and The Borders'. John Thomas 1971

'Broughty Ferry—Village to Suburb'. Nancy Davey & John Perkins. Museums and Art Galleries Department, City of Dundee District Council. 1976.

'Steamers of the Forth'. Ian Brodie, David & Charles Ltd., 1976.

'Crossing the Forth'. Hugh Douglas, Robert Hale Ltd., 1964.

'The North British Railway'. Vols. 1 & 2., John Thomas, David & Charles Ltd.

"Early Scottish Colliery Wagonways'. George Dott, St. Margaret's Technical Press Ltd., London, 1947.

'The Fordell Railway'. J.E. Inglis and F. Inglis, The Colony, Larbert, 1947.

'Forgotten Railways of Scotland'. John Thomas, David & Charles Ltd., 1976.

Locomotives of the NBR 1846-1882'. The Stephenson Locomotive Society, 1970.

'Glimpses of Modern Burntisland'. ex-Baillie Erskine, The Fife Free Press, c 1930.

'British Railways Locomotives and Locoshed Book', 1948-50, 1955 & 1959, Ian Allan Ltd.

'Scottish Motive Power 1953'. Angus Railway Group.

'Industrial Locomotives of Scotland'. Industrial Railway Society, 1976.

'Passengers No More', Second Edition, G. Daniels & L. Dench., Ian Allan Ltd.

Newspapers and Periodicals:—
The Fife Herald, The Fife News, The Fife Free Press, The Perthshire Courier, The Dundee Argus, The Dundee Courier, The Scotsman, Railway Magazine, Railway World, Modern Railways.

Index

L. Tawers
Ardta'naig
L. Freuchie
Amulree
MURTHLY
BANKFOOT
STANLEY
STA. & JUNC.
STRATHOR
LUNCART
Scone
Palace
LOCH Ardeonaig

E R T H

Ben Chonzie
R. Almond
RUTHVEN ROAD
ALMOND BANK
TIBBERMUIR
METHVEN
METHVEN JUNC.
ALMOND
PRINCES
STR.
PERTH
GOODS
GENERAL STA.
HARBOUR
HILTON
JUS.

St. FILLANS
HEARNHEAD
L. Earn
COMRIE
ABERCAIRNY
MADDERTY
BALGOWAN
INNERPEFFRAY
FORGANDENNY
FORTEVIOT
BRIDGE OF EARN

HIDDER
USE
B. Vorlich
Glen Artney
CRIEFF
HIGHLANDMAN
Drummond
Castle
R. Earn
DUNNING
MUTHILL
Uamh Bheag
TULLIBARDINE
AUCHTERARDER
GLENFARG

naig
s of Leny
CALLANDER
Braco
GREENLOANING
GLENEAGLES
BLACKFORD
MAWCAR
MILNATHORT
KINROSS
BALADO

KINBUCK
CROOK OF DEVON
RUMBLING BRIDGE
LOCH LEVEN GOODS

R. Teith
Lanrick Cas.
DOUNE
Blair Drummond
DUNBLANE
CLACKMANNAN
TILLICOULTRY
DOLLAR
R. Devon
BLAIRADAM

nteith
R. Forth
BRIDGE OF ALLAN
MENSTRIE
ALVA
SAUCHIE
LETHANS No 1 COL.
STEELEND
BLAIRENBATHIE
COL. KEI.

PORT OF MENTEITH
KIPPEN
GARGUNNOCK
CAUSEWAY-HEAD
SHORE RD GOODS JUNC.
ALLOA
PASS.
FOREST MILL
LETHANS No 2 COL.
OAKLEY COL.
GOODS
EASTGRANGE
OAKLEY COL.
BALMULE COL.
UPPER
LILLIE

sie Fells
STIRLING
CAMBUS CENTRAL GOODS
DOCK GOODS
CLACKMANNAN
KILBAGIE
BOGSIDE
WHITE TYRE

BLANE
CAMPSIE GLEN
BANNOCKBURN
THROSK
PLATFORM
SOUTH GOODS
KINCARDINE
CULROSS
DUNFERMLINE
LOWER

MILTON OF CAMPSIE
LENNOX TOWN
TWECHAR
PLEAN PASS.
PLEAN PITS
AIRTH
ALLOA JUNC.
TORRYBURN
CAIRNEYHILL
CHARLESTOWN

RANCE
BALMORE
KILSYTH
COLZIUM
INGLISTON GOODS
STONEYWOOD GOODS
DENNY
LARBERT STA.
CAMELON PASS.
FALKIRK
ALDERSE
GRANGEMOUTH
BO'NESS
NORTH QUEENSFERRY
FORTH BRIDGE

BISHOP BRIGGS
STEPPS
KIRKINTILLOCH
LENZIE
CROY
BONNYBRIDGE
DENNYLOANHEAD
BANKNOCK
BONNYWATER
CAMELON CENTRAL
FALKIRK HIGH
POLMONT
KINNEIL
BRIDGENESS
S. QUEENSFERRY GOODS
DALMENY

CHRYSTON
GARNKIRK
DULLATUR
CASTLE CARY
GREENHILL
ROUGH CASTLE GDS
SHIELDHILL GDS
REDDING
CAUSEWAY-END
MANUEL
LOCHMILL GDS
LINLITHGOW
PHILPSTOUN

W
GARTSHERRIE
COATBRIDGE
BARGEDDIE
CUMBERNAULD
STRATHAVON COL.
ROUGHRIGG COL EAST
ALMOND
BOWHOUSE
WESTFIELD GOODS
BROXBURN
WINCHBURGH
KIRKLIS TON

QUE
STR
LOCH
RUTHER
GLEN
EASTERHO
DYKEHEAD
GREENGAIRS GOODS
LONGRIGG END
SLAMANNAN
BLACKSTON
AVONBRIDGE
ARMADALE COL.
WOODEND COL.
POLKEMMET WEIGHS
SEAFIELD
OIL WORKS
HOLYGATE
UPHALL
DRUMSHOR LAND
CAMP

AIRDRIE
GLENBOIG
RAWYARDS
CALDERCRUIX
WESTCRAIGS
ARMADALE
BATHGATE UPPER
E. CALDER GOODS
LIVINGSTON

LANG LOAN
BELLSHILL
WHIFFLET
CLARKSTON
CALDERBANK
CHAPELHALL
PLAINS
FORREST FIELD
WHITBURN
BENTS
POLKEMMET COL.
BENHAR EAST
HARBURN
WEST CALDER
MIDCA

SHOTTS
NEWHOUSE
FORTISSAT COL.
WARD
DEWSHILL PIT
HASSOCKRIGG COL.
DUNSTON COL.
N PARK
ADDIE
MIDCALDER JUC.

LITHGOW